1983

Heroes & Heroines

LEFT TO RIGHT
Theseus and the Minotaur
Cleopatra as the Goddess of Love
Robert Bruce
George Washington
Charles Lindbergh

Heroes &
Heroines

Edited by
ANTONIA FRASER

A & W Publishers, Inc. · New York

First published in the United States of America in 1980 by
A & W Publishers, Inc.
95 Madison Avenue
New York, New York 10016
By arrangement with George Weidenfeld and Nicolson Limited

Library of Congress Catalog Card Number: 80-7821
ISBN: 0-89479-070-6

Printed in United States of America

The illustrations in this book are supplied or repro-
duced by kind permission of the following:

Copyright reserved 157, 158
J. Allan Cash Ltd 30, 52
Antikenmuseum Staatliche Museen Preussischer
   Kulturbesitz (Hamlyn Group Picture Library) 23
Antikvarisk Topografiska Arkivet, Stockholm 43, 48
Ardea, London 51 (photo John Mason)
Ashmolean Museum 114
Athens Museum 24, 25
BBC Copyright Photograph 240
Bibliothèque Nationale, Paris 125
Bildarchiv Preussischer Kulturbesitz, Berlin 194, 221,
   223
British Museum 20, 94, 128, 159
Camera Press 242
Chicago Historical Society 193, 194
Congregational Council for World Mission 195, 196,
   197
Mary Evans Picture Library 46, 77, 165, 173, 228
Fotomas Index 166, 188
Giraudon 14, 18, 82 (Hamlyn Group Picture Library),
   106, 139
Sonia Halliday Photographs 63
Michael Holford 101
Illinois State Historical Library 192
Illustrated London News 214
Imperial War Museum (Robert Hunt Library) 245
Lambeth Palace Library 134
Library of Congress 191 (l & r)
Local Studies Library, Nottinghamshire Country
   Library 187

Louvre (Hamlyn Group Picture Library) 13
Mansell Collection III, 10, 16, 22, 26, 29, 39, 67, 68, 72,
   74, 78-8, 88, 90, 92, 98-99 , 107, 109, 127, 130, 136-7,
   142-3, 145, 147, 163, 170, 203, 213
Metropolitan Museum of Art, New York (Gift of
   J. Pierpont Morgan, 1900), 141
NASA 256
National Army Museum 202
National Maritime Museum 177, 178-179
National Museum, Iceland 42, 44
National Portrait Gallery 131, 149, 176, 200
National Trust 164, 186, 204-5 (photo John Bethell)
Peter Newark's Western Americana 184
Ny Carlsberg Glyptotek, Copenhagen 50
Olympia Museum 12
Photo Research International 171, 174, 182, 185, 252
   254, 255 (NASA)
Popperfoto 210, 212, 226, 230, 234, 236, 237, 238, 243,
   247, 249, 250, 251
Radio Times Hulton Picture Library 36, 116, 161, 168,
   215, 216, 217, 219, 224, 225, 232, 241
Rheinisches Bildarchiv, Cologne 59
Roger-Viollet 32-3
Royal Geographical Society 197-8
Scala (Hamlyn Group Picture Library), 56
Ronald Sheridan 60, 121
Edwin Smith 19, 27, 70
Tate Gallery, London 61, 151
Vatican Library (Hamlyn Group Picture Library) 55
Vatican Museum 21, 84
Weidenfeld & Nicolson Archive II, 86, 96, 111, 118-9
Roger Wood 95
Picture research by Caroline Lucas.

Contents

Introduction

by ANTONIA FRASER

The Age of Myth and Legend

by MICHAEL SENIOR

Classical and Biblical Times

by JAMES CHAMBERS

The Age of Chivalry

by JOHN GILLINGHAM

The Age of Patriotism

by GILA FALKUS

The Modern Age

Index

Introduction

by Antonia Fraser

'The living rock amid all rushings-down whatsoever; – the one fixed point in modern revolutionary history, otherwise as if bottomless and shoreless' – thus Thomas Carlyle on Hero-Worship. The date was 1840. In the course of his mighty disquisition on the subject, Carlyle lambasted his own age for denying the desirableness of great men ('I am well aware in these days Hero Worship, the thing I call Hero Worship, professes to have gone out, and finally ceased') before going on to charge his imagined foes at full tilt, grandiloquent sword in hand. He claimed, in a famous phrase, that 'Universal History, the history of what man has accomplished in his world, is at bottom the History of the Great Men who have worked here'.

Nearly one hundred and fifty years later, the shade of Carlyle must be satisfied by the fact that hero-worship is alive and well – even if many scholars today would deny furiously his proposition concerning the nature of Universal History. Perhaps Carlyle was needlessly concerned. The truth is that hero-worship is an emotion so primitively strong that it is doubtful whether it will ever be eradicated in human nature. For one thing, like many such passions, it often makes its first – and formative – appearance in early childhood. Of course we do not always carry our infant heroes or heroines with us into adult life. Nevertheless the memory remains, and lurks deep.

Adulthood does not necessarily mark the passing of hero-worship altogether, but it often brings with it a change of hero-object. Let us divide our heroes and heroines, roughly speaking, into two categories, the Inspirational and the Challenging: those we admire just because we know we could never emulate them, and those we admire and wish to emulate. An Inspirational heroine might be Odette Sansom: while no-one could possibly aim to find themselves in her unfortunate situation, imprisoned and tortured, anyone can be impressed and encouraged by the courage and tenacity she showed in surviving it. A Challenging heroine, on the other hand, is Florence Nightingale, whose example could lead a young girl to take up nursing (or equally to reorganize a corrupt and inefficient government service).

In childhood, unaware as we are of our capacities and the lack of them, our heroes tend to be

I

Challenging: 'all I could never be' has not yet proved such a despairingly large category compared with 'all I might be one day with luck'. With self-knowledge comes the switch to Inspirational heroes; and in certain instances the same type of hero, once Challenging, moves on to become merely Inspirational. I am thinking of the enormous and life-enhancing category of Sporting Heroes: Don Bradman – Challenging to the eager boy – becomes Inspirational to the middle-aged man.

As I grow older, my own tendency is to choose Inspirational heroines more relevant to my way of life than the glamorous idols of my youth. The love objects of my childhood were ninety per cent tragic and one hundred per cent romantic: Mary Queen of Scots epitomized them all; her colourful but sad destiny proved a delightful contrast to life in my parents' happy and high-minded (but not romantic) North Oxford home. Latterly St Teresa of Avila has replaced Mary Queen of Scots, not merely for her Inspirational mysticism, but for combining in her own way – as an organizer of convents – the life of the world with the life of the spirit. Mrs Gaskell, the good mother, good wife, good housekeeper, good friend (and good writer) has replaced poor Charlotte Brontë – a great writer but one whose tragic personal life is irrelevant to my own. I do not however identify myself with either lady: to do so would be both presumptuous and unnecessary. Perhaps there is something essentially childish about such identification. In the clear light of adult reality, this element passes away from our hero-worship. Something humbler but equally able to transform our own ordinary lives remains.

I have assumed in all this that our heroes and heroines are leading us towards something higher than ourselves. Must it necessarily be so? Is it implicit in the very nature of a hero that he represent good rather than evil? Sir Thomas Malory in the *Morte d'Arthur* optimistically suggested that those who 'go after the good and leave the evil shall be brought to good fame and renown'; but the more depressing lesson of history is that these two categories of the good and the renowned are not always coincidental.

Certainly heroes are not to be equated with saints, although certain individuals can be both – St. Paul is included in this volume. Heroes, like saints, can also be chosen to illustrate particular virtues. Roland dying at Roncesvalles symbolizes the man who stands firm to the last rather than break his oath – 'Every man should be ready to die for his lord'; just as St Catherine, for example, martyred on a wheel after deliberately confessing the Christian faith at a public banquet of the Emperor Maximus, stands for another type of heroic testimony. Both Roland and St Catherine were, in so far as we know about their distant lives, morally irreproachable.

But there are tragic heroes whose qualities and destiny have nothing to do with sanctity. Part of the complex Japanese culture includes a special feeling for those heroes who are 'noble failures'. As Ivan Morris points out in a study of the subject, the Japanese not only admire historical figures like Admiral Togo – 'the Nelson of Japan' – who took on and defeated the forces of the West, but other very different types of hero. These are the men whose single-mindedness will not let them compromise, and who are thus inevitably vanquished: in short, the hero as loser, as described by Yeats, 'Bred to a harder thing than Triumph . . .'.

Death is often the harbinger of a heroic reputation. The great Spartacus, leader of the slaves who threw off their bondage, knew what he was about when he killed his horse during the final battle so that he could not escape. Our esteem for a certain type of hero – frequently if not essentially a poet or writer – is often bound up with his or her tragic early death. The premature deaths of Keats, Thomas Chatterton and Lermontov, to take but three examples, are inseparable from the romantic aura which surrounds them. To illustrate this point, Maurice Baring described a witty reversal of historical reputations in *The Alternative*: he suggested that if Shelley had survived to old age, he would have turned into a stuffy club bore, a pillar of the establishment, deeply ashamed of the radical poetry of his youth; Wordsworth, on the other hand, dying young on the barricades, would have had statues put up to him as a hero cut off in his prime. Fortunately longevity has not robbed Wordsworth of his serious-minded worshippers, although the dreamers will continue to prefer Keats, and the radicals Shelley.

However noble their deaths, it will be evident that many of the heroes in this book were morally ambivalent during their lifetime. Indeed, the importance of Achilles as a character is that he expresses this ambivalence, something which the Greeks held to be inseparable from the nature of war itself. In other cases, the deeds of certain heroes of myths and legends, descendants of the gods as they may be, do not pass muster by today's standards: Theseus's cruel abandonment of Ariadne is a notable example. The merit of Odysseus (the hero I would most like to meet, envying Princess Nausicaa her encounter, however, rather more than Penelope her marriage) is specifically stated to be his native sharpness. 'How like you to be so wary!' exclaims his patron Pallas Athene of some particular piece of cunning; 'And that is why I cannot desert you in your misfortunes: you are so civilized, so intelligent, so self-possessed.'

Other clay-footed candidates, those whose private lives would militate against them – rightly or wrongly — today, include Pericles, who would find it more difficult to stand for probity now than he did in his own lifetime. Sometimes the scandalous private life of a hero is actually interwoven with his public virtues, to his own advantage: in the present volume, Gila Falkus refers to Byron, in a felicitous phrase, as having 'heroism spiced with debauchery'.

Moral ambivalence, the private weaknesses which in themselves constitute evidence of humanity, are, however, a far cry from evil. It is surely by definition impossible for a hero to be totally evil. It is true that, as Lucifer was the fairest of the archangels before he fell, outshining 'myriads though bright', traces of this attraction remain in evil's face. Thus wicked people may from time to time in history, alas, be hero-worshipped. It is this possibility – regrettable but part of the human condition – that can cause a periodic revulsion against the very notion of a hero in our society: the profound shudder which follows on the regime of any one of history's magnetic tyrants. But in such a case it is the emotion of hero-worship which is responsible, not the concept of a hero.

Like all primitive emotions, hero-worship has its reverse side, inevitably according to the calibre of the man or woman admired. There are certain appalling manifestations, such as the public adoption of the Nazi philosophy, which have to be ascribed to the guidance of one man – Hitler – a monster, but once some form of national hero. Nevertheless, taking this extreme example, I would firmly contend that Hitler was not a hero, and furthermore that there was nothing of the heroic about him. In this sense, it can be argued that those in Germany who made Hitler their hero before the Second World War were deluded, and attributed to him qualities which he did not happen to possess. Despots and dictators can be benevolent or malevolent, both in themselves and in the effects of their regime. But there can be no wicked heroes.

What our heroes and heroines do have in common, beyond some form of virtue, however masked, is an ability to capture the imagination. And this romantic assault is carried through by means of a particular kind of heroic quality, an unmistakable attribute in the eyes of the outside world. In certain cases, the subject himself has been aware of it. Nelson wrote in his memoirs: 'I know it is my disposition that difficulties and dangers do but increase my desire of attempting them.' It is an attitude of mind summed up by Alexander the Great when he was urged to attack the enemy by night: 'Alexander does not steal victories.'

Heroism in this volume is however by no means confined to the martial, that vision of Richard the Lionheart quoted by John Gillingham:

> O, still, methinks, I see King Richard stand
> In his gilt armour stain'd with Pagan's blood,
> Upon a galley's brow, like war's fierce God . . .

We have also borne in mind the secondary dictionary definition of those exhibiting 'extraordinary bravery, firmness, fortitude, or greatness of soul, in any course of action'. David Livingstone, Gladys Aylward and Martin Luther King find their place as well as Hannibal, Henry v and Montrose. Wolfe, one of our heroes, went on record as saying that he would rather have written Gray's *Elegy in a Country Churchyard* than stormed the heights of Quebec. Nevertheless in their different ways, all these heroes and heroines appeal to the fires which lie damped within us all, and set them ablaze.

Carlyle followed through the idea of a special heroic disposition to its limits. He insisted that a given individual would always emerge as a hero, although the form his heroism took might and would vary from age to age. He was concerned to refute the notion that the age threw up the man. I believe that it is possible sensibly to combine both points of view. There is a special quality of heroism in some individuals, denied to others, but which, given certain circumstances, can remain latent throughout their lives. St Thomas More is a case in point. No-one can deny that he has emerged as one of the peaceable (as opposed to martial) heroes of our history. In our own century alone he stands as an Inspirational example to all those who have upheld their own consciences above the demands of the state. Yet St Thomas More did not seek a heroic role or a martyr's death. Had the matrimonial affairs of Henry VIII taken another course, he could well have ended his life trusted and honoured, the King's good servant. It needed the crucible to test his gold.

The present book is divided chronologically into five sections. This seemed the most helpful arrangement to the reader, bearing in mind that one of the primary purposes of this volume is to act as a kind of reference book. It is intended to trace the distinction between myth and reality in the lives of heroes and heroines, casting a little cold water where necessary: Edith Cavell was not a lovely young woman, Saladin was not a Christian Frankish gentleman! On the other hand, Joshua did exist as a war leader in the thirteenth century BC, even if his true story is not identical with that told in the Bible; the facts concerning Joan of Arc are fascinating in themselves, not merely as a corrective to George Bernard Shaw's dominating dramatic picture.

As a result of this planning, certain patterns did emerge amongst the heroes and heroines. I use the word emerge deliberately, since these patterns were not imposed from above; we chose our fifty-two heroes and heroines on their individual merits, after agonizing debate (the reader will undoubtedly have his own candidates for both admission and omission). In the first section, Michael Senior writes of the interrelation of common themes in European mythologies. One of these is the long journey and return of the hero, the most poignant version being the visit of the hero to the kingdom of the dead. But the early heroes are also close to the cycle of nature, as society then was: the classic exposition being the legend of Demeter and Persephone. In the second section on Classical and Biblical heroes, James Chambers points to the vital distinction between the two categories. Classical heroes could and frequently did meet a tragic end, from Leonidas to Cleopatra. The Biblical heroes such as David were on the contrary basically triumphant.

The Age of Chivalry brings us, as John Gillingham points out, a preponderance of sovereign princes and only one heroine. Both weightings illuminate for us the nature of the times. On the one hand, this was a highly 'established' society, the heyday of the Christian military aristocracy, and to be outside it was to be outside the pale of heroism, as it was then understood. Even Hereward the Wake was a member of an establishment – even if it was one in the process of being destroyed. On the other hand, the status of medieval women was extremely low.

The Age of Patriotism brings with it a series of quite different heroes, who, as Gila Falkus expresses it, have to be seen 'in the context of the aspirations of whole nations', now that the feudal ideals have vanished. Even Bonnie Prince Charlie, at first sight the hero as loser, stands for the nostalgic side of patriotism; for he represents a country which felt itself to be rapidly losing its national identity at the expense of its English neighbour. Abraham Lincoln is an obvious example of a high-minded and patriotic hero; but Davy Crockett stands for another aspect of the American nineteenth-century emergent nationalism – that of the settlers in the west.

Lastly, in the twentieth century, Alan Palmer points to the significant fact that so many of the modern heroes and heroines spent time in confinement, from Rosa Luxemburg to Douglas Bader. The prisoner has replaced the king as a symbol of the age. As a corrective to this sad commentary, at least women make their appearance on equal terms.

The special nature of a heroine (merely a female hero or something different?) was one reflection provoked by the editing of this book. I am inclined to believe that there was a distinction in the past: with the idea of a heroine came the notion of a particular frailty overcome. We all know what we mean by a Shakespearean heroine and she is not at all the obverse of a Shakespearean hero. Witty, delightful, bold, a Beatrice, Rosalind, Viola – she must yet prove to have a romantic feminine heart beating softly somewhere beneath the gown or doublet at the end. About an operatic heroine there used to be an even greater hint of frailty – lethal illness at times, as Mimi and Violetta cough their way to the final curtain – and also more than a hint of melodrama. And this carries with it an implication of self-indulgence, a lady going mad in white satin to the sound of her own High C, as Sheridan had it in *The Critic*.

More genuinely, Brunnhilde is a heroine, not merely because she sacrifices herself unselfishly for love, but because she shows greater nobility and greater strength than the males around her (personally, I have never found anything the slightest bit heroic about Siegfried's conduct but perhaps that is sexual prejudice). Queen Elizabeth I, with the 'heart and stomach of a king' but the glittering costumes of a delicate woman, knew just how to exploit this combination in the minds of her subjects. No mere king could have done so.

Will the distinction vanish in the future with the improving status of women? The trouble is that equal opportunities, if granted, still cannot guarantee equal physical strength. Grace Darling will always be rated a heroine, and her male equivalent merely expected to do his duty. We shall have many more heroines, in sheer numbers. But heroism has enough of the physical about it, I suspect, for a heroine to remain in some ways in a special category.

Finally, the experience of editing this book was in itself an uplifting one. It was not only a question of encountering the familiar favourite stories of courage from Boadicea to Captain Scott, and thrilling to them again. I was also introduced to new heroes, foremost amongst them two from Celtic myth, Lleu 'the bright one', whose wife was fashioned from the native wild flowers of his country; and CuChulainn, of the Ulster Cycle, who passed some women washing a blood-stained garment in a stream on his way to battle and, recognizing it to be his own, knew that he had seen into the future, and foretold his own death.

The real lesson of this book must be the imperishability of heroism, as a manifestation of the human will. The running vein of evil in every society is often stressed; these stories of the heroism of others remind us that even in the most terrible circumstances some kind of choice may remain. In the words of Matthew Arnold:

> The will is free;
> Strong is the soul, and wise and beautiful;
> The seeds of godlike power are in us still;
> Gods we are, bards, saints, heroes if we will.

The Age of Myth and Legend

by Michael Senior

THE AGE OF MYTH and legend is not a historical period; rather it is a stage in the development of a people's culture which in Europe alone has occurred at very diverse times. It is a step lying between one way of thinking and another; one might say it occurs in the spectrum of belief somewhere between religion and science. Myths often come from religion, in the sense that they are one form taken by the figures of a religion when it is no longer active. It is clear that in the myths and legends of Greece and Scandinavia, for instance, the characters of the stories are not the product of folk-tale or of fancy, but have once been believed in as deities. They tend to be derived from natural elements, such as the sky, thunder, the earth, and so on; and partly owe their identity to abstract ideas to do with human life, such as fatherliness, motherhood, war and love. At some earlier stage they had become personalized, and then believed in as real individual beings. By the time we meet them in myth and legend they have declined into the figures of tales.

These in turn come to us not in their original, oral form, presumably as told by generations of parents to their children, but as the product of a more literary imagination. Our sources vary greatly, both in age and in closeness to this earlier form. Homer composed his works in about 750 BC, the Icelander Snorri Sturluson wrote the 'Prose Edda' in the thirteenth century AD, yet both convey to us an authentic view of their country's traditional material. In Britain a group of stories which contained the remains of a mythology, much altered by folk-tale, became collected in medieval manuscripts which, translated in the last century by Lady Charlotte Guest, have come to be known as the Mabinogion. That is about as near as we can get to our native lore, but in Ireland, where there is evidence of the stories being written down as early as the seventh century, their authenticity as communal property has been strengthened by the survival of some of them as story-tellers' tales into quite recent times.

It is from such sources as these, from Homer, from the Norse Eddas, from the Mabinogion, that this selection of heroes and heroines from myth and legend has been made. I have chosen them for their authenticity, their character of belonging to a genuine tradition, and for their

7

representativeness within that category. I have tried, through the selection, to give a feeling of what myth and legend are. This is not a defined, or definable, area. There is, for instance, no clear boundary between those two subjects, myth and legend; they merge into each other, but between them they cover the zone stretching from religion on the one hand to history on the other. There is no firm distinction, similarly, between gods and heroes. In some cases it is as if a figure has, over a long period, moved backwards and forwards between the two statuses. Ambiguity, paradox, blurred dividing lines: these are essential qualities of this subject.

Although myth and legend have no firm defining qualifications and merge bewilderingly into other subjects, they do have several typical characteristics which make them identifiable in the central ground. One remarkable thing about them is that they appear, across the continent of Europe and into India, to be closely inter-related. The same types of characters crop up, the same things happen to them, the same ideas are expressed in the same images. This is remarkable enough to be quite disturbing at times, since there seems no reason why (for instance) a Hindu wind-god should reappear in Iceland. Part of the explanation seems to lie in the existence of an original common stock of Indo-European peoples, a clue to which is given by the relatedness of the languages themselves. But the continual cross-references in such matters are, in world terms, both wide and deep, and this relatedness has given rise to a continuing and stimulating debate. The 'diffusionists' trace the steps by which material might have passed, changed and joined with other material, over the face of a continent and over the considerable period involved. The 'evolutionists', on the other hand, those who believe that the themes and figures developed separately, have to explain in terms of innate psychological tendencies how the separate material came to look so alike. There is a strong case for their argument that like conditions must produce like results, common themes arising inevitably from common interests. As always the rational conclusion would appear to lie in a compromise. There has undoubtedly been influence; but influence only takes effective root where circumstances favour the result in the way they favoured its original appearance.

We shall be coming across a number of these common themes, as well as the constant network of relationships both within and between Europe's mythologies. Some of them – the father–son relationship, for instance, or the husband–wife–lover one – are natural results of the combination of the social and biological forms of human life. Others, such as the withdrawal of vegetation and its vernal return, are clear expressions of our inevitable relationship with the natural world. If mythology is 'about' anything, it is about the perpetual human predicaments; and another of these is death. Starting from the knowledge that we are mortal, our remote ancestors have constructed in their imaginations a compensating world of immortality. That seems to have been one factor in the making of the gods, most of whom, unlike us, do not die. It has also given rise to another constant theme in myth and legend, the visit to the otherworld kingdom of the dead. Typically the hero makes the journey and returns; and this is part of his special, literally super-natural, status as a hero.

The great success of myth and legend over the course of several thousand years, and their continuing popularity and fascination for us today in our rather materialistic world, tempts one to ask what they owe both this success and this survival power. If there were an original explanatory function, we clearly now no longer need it; we know what causes the thunderstorm and the seasonal cycles. Yet the stories seem to contain for us something more than mere narrative interest, and perhaps this is because they permanently present a distilled image of experiences which are still (and always will be) part of our lives.

Michael Senior

~ *Heracles* ~

If there is a perfect example of a hero, it is Heracles. Demi-god, monster-slayer, lone traveller on tremendous journeys, he is the doom-driven, task-achieving superhuman who occupies a central spot in the imaginations of all periods and peoples.

His mother was the daughter of the high-king of Mycenae, and on that maternal side he was therefore a descendant of Perseus. His father was Zeus, the king of the gods, who made a habit of seducing mortal women. It is to this preliminary episode in his story that much of the rest of his career is attributable, since it meant he was, like Theseus, a divine hero: man, but with an element of the supernatural in him. It meant that he had a claim to the Peloponnesian kingship. And it meant that as the offspring of an illicit liaison he was to bear the implacable antagonism of Hera, Zeus's wife.

This jealousy of the queen of Olympus took effect early. Zeus rashly boasted that the child about to be born into the house of Perseus would become high-king of Mycenae, and Hera, knowing of his infidelity, revenged herself by delaying the birth of Heracles. Another of Perseus's descendants, Eurystheus, was born first. Zeus's oath was irreversible, and thus Heracles found himself landless, and subservient to Eurystheus.

Like so many heroes of myth, he developed his amazing abilities precociously. He killed serpents while still in his cradle and a lion in his youth, during the hunting of which he slept with the fifty daughters of King Thespius. The central section of his story then consists of the twelve famous 'Labours', but these themselves are

The Theban usurper, Lycus, clutches frantically at Heracles' lion skin before being dashed to the ground. It was thought that Lycus had murdered the previous king, Creon, whose daughter, Megara, Heracles had married and later murdered.

grouped into two phases. The first six are localized, and indicate that he was, to begin with, a specifically Peloponnesian hero: they all take place within a quite small radius of Mycenae. The second six are very widespread, and perhaps reflect the almost universal spread of the cult of Heracles in the Greek world.

The sequence opens with a spell of madness, said to have been caused by Hera, during which he kills his children by his wife Megara, daughter of the king of Thebes. On recovering sanity he seeks the judgment of the oracle at Delphi as to how he might expiate this crime. The oracle makes him subject to the commands of his cousin Eurystheus, a bond which is to last twelve years; and thus he comes to Tiryns, near Mycenae, the ancient seat of Perseus's kingdom, to receive the orders of his overlord and cousin.

The list of apparently impossible tasks is a common theme in folk-lore and mythology. We find it in Ireland and Wales, and elsewhere in Greek myth. The tasks now given to Heracles are simply the clearest representatives of this ancient idea: the testing of the hero's supernature, the paradox of the achievement of the impossible. The story has compulsive narrative power because we, the audience, know that he will do it, but cannot see how.

The first task occurs in the hill country near Argos, where the lion of Nemea is depopulating an area uncomfortably close to Mycenae. Heracles strangles it with his hands, its skin being too tough for any blade to penetrate. The second monster is worse: a 'hydra', a water-serpent in the low-lying area of Lerna, to the south of Tiryns. It has nine heads and the additional ability to grow new ones if any are cut off; Heracles cauterizes the roots with a fire-brand. But this particular monster has been destined by Hera to be his ultimate downfall, and so, in the distant end of his story, it is. He dips his arrows in its poisonous blood to use in later adventures: and he himself dies of this poison.

Though the order of the labours varies in different accounts, the next is usually said to be the hunt for the boar of Erymanthus, in the wild hills of the northern Peloponnese. He catches the boar by driving it into a snowdrift, and takes it home alive to Tiryns. Two more encounters with supernatural creatures follow: the catching of a bronze-hoofed, golden-horned stag, and the destruction of a flock of man-eating birds with metal claws – the Cerynian hind and the Stymphalian birds.

After these he is allotted a different sort of task; instead of chasing and destroying some dangerous creature, he has to devise a way of cleaning out the cattle-sheds of King Augeas in a single day. This is more the cunning, trick-playing aspect of the hero than the display of power which we have so far seen. Heracles achieves it by diverting two rivers, which wash away the apparently enormous quantity of dung in the Augean stables. It appears to have been more a commission than an imposed task, since when Augeas refuses to pay the agreed price a war breaks out between them.

Next Heracles is sent to deal with a mad bull which is terrorizing the population of Crete. We will come across the bull theme in connection with Crete in the story of Theseus, and no doubt this is a version of the same idea. Then he has a similar task in Thrace, capturing the man-eating mares owned by Diomedes. Two of our heroes meet here, since after the conquest of the mares Heracles joins Theseus in an expedition against the Amazons, his task this time being to bring back the girdle of Hippolyte, the Amazon queen.

The adventures begin to range more widely, and less specifically, through the Mediterranean world and beyond. The cattle of the three-headed monster Geryon, which he fetches next, are said in some accounts to have been found on the Iberian peninsula, and the journey to fetch them involves events in areas as far apart as Gaul and Sardinia. Probably what we find now, in these later labours, is a reflection of the spread of the cult of Heracles, particularly in his later Roman form, Hercules, into various parts of the Greek colonies and the Roman empire.

The last two labours take the matter further still, out of the Mediterranean world and into the realm of the supernatural, reminding us that the semi-mortal became a god and was viewed increasingly as an abstract idea, the generalized representative of the universal hero.

The Apples of the Hesperides, which Heracles now has to fetch, are a golden fruit guarded in their orchard at the western end of the world by the daughters of Atlas and Hesperus, the Hesperides. It is on this journey that Atlas himself helps him, gathering the apples while Heracles performs Atlas's task of bearing up the world on his shoulders. The giant Atlas is understandably reluctant to take up his burden again, and it is only by a trick that Heracles escapes.

Finally Eurystheus sends him on the most fearful journey of all, to fetch the watchdog Cerberus from the gates of Hell. Interestingly it is said that he first takes the precaution of going through the initiation at Eleusis, the purpose of which, it seems, was to ensure rebirth after death. Once in the underworld he encounters Theseus again, since the latter is trapped there and needs Heracles' assistance to escape. Overcoming the three-headed Cerberus with his bare hands, he returns – one of the select band of mythic heroes to have been to the land of death and come back into the light.

The further adventures of Heracles are partly again located in the Peloponnese. In particular his cult seems to have flourished at Olympia, where he was said to have measured out the stadium and instituted the Olympic Games. After a second murder he is subjected to a second purification and enslaved to Omphale, queen of Lydia; and even after that his life continues to be one of tragedy. Married again, living in Trachis, he incurs the jealousy of his new wife. Some time before, a dying centaur shot by Heracles had given her a phial of his blood, saying that it was a love potion which would ensure her husband's fidelity. Circumstances prompt her now to use it, and she smears some on a shirt which she sends to

Atlas brings the golden apples of the Hesperides; Athena, who took a particular interest in the exploits of warriors, stands behind Heracles, who was one of her favourites. Remains of a relief from the Temple of Zeus at Olympia.

her husband. But the arrow which shot the centaur was poisoned with the blood of the hydra sent by Hera to be Heracles' downfall, and the poison is so strong that it continues its work. The shirt corrodes his flesh and, driven wild with pain, he decides to die. Having built himself a funeral pyre on Mount Oeta, above the Gulf of Lamia, he is transported to Olympus in the smoke and flames to join the family of the gods. In some versions of the story we are told that he flies into the sky in the form of an eagle, a bird sacred to his sky-god father, Zeus.

The myth then tells that his descendants later invade the Peloponnese, a reference, it is assumed, to the Dorian invasion of the twelfth or thirteenth centuries BC, which effectively brought the Iron Age to Greece, when the peoples of northern Greece spread southwards into the land formerly governed by the Myceneans. Perhaps it was in some such invasion that this cult of the hero, the son figure, began to rival that of Zeus, the father, in places such as Olympia. We often find this sort of movement taking place in mythology, the god of a later culture overcoming that of an earlier, with the shift of emphasis from the father-figure to the son. In a context in which man is increasingly regarded as the hero, the more abstract gods become less meaningful, and the cult of Heracles flourished in the world of imperialist leaders such as Alexander the Great. It was natural that he should then be adopted, in his Latin form of Hercules, by the military power of Rome.

Heracles, watched over as usual by Athena, advances cautiously, chain in hand, to capture Cerberus.

~ *Odysseus* ~

Some of the Greek heroes are too superhuman to be entirely likeable, but this is far from being the case with Odysseus. Led by his own weaknesses into prolonged misfortune, pitting very mortal wits against elemental forces, he is nothing if not human. With characteristic confidence he talks, as if on equal terms, with kings and gods – yet his emotions and desires betray his nature. We admire him for his powers of survival, and for his eventual surmounting of his own faults. We admire him with a sneaking feeling of guilt at doing so, and in this ambiguity which his character raises one can see the genesis of the eternal anti-hero.

Odysseus owes his existence as a personified character to Homer, but this type of hero, the trickster, the embodiment of deceit and cunning, exists in myth and folk-tale in many countries. So too does the theme most closely associated with Odysseus, the long episodic voyage. What differentiates him from numerous similar folk-figures is the care and detail with which Homer characterized him; and it is this which has given him a permanent place in European culture.

Odysseus occurs in both great sagas composed by Homer in about 750 BC, the *Iliad* and the *Odyssey*, and in the development of his personality from the first book to the second we can infer an increasing fascination on the part of the poet with this complex character. Even to begin with, he is highly defined; what comes out later is the tension in him between good and bad, between the hero and the man.

It is interesting that, as so often, Homer gives us first a visual impression. We learn that Odysseus is a short man: when sitting beside

King Menelaus he looks the more impressive of the two, but is dwarfed by the king when they both stand up. He has too that element of aggressive confidence which is conventionally thought to accompany shortness. It is clear that people are a little afraid of him. Even Agamemnon, the High-King and commander-in-chief of the Greeks, apologizes quickly when told by Odysseus that he is talking nonsense. In the *Iliad* we find him taking an interest in the more devious aspects of politics. And there too the particular quality which is later to be his trademark, that ability to straddle the boundary of good and bad, is brought out by the attitudes of those around him, who use terms of ambiguous ethical value: wily, resourceful,

'Odysseus of the nimble wits'. These attitudes reflect the balance which the story-teller carefully maintains, and they infect our own responses.

The *Odyssey* as a work has many contradictions: deceptively easy to read, it reveals an impressive intricacy of structure when one looks more closely. Its form is a series of flashbacks, and in effect we start the story near its end.

The gods, assembled at the court of Zeus on Mount Olympus, express their concern at the delayed homecoming of Odysseus, and send the

On this terracotta from Tanagra, Calypso, ordered by Zeus to release her beloved captive, tells Odysseus that he may leave.

goddess Athena to his island of Ithaca to stir his son Telemachus to attempt to find him. When at last we join Odysseus himself, on the island of the enchantress Calypso, we find him pining for home. Eventually Calypso is persuaded to let him go, and a shipwreck then lands him naked and helpless on another island. It is there that he tells his story to the hospitable king, and the main section of the *Odyssey* consists of this tale within a tale.

After the end of the Trojan War he had set off with a company of followers to sail home to Greece. It should have taken him a few days; yet that was years ago, and he is still far from home. When rounding the bottom of the Peloponnese he had drifted off course, and drifted, it is clear, into another sort of world. It is no longer a world identifiable on the map of the Aegean, but seems more one in which strange, dreamlike things happen. First there is the land of the lotus-eaters, a people who have been drugged by an addictive fruit into abandoning their responsibilities. His men are tempted by this life of ease, but he forces them back on to the ships and they sail on. At their next landfall they encounter the opposite sort of peril: at least the lotus-eaters had not tried to harm them, but on the island of the Cyclops they come close to being killed and eaten.

These one-eyed giants are the familiar horror-figures of many folk-tales, yet they are dealt with by Homer with a characteristically balanced judgment. They live in a lovely land, tend their flocks, and would, we feel, leave the visitors alone unless provoked. It is greed which leads Odysseus into their power, nearly costing him his life. He enters the cave of the leading Cyclops, Polyphemus, hoping to be given generous gifts by this evidently prosperous farmer.

When the giant finds the Greeks making themselves at home in his cave he reveals a side of his nature which they had not anticipated. Having blocked the entrance with a huge stone, he picks up two of Odysseus's men and eats them. They are then in a double quandary, since even if they overcome him, and thus survive,

they will not be able to move the stone to escape. In this apparently impossible situation it is Odysseus's cunning which gets him out of the predicament his greed and rashness have got him into. He makes Polyphemus drunk, blinds him with a hot pointed stake, and he and the remaining men escape by clinging to the underside of the giant's fat sheep when he drives them out of the cave to pasture.

It is only a partial escape. The Cyclops is the son of Poseidon, god of the sea, and he calls to his father to bring a curse on this small and wily mortal. The god grants it, and it is that which gives rise to the rest of the long and painful voyage. The curse is to the effect that if Odysseus ever reaches his home it will be in a sad state, alone, and with trouble awaiting him.

After a brief and deceptive respite on the island of Aeolus, guardian of the winds, and a contrasting brush with the man-eating Laestrygonians, they come to yet another island, the home of the goddess Circe. The lovely Circe lures travellers into her castle where, like many another witch in fairytale, she magically changes them into animals. Such a fate occurs to several of Odysseus's men, but he is provided with a drug by the god Hermes which makes her spells powerless against him. He then bargains with her: his men are to be turned back into humans, and she is to give up her witchcraft. At this point she adopts another familiar aspect of the witch-figure of folktale, the seductress.

They tear themselves away in due course from the banquets and leisure of Circe's enchanted castle, and sail on. A few further memorable images complete the voyage: the journey to the land of the dead, the luring Sirens, the double danger of Scylla and Charybdis which forces them to navigate a perilous middle way. And in due course Odysseus's retelling returns us to Calypso's island, and thence to his present position. When he has told his tale the compassionate king provides him with ships, and at last he sails for Ithaca.

But the Cyclops' curse prevails. Alone now,

after his last shipwreck, and in someone else's ship, he returns to trouble. His faithful and hopeful wife Penelope has been beleaguered by suitors, who evidently expect to gain the kingdom by marrying the ruler's widow. He has to arrive at his own palace in disguise, and only by waiting for his chance does he eventually outwit the suitors and regain his kingdom.

Homer describes Ithaca in its real geographical form: a small and rugged island, not the sort of place (he says) where one can drive a horse.

Odysseus is presumed dead, and his wife Penelope is importuned by a horde of suitors. She promises to choose her new husband once she has finished weaving a shroud for her father-in-law – a decision which she intends to avoid by unpicking, each night, the work of that day. By the Umbrian painter Pinturicchio (Bernadino Betti), 1454–1513.

The time to which he refers is, we assume, the Mycenaean age, the great Bronze Age civilization of the kingdoms of Mycenae and Pylos. And recent archeology has confirmed that at that time

Ithaca, for all its later poverty, was the seat of a kingdom which probably controlled the coastline of the nearby Peloponnese. This does not mean that there was an identifiably historical Odysseus there, and his strong qualities of folk-hero indicate that the tale could as well have been placed elsewhere. It is sometimes suggested that the long voyage bears some reference to a memory of the Mycenaean trade routes, and certainly sea communications have always been of crucial importance to the Greeks. But the theme of a voyage amongst mysterious islands, a perpetually intriguing image in itself, occurs in other mythologies.

Better known now by the western and therefore the Latin version of his name, Ulysses, this figure has come to represent in modern culture the wandering hero, an idea which lies behind his most recent reincarnation, in James Joyce's *Ulysses*. The themes which Odysseus embodies remain of permanent fascination: the journey, the quest, the narrow escapes – and particularly the hazards of picking one's way through a minefield of moral choices.

~ *Theseus* ~

Theseus is the local hero of Athens, the archetype of the ruler of a city-state to whose example politicians such as Pericles would have been proud to refer. But though its main focus is in Attica his tale ranges widely, and includes in its several phases parts of the stories of other mythic figures.

His father was king of Athens, his mother princess of the small town of Troezen, on the coast of Argolis. Like several other heroes, however, he had a second father, the god Poseidon, who had seduced his mother and thus gained a share in his conception. Already distinguished in his youth by the defeat of bandits and giants, he came in due course from Troezen to his mortal father's city, and there his main story starts. It happened that at the time King Minos of Crete was imposing on the Athenians a terrible form of tax: at fixed intervals they had to send him a tribute of their young men and maidens, to be sacrificed to the Minotaur, the half-human bull which roamed Minos's labyrinth at Knossos. This monster was the offspring of Pasiphaë, the Cretan queen, and a bull sent to Minos by Poseidon as a sacrifice; Poseidon had made the queen fall in love with the animal to punish the king who, impressed by its beauty, had kept it for his herd and sacrificed an ordinary bull instead.

The prince joined the pitiful troop of young people sent to the Cretan sacrifice, his intention being to put an end to the dreadful payment. He arranged with his father that if he succeeded in his mission he would change the usual black sail of the tribute ship to a white one on his return. If the ship came back with a black sail he had failed.

On his arrival in Crete Theseus, outstanding among the Athenians, caught the attention of the king's daughter, Ariadne. She promised him her help, if he would take her back to Athens as his wife. Part of the difficulty of his task was the labyrinth itself, in which the monster was kept. Even if Theseus overcame the Minotaur, he would be unable to find his way to safety. Ariadne's aid took the form of providing him with a ball of string, so that by unrolling it as he went in he would be able to retrace his steps by winding it up again.

It is clear that what the tale has in mind here is a labyrinth in the sense in which we understand it, a series of passages. The basements of Knossos (we may guess from the present ruins) might well have seemed like such a maze to a visiting stranger. Perhaps the word *labyrinthos* came to have the meaning of a maze through this connection; but the palace itself had as its emblem the *labrys*, a double-headed axe, and this is what originally gave it such a name. Carved on the walls, carried in procession, perhaps used at sacrifices, this symbol of Knossos (examples of which one may now see in the museum at Heraclion) was everywhere in the complex building. And if we may judge by the frescoes from Knossos in which young men are seen leaping over bulls, the Minoan bull ceremonies were in later times a form of spectacular game. The story, however, seems to refer to a primitive habit of human sacrifice to a bull-god. At any rate it shows the end of this, since the heroic Theseus, needless to say, succeeded in destroying the Minotaur.

With the help of Ariadne's string he found his way back out of the labyrinthine passages of Knossos. The Athenians sailed away at once, taking Ariadne with them, and broke their journey on the island of Naxos. Here, in a strangely unheroic moment of treachery, Theseus abandoned his protectress, contravening his promise to make her his wife. Why he did so the story oddly enough does not make clear, though some versions suggest that he was under the influence of a spell which caused him to forget her. She for her part was understandably dismayed, and was only comforted by the arrival of the god Dionysus, who became her husband instead. We can still see a part of her wedding regalia: a half-circle of stars, now called the Corona Borealis, near to the constellation of Hercules.

Perhaps the same forgetfulness which caused him to leave his bride on Naxos continued to

Theseus is fêted by fellow Athenians after he has slain the Minotaur. From a fresco in Pompeii.

influence him. At any rate the next episode seems to be a moral requital, since he arrived home to tragedy. His father had been watching from the Acropolis above Athens for the returning ship. But Theseus had omitted to change the black sail, and the king assumed that his son was dead, sacrificed to the Minotaur. He leapt to his own death from the ledge of rock where the pretty Nike temple now stands.

Theseus then became king of Athens, where he had a stormy but forceful reign. The story attributes to his time the origins of social and political institutions, and of the expansion of the city-state of Athens. In the meantime he gained a son by the Amazon, Antiope, yet married not her

The temple of Nike, site of the death of Theseus's father.

using her powers to make his stepmother fall in love with him.

When Phaedra disclosed her love to Hippolytus he was naturally horrified. He angrily rejected her approaches, and she reacted by accusing him publicly of attempting to seduce her. When this false news reached Theseus he believed it, banished his son in anger, and in doing so called to his father Poseidon to send down his anger on Hippolytus. As the youth drove his chariot along the shore the sea-god sent a monster from the waves, and the terrified horses dragged Hippolytus to his death. He died by means of the animals for which he had lived.

The name itself, Hippolytus, proclaims a connection with horses, and probably the story is descended from a remote memory of a horse-cult, perhaps involving a sacrifice to a horse-god, just as the previous episode may have been distantly derived from a sacrifice to a bull-god. The gods of Greece in their early form were not distinctly specialized, and Poseidon is one who has overlapping functions. Though god of the sea, he was also a god of bulls and of horses; in one episode of his story, he himself became a horse.

Theseus's other adventures, like those of Odysseus and Heracles, included an expedition to the land of the dead (his intention being to carry off Persephone, queen of Hades) from where he escaped only with the aid of Heracles. The journey to the other world is a common feature in Greek and other mythologies, the notable sign of the hero being that, unlike the rest of us, he returns.

When Theseus came back to Attica he found his position as king endangered. One of his escapades had been to abduct Helen, daughter of the king of Sparta, and her brothers had come to demand her return. Ageing now, he found it safer to retreat, and went to take refuge on the northern island of Skyros. There the king, Lycomedes, in an outburst of jealousy, lured him to the top of the cliff which rears over the town and the bay, and threw him over. It was an

but Ariadne's sister Phaedra, now the sister of Minos's successor, with whom Theseus formed an alliance. Another phase of his troubled life then began.

The son Hippolytus had inherited his mother's love of horses and hunting, and devoted himself to Artemis, the virgin goddess of the hunt. He remained chaste, and paid no homage to the love-goddess Aphrodite. The two goddesses are contrasted in the mythology: Artemis hard and lacking in sensuality, Aphrodite gentle and lovely. On this occasion, however, the latter took offence; it did not seem natural to her for the youth to ignore her so completely, and her jealousy overcame her. She took her revenge by

ΠΕΙΡΙΘΟΟΣ   ΛΑΟΔΑΜΕΙΑ

The lovesick Phaedra (seated). Hovering in front of her is the winged figure of the god Eros.

undignified end for so great a hero.

As the founder of Athens' political dominance, Theseus had a role to play in later times; and when the new stability provided by the democracies of Cleisthenes and Cimon permitted thoughts of territorial expansion, *c.* 478 BC, it was time for Theseus to make a come-back. This was arranged by the Athenians in characteristically literal terms. Cimon ordered the return of Theseus's bones from Skyros, in 474, and the bones were duly discovered there and brought to Athens. At the same time the story was resurrected, and Theseus became established as conqueror and king. So firmly was he thus embedded in the history of Attica that Plutarch, writing in the early decades of this era, included the life of Theseus among his historical biographies.

~ *Achilles* ~

It is a curious feature of many of the Greek heroes that some of their deeds are rather less than heroic. Perhaps this reveals a desire in the minds of those who moulded them to reassure themselves that their human fallibility was shared by the figures they reverenced.

Achilles, portrayed on a Greek amphora, *c.* 455 BC.

Achilles was the son of the sea-nymph Thetis and Peleus, king of a northern area of Greece. His mother wished him to be immortal like herself, and for this purpose held him in the river Styx, a process which inevitably left a fatal mortal portion, the heel by which she held him. The child was coached by the wise centaur Cheiron, and grew at the usual heroic prodigious rate. Thetis knew from the start what his fate would be, but even so, with a foolishness more suited to a mortal, tried to prevent it.

Achilles was destined to die at Troy, and events began to move steadily in that direction. At the marriage of his parents all the gods had been present, among them the goddess of discord, Eris. She had chosen this opportunity to create long-lasting havoc by throwing down in front of the distinguished guests a golden apple bearing the inscription 'To the fairest'. This had inflamed the smouldering jealousy of the three main goddesses, Hera, wife of Zeus, Athena, goddess of wisdom, and the love-goddess Aphrodite. Which of them would win the prize?

Zeus wisely refused to act as judge, and an impartial arbitrator was found in the person of Paris, prince of Troy. The goddesses approached him unashamedly with appropriate bribes, and he finally rejected both Hera's offer of wealth and Athena's offer of wisdom. As events proved, he could have found a use for the latter. But Aphrodite had offered him a woman as beautiful as herself, and he gave her the prize.

The woman in question was Helen, queen of Sparta. A minor inconvenience was that she was somebody else's wife, but Aphrodite undertook to make the necessary arrangements. Helen fell in love with Paris while he was on a visit to Sparta, her husband, Menelaus, being conveniently away. They eloped to Troy, and it was as a result of this that the gathering of forces took place which led to the long and eventful Trojan War.

Menelaus and his brother Agamemnon began to call on the assistance of their allies, but one of

'The Judgment of Paris': a 15th-century painting of the Tuscan School.

them, Achilles, could not be found. Ever fearful for his safety, and knowing what she did of his future, his mother Thetis had hidden him. It is one of the least heroic aspects of his career that we then find him dressed as a girl and living among the maidens at the court of Lycomedes, king of Skyros. Greek mythology, like many others, is densely intertwined, and even in this short expedition into it we keep encountering old friends: it was this same King Lycomedes who pushed the hero Theseus to his death; and Achilles was tracked down and identified by none other than Odysseus, not above such tricks himself. Odysseus trapped the hero into revealing himself by laying before the maidens of the court an assortment of feminine gifts with, among them, a shield and a spear. Achilles, evidently not as devious, chose these; and thus he found himself involved in the Trojan War. It is a common theme in the biographies of mythic heroes that destiny can never be avoided.

Achilles, being almost immortal, became the main champion of the besieging Greeks. He figures as the hero of Homer's *Iliad*, but characteristically Homer does not present him without criticism. It is no coincidence, but rather part of the plan of the story-teller, that what we remember most about him is his bad temper. Rather arrogant and conceited, he was disposed to take any opposition to his will as an attack on his dignity.

Achilles brought with him a valuable fighting force known as the Myrmidons, from the word for ant, since Zeus had created men out of ants to provide troops for Achilles' father, Peleus. The *Iliad* opens with the episode which caused him to withdraw this force from the field, crucially affecting the balance of power.

No progress is being made by the Greeks in the long war, and it appears that Apollo is against them. The reason is revealed by the prophet Calchas: Agamemnon has taken as mistress the daughter of Apollo's priest, and refuses to return her. Achilles advises him to give her up; but the matter develops into a personal quarrel as Agamemnon, while complying, points out that Achilles intends to retain his own captured mistress. The enmity between the two erupts when the high-king takes Achilles' girl to replace his own. It seems that for the remainder of the war the angry Achilles and his men will sit by their ships and refuse to help Agamemnon. The effects of this dudgeon, and the events which overcome it, form the central story of the *Iliad*.

Warned by his mother that to stay and fight would be fatal to him, Achilles is determined to go home. But he does not do so, and the plight of the army is finally so severe as to move him to help. The Greeks have been beaten back to the

Achilles binds Patroclus' wounds after an earlier battle. 5th-century BC Greek bowl.

beach, and their ships, the lifeline to home, are in danger. Though he will not go into the fight himself he sends his friend Patroclus in command of his Myrmidons. Spurred by an initial success, Patroclus is tempted to pursue the fleeing Trojans towards their city, where he is killed by their champion Hector through the intervention of the god Apollo himself, who joins the fight on the side of Troy. Achilles is moved by this to re-enter the conflict, and in due course settles his account with Hector. His own death is foretold, but the *Iliad* ends before it takes place.

The most famous event of the Trojan War also lies beyond the end of the *Iliad*: the story of the wooden horse and the taking of Troy is told later, in Homer's *Odyssey*. The death of Achilles too is told there by the ghost of Agamemnon, and when Odysseus visits Hades and talks with the famous dead he finds among them the great hero Achilles. He was killed, inevitably, by a wound to his only mortal part, his heel, which was struck

The gold mask of a Mycenaean king, discovered in 1876 by Heinrich Schliemann.

him is part of a general criticism of the values of war, the ultimate pettiness of all quarrels and of all attempts to preserve inflated dignity. Achilles, as the hero of the *Iliad*, is a representative of the theme embodied in the idea of the Trojan War.

As so often, this sequence in Homer and in myth seems to have had a historical counterpart. There has always been tension between the eastern part of Europe and the coasts of Asia Minor, and Greek history from the age of myth and legend to the present day is beset with conflicts very similar geographically and politically to those which smouldered between the realms of Agamemnon and Priam of Troy. When the enterprising German archeologist Heinrich Schliemann excavated at the reputed site of Troy in 1872 he revealed a long succession of cities on the same spot, and no doubt these had been destroyed by enemies on several occasions. Troy seems to have been in existence from about 3000 BC, and to have persisted until about the fifth century AD. There was a city there during Mycenaean times, and it came to a violent end at about the time, around 1250 BC, when the events described in the legend are traditionally held to have occurred. Homer was not writing history; in telling the story of Achilles he was expressing on several different levels a range of general, even perpetual, ideas. But myth and legend often hang their themes on a historical hook, and the fact that Achilles at Troy may well have had a historical original is an interesting illustration of this process.

by an arrow shot by Paris with the aid of Apollo. Expressing Homer's view of death as a shadow half-state, he says pitifully, 'Let me be on earth again, and I would rather be a poor man's serf, than be king of all these dead.'

The playwright Euripides perhaps extracts from Homer the essence of the character of Achilles, when he portrays him in his play *Iphigenia* as boastful, conceited and ultimately morally weak. Yet in the *Iliad* we find him displaying occasional moments of nobility, as in his grief over the death of Patroclus, and the ambiguity of judgment which Homer directs on

ᕽ Demeter & Persephone ᕽ

Elevsis now is a dirty cargo port on the oil-stained coast opposite Salamis. Once it was the centre of a religion which spanned the civilized world and survived for about 2,000 years. The

cult of Demeter at Elevsis was as dominant in its time as Christianity has been since.

Just as myth and legend have a relationship with history, so they also have links with religion.

And the religion of Demeter was firmly based on a fable, itself expressed in an official scriptural form, the so-called 'Homeric Hymn to Demeter'. This was not in fact composed by Homer, dating possibly from about 600 BC, but it records old and traditional material expressed in a Homeric style of detailed realism.

The story tells of a time when the deities used to appear in the countryside of Greece, and the goddess Demeter and her daughter Persephone were walking there in the fields one spring day. The daughter had strayed from her mother, gathering flowers. She stooped to pick a blossom even more lovely than the rest, and as she reached for it the earth gaped at her feet. Hades (later known as Pluto), the god of the underworld, the land of the dead, appeared from the ground in his chariot and carried her away. Hearing her call for help, her mother searched for her, but in vain, for the earth had closed again. After wandering in dismay for nine days she was told by Helios, the sun, where her daughter had gone. It appeared that Zeus had permitted the rape, and Demeter angrily refused to attend his court on Mount Olympus. She went to live among mortals, disguised as an old woman, and eventually came to the city of Elevsis – or, as it is spelt in classical form, 'Eleusis'.

The royal family of Elevsis were hospitable and kind to the old woman, giving her the job of caring for their infant. The child, however, grew so unnaturally quickly under her divine influence that it became clear that she was not an ordinary mortal. She revealed her identity, and they built a temple for her to dwell in below their citadel.

Demeter was still inconsolable about the loss of her daughter. As a result of her refusal to join the other gods, the earth turned barren. A disastrous famine spread, which threatened to extinguish mankind. The gods of Olympus were fearful of the possible results, since men provide for gods the sustenance of sacrifice and worship. They came to Elevsis to beg the goddess to rejoin them, but she made the condition that her daughter should be returned. Zeus then in-

Demeter (left) and Persephone, also known as 'Kore' (the Virgin), with Triptolemus, an Eleusinian prince whom Demeter instructed in the arts of agriculture.
5th-century BC bas-relief.

tervened, and sent his messenger Hermes to Hades to bring Persephone back.

They burst out into the sunlight in the chariot in which she had been abducted, and an emotional reunion between mother and daughter took place outside the temple at Elevsis. With Demeter's decision to return to the Olympian gathering, the flowers bloomed again, the leaves came back to the trees and the land regained its fertility. But there was still a qualification to this pleasure. It was a peculiarity of the land of the dead that anyone who took food there must return; and although Persephone had been careful not to eat while she was there, she had been persuaded by Hades to swallow the seeds of a pomegranate. That was enough to ensure that she was never to be free of the bonds of the

Hades abducts Persephone: by the Italian sculptor, Gian Lorenzo Bernini, 1598–1680.

Elevsinian princes the principles of cultivation, and told them to travel the world teaching it to men. With that new science, it is perhaps implied, some precaution can be taken against both the repetition of failures of fertility and the annual withdrawal of the earth's vitality.

Before she left for Olympus, Demeter taught the king and his court something more, not unconnected, we guess, with these great themes of death and renewal. She showed them the mysteries, the rituals which they were to practise in her temple there. These were to remain permanently secret, known only to the initiated. Although these rituals were practised at Elevsis for such a long period – they only came to an end with the effects of the hostility of the Goths on the one hand and the Christians on the other, in the fourth century AD – and a period too which is otherwise highly documented, and although many famous people in the Greek and later the Roman world became initiates, nothing of their secret has ever been revealed. It is known that the rites involved the showing of certain objects and the speaking of certain words. What these objects and words were will probably never be known.

We know that the initiation and the ceremony in general gave those who experienced them a feeling of hope. From what they say, and what little we know of the form the ceremony took, we may reasonably guess that the religion was centred on the hope of survival after death. It would be in keeping with other such mysteries if a dramatization of the story of Persephone's descent and return were enacted, and if the initiation correspondingly symbolized the death and resurrection of the participants. It is significant, as has been mentioned, that before his descent into the underworld the hero Heracles was said in his story to have undergone initiation at Elevsis.

There seems little doubt that Demeter's tale is partly about the need to reconcile oneself to death, a problem it solves through the hope of renewal, on the model of the annual renewal of nature. Demeter has counterparts in this role in

underworld. Consequently it was arranged that she should spend a third of the year below the ground, and the remainder with her mother.

There is a clear reference here to the cycles of nature, the barrenness of winter occurring while Demeter mourns for her daughter's temporary absence, spring returning with Persephone's re-emergence. The overall story seems to contain a summary too of the experiences of great droughts and famines. And some confirmation of these connections is given by the tale's addition of the theme of the introduction of agriculture. Before she left Elevsis, it says, Demeter taught the other mythologies, and the story of Persephone is particularly closely paralleled by one of Middle Eastern origin. It is significant that Demeter reveals by her name itself that her role is even more general than her story implies, since the 'meter' part is none other than the base-word for 'mother' in the common source of European languages. It gives us such words as the German 'Mutter' and Latin 'mater'. The 'de' of Demeter's name is thought to mean 'earth', in which case as earth-mother she would originally have represented the providing function of the natural world, a recognition that we are sustained by the ground we live on. In such a role she is one aspect of the universal goddess worshipped very widely in primitive times.

Persephone, for her part, reappears in mythology as queen of the dead, a more dreadful figure than her innocence in the original story would suggest. Demeter's story too has episodes unconnected with this central doctrine, revealing other aspects of her nature. In particular she seems to have been associated with horses. Greek mythology is accumulated from different sources, and as a result functions often overlap. Poseidon, too, appears to have been in part a horse deity. And one story seems to make this link between the two: when Demeter is at one point wooed by Poseidon, she hides from him by becoming a horse and grazing among a herd. The god becomes a stallion and mates with her, and presumably this episode of evasion and pursuit results from a mistaken memory of the symbolism of a horse cult.

Not much remains of the great sanctuary at Elevsis which housed the celebrations of Demeter's cult. The temple which at one time held 3,000 people is a level platform now, and the area of excavations around it presents a confusing maze of structures representing the uncovering of many phases of the place's use. Archeology has revealed that the same central site had been continuously sacred. The earliest of the successive temples on that spot, a small structure of the Mycenaean age, dates from about 1500 BC.

Ruins of the Sanctuary at Elevsis.

That was the physical equivalent of the temple in the story which the king of Elevsis built at the command of the goddess herself, and it gives us a clue as to the age of the cult of Demeter.

~ *Gwydion* ~

Although it is a small country, Britain has a population made up of several different elements drawn together over a long period. The Continental influences have been so strong that it is hard to find features in the culture of the nation which are specifically British, and partly because of this confusion the true mythology of Britain is very little known. Yet the later legendary heroes, such as Arthur and Merlin, developed from a basis which, when isolated, is both clearly mythological and clearly British.

The pre-Roman inhabitants of Britain were one branch of a large group of peoples who had a material culture and a language-family in common, usually referred to as the Celts. When they came to Britain from Europe during several centuries of the first millennium BC, they probably brought with them a form of religion which developed in their new island home into something which was in later years to be particularly associated with Britain: Druidism. It was still flourishing here at the time of the Roman invasion of Gaul, which is the date of Britain's first recorded history.

We do not know for certain that the mythology which has survived reflects elements of that important British religion, but it does have recognizable religious aspects. We can speculate that when the national religion had been suppressed by the Roman occupation it was preserved in the form of tales, and when it re-emerged in the context of Christianity it was as tales that it remained. The gods had become the heroes of fables. Such a figure, it seems, is Gwydion.

Gwydion is probably the earliest example of a type which has remained strong in British myth and folk-lore: the wizard, the prophet, the spell-weaving plotter who protects his friends and destroys his enemies. His successor in this role was Merlin, who became one of the most popular and famous British mythic conceptions. The character inhabits a world of magic and enchantment which brings with it, in the stories, a marked feeling of its antiquity.

Gwydion is known as the son of Don; and although he himself occurs in no other mythology, this person, Don, provides a recognizable link both with Continental origins and with the related ancient culture across the Irish Sea. In Ireland this Don is the goddess Danaan or Danu, mother of the gods, and since we find the name recurring throughout Europe we may guess that we have found a deity belonging to a time before the period of diffusion. Several rivers were called after the goddess, including the great Russian river Don, and the Danube. References to the same name are found as far apart as Greece and Scandinavia, and even spread into India, where Danu, mother and wife of major gods, appears in the ancient Sanskrit scriptures. Gwydion therefore has an impressive pedigree.

The story as we have it seems to refer to a local cult centred in an area of north-west Wales. It tells of the disputes of tribal groups, perhaps representing the conflict of rival religious

Gwydion's successor in the role of mythical wizard was Merlin, seen here in an engraving of a drawing by Gustav Doré.

A mountain stream in north-west Wales, home of the stories of Gwydion and his son, Lleu.

what is now Wales, the north and the south. He steals the sacred swine of Pryderi, king of south Wales, and carries them north. During the war which ensues between Pryderi and Math, king of the north, Gwydion and his brother achieve their aim of gaining access to a maiden in Math's court. When this is discovered, Math (who is also a magician of some power) inflicts on the brothers a strange and severe punishment. He turns them each into an animal of the opposite sex – Gwydion a stag, his brother a hind – condemning them to live together and produce offspring. This, with successive changes to a wild boar and sow, and so on, is repeated, with reversed roles, so that each has young by the other. It is hard not to see in this sequence a reflection of the belief in transmigration of souls, by which the Hindus consider that misdeeds in this life will result in reincarnation in animal form, which is a belief said by Caesar to have been held by the Celts of Gaul. In accordance with this principle of punishment, Math considered they had expiated their sin at the end of several rebirths, and restored them to human form.

The story turns then to a new figure, Gwydion's sister Aranrhod, daughter of Don. She too is something of a fearful figure, and the tale tells of her attempts to thwart the rearing of her son, whom Gwydion treats also as his. Although the story is not explicit it seems to refer to a case of brother–sister marriage, such as that of Cronus and Rhea and of Zeus and Hera in Greek myth. The struggle between the parents for domination of the child is also paralleled in other mythologies.

Aranrhod swears on the boy, Lleu, a number of destinies, which Gwydion then has to circumvent. He shall not have a name until he gets one from her – but a trick of Gwydion's startles her into an exclamation, which gives him a name. He shall not have weapons until he is given them by her; but Gwydion causes an apparent battle outside the castle, and Aranrhod hurries to arm her disguised son. Gwydion's role

factions. Since it survived only in medieval manuscripts, it is clearly much distorted even from the disguised form in which it may have emerged after the Roman withdrawal. But for all that, it conveys a powerful sense of the mysterious.

Gwydion is a magician of great power, and he uses his arts to stir up a war between two areas of here confirms him as the figure of the trick-playing magician, but the struggle between him and Aranrhod had an aspect of a general theme which seems to occur again and again in myth: the conflict of a matriarchal principle with a patriarchal one, a concern which may reflect a change in social customs with the movement of people in Europe at some very remote time. There is plenty of evidence that mythology does perpetuate some extremely ancient memories.

Gwydion wins, and Aranrhod retires from the narrative. She, like the other figures in the story, is not a fanciful invention, but seems to have been another major deity in her own right. Her castle, where the events take place, is said in legend to be a submerged reef of stones, once supposedly dry land, off the North Wales coast. But it is also the Celtic name for a heavenly constellation, Caer Aranrhod, Aranrhod's Castle; and as such it gives us a link to an event mentioned in the story of Theseus, since this is the same constellation as that supposed to be Ariadne's coronet, the Corona Borealis. This, together with the possible connection of their names, may make us wonder whether the two heroines have evolved from a common source.

What of Gwydion himself? As so often in myth, it is his name which reveals his true identity. It appears to be the British form of Woden, the Teutonic god re-imported into Britain by the Anglo-Saxons to give us the name of the day in the middle of our week, Wednesday (Woden's-day). Also known in Scandinavia as Odin, this figure was a god of storm, trickery and battle, essentially, like Gwydion, a magician, an intriguer and intervener by spells and sorcery in other people's lives. As such he is associated at least by affinity with the Roman god Mercury, and this was sufficiently recognized in Roman Europe for the Germans to translate the Latin day named after Mercury, *Mercurii dies*, as Woden's-day. Julius Caesar noted that the Celts of Gaul worshipped above all others a god equivalent to the Roman Mercury. Was that, then, the Continental prototype of the later British god whom we now meet as the wizard-hero Gwydion?

Gwydion's story offers much room for speculation. It gives us some insight into the possible links of myth with religion, and shows something of the development of independent British tradition from its distant Continental Celtic origins. Perhaps what it does most is preserve for us in our scientific and practical world a little of the tension of mystery and puzzlement of a world where the unknown dominated the understood.

~ *Lleu* ~

If Gwydion is British myth's representative of the paternal figure, the wise old man, then Lleu is a typical example of the younger hero. In many mythologies such a figure arrives in the story of an older generation and begins to dominate it.

Lleu's story begins, in fact, where we left Gwydion's. The old wizard had brought him up, tricked his mother into giving him a name – Lleu Llaw Gyffes, which means something like 'Fair deft hand' – and weapons; but there remained a third curse. He was not to have a wife of any race then on earth. The two magicians, Math and Gwydion, set about overcoming this destiny, and in doing so give rise to one of British mythology's

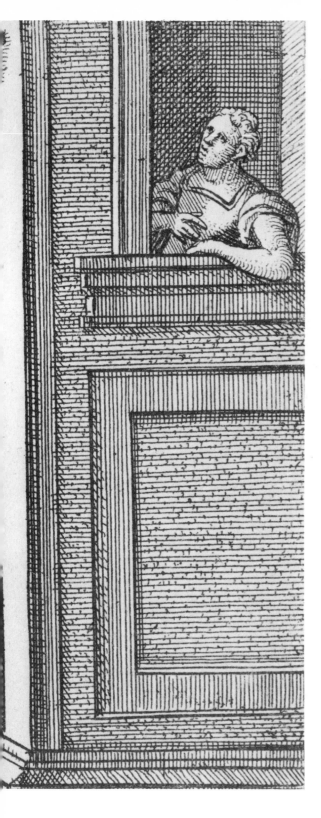

most memorable images. They make for him a wife out of flowers. The story tells that they used wild flowers native to the country, common still on our hillsides in the first burst of early summer: the flowers of the oak, the meadowsweet, and the broom. They called the resulting woman Blodeuedd, from the Welsh for flower.

She and Lleu settle to married life; but Blodeuedd's role in the story is to be that of the unfaithful and conspiring wife. While Lleu is away visiting Math, she invites into their castle a neighbouring lord and the two become lovers. They plot to destroy Lleu on his return, but this is a matter complicated by Lleu's heroic status. Like several other heroes of myth, he can only be killed under certain circumstances. The same theme of near-immortality occurred in the case of Achilles, and Shakespeare uses it in the witches' prophecy to Macbeth. We, the audience, know that the hero will die, however impossible it appears to be. Achilles will be struck in the heel; Birnham Wood will come to Dunsinane. The story uses the tension of the situation by making us wonder how the paradox will be resolved.

In Lleu's case there is a list of apparently contradictory conditions. He can be killed neither in a house nor outside, on horseback nor on foot, and evidently (from the outcome) neither on water nor dry land. Like Delilah and Samson, Blodeuedd persuades Lleu to tell her how, then, it can be done. Lleu is naive enough to demonstrate the circumstances, and consequently we find him (in yet another memorable image) standing with one foot on the back of a goat, the other on the edge of a bath-tub, under a canopy of thatch on the bank of a river. Destiny is sometimes obliged to take bizarre forms.

The lover in ambush strikes him then with a specially-made spear, and sure enough the blow is fatal. But Lleu does not simply die; instead he flies upwards in the form of an eagle, a detail

Mercury, the Roman god to whom Lugh and thus Lleu may be related. Engraving by Peter van der Borcht.

which seems to relate this story to that of Heracles, who also left for the home of the gods as an eagle when he died. Perhaps this represents another reflection of the ancient Celtic belief in transmigration of souls. The eagle is a familiar emblem in myth, being particularly connected with the sky-god Zeus, and Lleu's transformation, like Heracles', is thought by some to mark him as a sun-hero.

His mentor Gwydion devotedly searched the forests for him in his metamorphosed shape, and found him perched in an oak tree – a tree both sacred to Zeus, like the eagle, and connected with the Celtic religion of the Druids. Using his magic powers, Gwydion returned Lleu to human form, and in due course the two set off to take their revenge on Blodeuedd. Hearing they were coming, she left the court with her maidens, the latter so afraid of Gwydion that they walked looking backwards. In this way the maidens all walked into a lake and drowned; Gwydion then caught Blodeuedd alone, and wrought his revenge by once again using his spells. Blodeuedd became an owl, and you can hear her still bemoaning this fate.

Although the story as it appears in the medieval tales in the collection known as the Mabinogion has now all the appearance of being a popular traditional tale, its choice of hero ties it to matters of wider significance and greater import. Just as Gwydion and Don carried with them into the earlier part of the same narrative (known as 'Math, son of Mathonwy') some mythic ramifications which seem to stem from the Indo-European roots of the peoples of Europe, so Lleu is far from being the simple hero-figure which he appears.

Firstly he has a direct counterpart in Irish myth, and so illustrates the overlap between the British and Irish material, perhaps the result partly of a common origin, partly of many periods of mutual influence. Lugh, or Lug, is connected with Lleu not only linguistically but also by his attributes. He is characterized as skilled and inventive, qualities which Lleu

shared with Gwydion, and so, like Gwydion, might be related to the Celtic version of the Roman god Mercury. Lugh's name, which means 'bright one', and the fact that he is frequently described as having a brightly shining face, make it seem likely that he too is among other things some form of sun-representative.

In the Irish stories Lugh, like Lleu, plays the part of the younger hero arriving at the established court of an older order. This sort of arrival seems related to a theme which we have seen already illustrated in another form in the story of Heracles, whose cult began to rival that of his father Zeus in classical Greece. Lugh comes to the king's court at Tara bringing his many skills and his superhuman fighting power, and before long he, rather than the king, is leading the people of Ireland in battle. Among other episodes one sequence of his story once again reminds us of Heracles, though with the roles reversed, when he sets some wrongdoers a long series of apparently impossible tasks.

Lugh is more clearly than Lleu on the divine side of that border on which gods and heroes merge. He is a god among men. And in fact this is probably closer to his original form, since we find that as Lugus he was a god of the Continental Celts. So prominent and widespread was his cult that his name is still recorded in place-names all over Europe. In France, Lyon and Laon both owe their names to him, in Holland Leiden, and further into central Europe so does Leignitz. Here in Britain the prominent Roman outpost Luguvalium became in post-Roman times the British Carlisle, which consequently is also connected with Lugus.

Names are among the most enduring of human constructs, and the god Lugus, the hero Lleu, continued to undergo reincarnation. It has been convincingly argued that it was from this source that the otherwise puzzling name Lancelot came, via the Celtic Llenlleawc and the Old French Lancelin; and if so then the character too has shown considerable powers of survival. Lancelot arrives at Arthur's court and begins to dominate it much in the way that Lugh takes over at Tara and Lleu becomes prominent in the story of Gwydion. They are related by their roles; but perhaps too they are an instance of the type of immortality which a divine hero, as the embodiment of a perpetual idea, possesses.

～ CuChulainn ～

CuChulainn (pronounced Ker-*hool*in) has been called the Achilles of Ireland. He is the central hero of the literature dealing with Ireland's heroic age, a body of stories known as the Ulster Cycle. There he figures as the doomed hero, the champion of his people who chooses for himself a short life with much fame, as Achilles did when he decided to stay at Troy.

Like so many other heroes of myth, CuChulainn had a double parentage. His mother was an Irish princess, his father both the god Lugh and Conchobar, king of Ulster, who, in some versions of the episode, was said to have sired CuChulainn on his own sister – a reference to brother–sister incest which we have met before in both the Greek and the British stories. His origins, in fact, are generally remarkable. At the time of his birth two foals (which will later become his chariot horses) are born to a mare standing outside the door. In many tales we find this close association of a child with an animal, and this connection in the story of CuChulainn perhaps indicates that he, like the Greek hero Hippolytus, may derive an element of his character from the hero of a horse-cult.

At the start of his life he had a different name, Setanta, and he only gained the one by which he is known through the episode which brought him into his heroic career. While playing ball one day, he was attacked by the monstrous hound which guarded the property of Culann, the smith. He threw his ball down the animal's throat, and destroyed the dog by hurling it with his bare hands against a pillar. The smith was so upset at the loss of his guard-dog that Setanta undertook to do the dog's work of protection. Thus he came to be known as Cu Chulainn, the hound of Culann.

His early adventures consist of the overcoming of the champions of his country's enemies, in the course of which he exhibits a notable characteristic, his battle-fury. CuChulainn becomes so heated in this state that not even his own side can go near him. When he returns successful from one adventure, the Ulstermen have to send their women out naked to meet him, causing him to turn away his face in embarrassment, whereupon they are able to seize him. They plunge him into three successive vats of water: the first bursts with the heat, the second boils, and the third, as he cools, becomes hot.

Like the *Iliad*, the Ulster Cycle shows us the world of a warring society, an idealized picture, in this case, of an independent Celtic state. The people of Ulster, under Conchobar, are at war against the kingdom of Connacht. Two main episodes stand out, known respectively as Bricriu's Feast and the Cattle-raid of Cooley.

On the latter occasion the men of Connacht have invaded Ulster to seize the bull of Cuailnge (for convenience transliterated Cooley, as it is pronounced), and at the critical moment the Ulstermen are rendered helpless by a strange disease, a periodic illness which overcomes them, perhaps the result of a curse. CuChulainn, who is immune to it, holds off the enemy single-handed

until his army recovers. The bull of Cooley is an enormous animal of mystical origin, a counterpart to a bull owned by the men of Connacht. These two had in previous existences been two kings, and had gone through various forms of rebirth before becoming these bulls. Here we have once more not only the theme of the sacred bull, as in the Cretan stories, but also the idea of reincarnation in animal form which is so common in the Celtic myths.

The other episode concerns a vast heroic feast in the hall of Bricriu, who is characterized as a stirrer-up of trouble. He invites the reluctant Ulstermen to this lavish spread, and they, in spite of their fear that tragedy will result, are obliged to accept. The dispute which breaks out is over who shall have the champion's portion, and CuChulainn fights with two rival heroes. The three contending warriors are tested by repeated encounters, CuChulainn eventually being judged the winner. But Bricriu is not satisfied with this dispute, and adds to it a contest for precedence among the champions' wives. The first to enter the hall will be the supreme lady of Ulster. The other champions make various attempts to speed the entry of their wives, but CuChulainn lifts the whole side of the hall to allow his wife to enter first.

The continuing rivalry is settled in favour of CuChulainn by means of a contest which forms one of the primary images of Celtic lore. The champion has to undertake a beheading test put by a giant challenger who arrives at the feast, a being who allows himself to be beheaded on condition that his opponent will do the same the following night. The giant picks up his severed head and walks out of the hall, and the other two champions rather reasonably shirk their part of the bargain. Only CuChulainn, when it comes to his turn, puts his head on the block. The giant

A medieval manuscript illustration: watched by King Arthur, the Green Knight holds up his head, which Sir Gawain has just severed.

reveals that his purpose was to achieve this proof of valour, and lets him go. This image proves its enduring effectiveness by forming the main sequence in the Middle English poem *Sir Gawain and the Green Knight*.

CuChulainn's death, like those of other heroes, is foretold. In his case too a complicated set of conditions must be fulfilled before it can take place, just as in the story of Lleu. There is a way that heroes must die – Achilles through his mortal heel, Heracles by the agency of the hydra's blood – and, however improbable it is, we know that the story will finally reach it. In several instances in Irish story the hero has a series of taboos, and his death is the result of the unlikely breaking of these, one by one.

When CuChulainn sets out on his last journey, a whole set of omens foretells his doom. Among these is the behaviour of his horse, the Grey of Macha, one of the foals born with him and so in a sense a spiritual twin. This supernatural animal now tries to prevent him leaving. We are told that he weeps tears of blood, as the wonderful horses of Achilles wept after the fateful death of Patroclus. As CuChulainn leaves he is begged by weeping women to desist, and on his way to his last battle he passes some women washing a blood-stained garment in a stream. The garment, it is revealed, is his; he has seen into the future.

Further on this same terrible journey he finds himself put in a quandary, faced with the paradox of having to break one or other of his rules of destiny, when he passes three crones cooking a dog. It is prohibited for him to eat dog, his namesake; yet it is prohibited for him to pass a cooking-hearth and refuse hospitality at it. This situation, where forces convene to produce a crossroads of conditions, a paradox in action, is a basic factor in many heroes' stories.

By playing upon his magical obligations, his enemies trick him into taking part in a fight he would have avoided, and into parting with his spear. Finally he ties himself to a pillar so that he may die standing up, and the battle-goddess and her attendants alight on his shoulder in the form of crows. His attackers know then that he is doomed, and dare to come near enough to cut off his head.

CuChulainn dies in a series of such striking images, his battle-light shining about him. He dies a hero, his nobility unscathed; and has survived as such in the culture and imagination of Ireland.

~ *Finn* ~

If CuChulainn is the epitome of the solitary champion, Finn is a perfect example of the leader of a war-band. He has much in common in this respect and in others with King Arthur of British legend. They are both characterized by the fact that they are seldom found without their troops. Finn occurs in a body of stories known, after him, as the Fenian Cycle, which contrasts in mood and style with the Ulster Cycle and its stories of CuChulainn. Finn (more correctly spelt Fionn) lives in a world less heroic and more down-to-earth than that of CuChulainn.

He and his men are associated particularly with the natural countryside, a feature which makes his stories equivalent in some ways to those of Robin Hood. The troop, called the Fiana, has strict rules of membership and only accepts those suited to its wild life. They are both a hunting and a warring band, and the wide range of their activities across the land of Ireland, together with their connection with local features in the landscape, points to their background in the folk culture of the ordinary people. The stories were popular in early times and remain so.

Just as Finn and the Fiana are to be found all over Ireland, so they give us a link too with the other Gaelic country of Scotland. Scotland was largely colonized from Ireland during early historical times, and as a result its mythology is partly the same as that of Ireland. Finn, in the form of Fingal, is thus to be found in Scotland too, where he has achieved fame through the Ossianic body of lore, called after his son Ossian, in Irish Oisin. Just as the overlap of the Celtic cultures of Wales and Ireland can be illustrated in the traditional material, so can that of Ireland and Scotland.

The Fiana, like the Arthurian knights, had the function of protecting their country against its enemies. In that role, though living a simple life almost equivalent to that of outlaws, they constituted a warrior élite. It was said that no girl could be married until she had first been offered to the Fiana. Their initiation tests included being buried up to the armpits armed with a shield and a hazel stick while nine warriors threw spears at them. If they were wounded, they were not admitted to Finn's people. Another test involved running through the woods pursued by the others: if a stick cracked under him, or if a branch disturbed his braided hair, the applicant would not be admitted to the Fiana.

Like CuChulainn, Finn started his career with a change of name, being previously known as Demne. He was brought up in secret, hidden from his enemies, by two women in the forest. He distinguished himself in his childhood by defeating monstrous warriors, such as the fire-

One of British myth's greatest figures, King Arthur, appears in the story of Finn. He is pictured here by Gustav Doré.

breathing creature called Aillen who burnt down the court of Tara once a year by first putting its warriors to sleep with enchanting music. Finn stayed awake by pressing a spear-point to his head, and saved Tara by beheading this attacker.

In his youth he became a poet, and through an early episode in his story he also acquired the gift of prophecy and total knowledge. He happened to be given the task of cooking the Salmon of Knowledge, and while doing so he burnt his thumb on the skin of the fish, and put it into his mouth. From that time on, if he sucked his thumb all knowledge would be revealed to him.

The central story of the Fenian Cycle is an elopement theme, a story of deceit and infidelity comparable to that which forms the centre of the Arthurian cycle, with its tensely balanced triangle of Arthur, Lancelot and Guenevere.

One of Finn's most loyal supporters in the Fiana is a man called Diarmaid. Finn's wife Grainne has fallen in love with him, and as early as their wedding feast she contrives to oblige him to elope. She puts the gathering to sleep with a potion, and informs Diarmaid that he is under a supernatural bond to take her away. This sort of powerful spell is a peculiarity of the Irish stories, and its effect, it seems, outweighs even the influence of the friendship and loyalty which Diarmaid feels towards Finn. A long pursuit begins, as Finn and the Fiana track the fleeing couple across the face of Ireland. Though Diarmaid is obliged by the bond to take Grainne away, he remains faithful to Finn by refusing any closer relationship with her. As a sign of this he leaves uncooked meat at each of their sleeping places. One day, however, as they cross a stream, some water splashes on to Grainne's leg. The water, she tells him, is bolder than he is. Such a rebuke to his daring is a reproach which he cannot support, and he becomes her lover.

A pact is eventually made between Finn and Diarmaid, which allows him to return to the Fiana. As a result, a further episode forms the separate story of his death. Together with Finn he goes to hunt the great boar of Ben Gulban, an

animal which (like so many special creatures in Celtic mythology) had once been a human being. In that form it was in fact Diarmaid's own foster-brother, and his destiny was that it would be through him that Diarmaid would suffer his downfall. In spite of this foreknowledge he goes to the boar-hunt.

One of the poisonous bristles from the boar wounds Diarmaid, and nothing can save him except water drunk from the hands of Finn, who has the power of healing. Finn is persuaded to carry water to him from a nearby well, but as he comes back he thinks of Grainne, and lets the water run through his fingers. A second time this happens; and the third time, as he reaches Diarmaid with the healing water, he finds it is too late: Diarmaid has died.

This death by wounding from a boar is bled to death after receiving a wound from a boar's tusk. Supernatural boars occur frequently in mythology, especially in that of the Celts. King Arthur is said in one story to be engaged on a great boar-hunt, and in one of these stories of Finn we find the two troop-leaders from either side of the Irish Sea together. Arthur, in Ireland on a visit, has joined Finn's hunting expedition. He takes a fancy to Finn's three famous hounds, and when he leaves he takes them away. Finn uses his divinatory powers to find out where they have gone, and he and a few companions then pursue Arthur to Britain. They overcome the British leader, bring him and the stolen hounds back to Ireland, and Arthur becomes Finn's liegeman for the rest of his life.

That is the Irish version of what happened. A Welsh tale also tells of a visit by Arthur to Ireland, with, as may be imagined, very different results. In that, the Irish end up begging for mercy. What both stories illustrate is the continual interplay of the culture of the two countries, a communication no doubt not always amicable but made inevitable by the sharing of a common seaway.

The tales of Finn, the Fenian Cycle, did not enter literature until the end of the twelfth century – some five hundred years after the Ulster Cycle had been written down. Before that they belonged to the oral art of the people, clearly their natural homeland. From the start, in their literary form, they have had a strong undercurrent of nostalgia, a longing for the past of an Ireland once great and strong of spirit. The form in which they were written is partly a result of this motivation, since it shows the son of Finn, Oisin, surviving into Christian times. Together with another son of the Fiana he meets St Patrick, and the 'ancients' (as the story terms them) accompany the Christian across Ireland. As they travel, the natural features of the land remind them of the adventures which took place there in the days when the Fiana was at its height, and they recount to the saint and his contemporaries the stories of Finn. It is hard to imagine a stronger image for the expression of the feeling of having outlived one's time.

But Finn's literary career was in fact only just beginning when he emerged from his origins in folk culture during the Middle Ages. The Fenian Cycle soon became more popular than the Ulster Cycle. If Finn is better known now than CuChulainn, it is partly because of this historical overshadowing. A more direct cause, though, is his resurrection by the eighteenth-century Scottish writer, James Macpherson, who published epics supposedly translated from poems by 'Ossian' himself. Although Macpherson invented much of the material, the groundwork of Gaelic ballad survived through his works to ensure Finn's survival, as Fingal, in European literature.

∼ *Thor* ∼

It is not surprising that men should always have been impressed by certain natural phenomena, and that in their puzzlement they should seek a way of making these things comprehensible. Among the most frequent and most obvious of these inexplicable and rather disturbing events is the thunderstorm. The Greeks explained this to themselves as being caused by the anger of Zeus, the sky-god. In the northern lands of Europe people came to much the same conclusion, although the god had a different name. That rumble across the clouds was Thor driving through the sky in his enormous chariot; that flash and bang shooting down the firmament was his hammer flung in anger at some enemy.

This connection between the Norse god Thor and the Roman god Jove, or Jupiter, their version of Zeus, in his role as Thunderer, was recognized by the Germanic people of the Roman-occupied lands of northern Europe. Jove's Day, the Latin *Jovis dies*, thus became Thor's, and so we have Thursday, one link with our ancestry as a nation which is with us still.

The stories and characters of northern gods come to us from some Old Norse poetry which largely originated in Iceland, and was conveyed from there to other lands colonized or influenced by the Viking voyages. The earliest pieces date from about 900 AD, and the body of work in general was collected by an Icelandic historical writer, Snorri Sturluson, in a work known as the 'Prose Edda', in about 1200. This was after the introduction of Christianity to Iceland, in 1000, but although Snorri's view of the matter is distorted by this and in any case must give us a view of paganism in its terminally declining state,

A bronze statuette of Thor, 10th century AD from Eyrarland.

comparison of his work with earlier sources shows him to be conveying a great deal of the essence of the old Nordic religion.

Thor, we are told, drove in a chariot drawn by two wonderful goats. These had the property that he could eat them if he felt hungry, preserving their bones, and in the morning bring them to life again. Besides his goats and his chariot his three main possessions consisted of his hammer, the iron gauntlets which he needed to grasp it, and a belt which increased his

strength when he buckled it on. It was the great stone hammer which chiefly distinguished him. This he could throw at his enemies with the confidence that it would return to him of its own accord. Clearly the hammer represented, to those who believed in these gods, the thunderbolt itself, and its stone nature may have originated in the supposition that a meteorite was the result of thunder. The Romans compared it to Heracles' club. And Thor, as a gigantic warrior figure, as the slayer of giants and monsters and an endless traveller on tremendous tasks, has much in common with that militant hero.

Thor is the protector of gods and men against the evil forces represented by the giants. He is pictured as something of a giant himself, with a large red beard, and in his manner appears as a simple warrior type, straightforward and courageous. His stories tell of his expeditions and his permanent campaign against the giants, without which both Asgard, the citadel of the gods, and Midgard, the world, would be in danger. Often he goes on these trips in company with the god Loki, the trickster among the northern gods, wily, cunning, not always trustworthy – the counterpart, in fact, of Bricriu in Irish myth, and incorporating not a little of the character of the Greek Odysseus. Loki acts as a sort of foil to Thor's bluff naivety. The thunder god occasionally borders on appearing a buffoon, particularly in one story, in which the giants belittle his talents and make him seem of scarcely more than mortal might.

Thor and Loki and two companions have set out once more on one of their expeditions to Giantland. On the journey they come across a huge hall whose entrance-door, much to their surprise, stretches the whole length of its wall. They shelter inside, spending a night disturbed by earthquakes and a sound of roaring. At dawn Thor ventures outside, only to find that the tremors and din of the night were the snoring of a recumbent giant asleep outside. When the giant awakes he reveals that the hall with the wide doorway was his glove, and the small room in which they had taken shelter when the noise began was the glove's thumb.

The giant accompanies them on their way, and rather rashly the gods pool their provender with him and store it in his bag. The next night when he has fallen asleep again they decide to eat, but are unable to undo the knots with which he has tied the bag. Thor's anger gets the better of him, and he strikes the giant with his great stone hammer. Waking, the giant wonders if a leaf has fallen on his head. The second time Thor tries the blow is harder, but the giant mistakes it for a falling acorn. The third time the hammer appears to sink deep into the giant's skull – but he only wonders when he wakes if the birds in the tree above him have been littering him with droppings.

Things are not much better for Thor when he reaches the castle of the giant-king. Challenged to test his ability against the occupants, he first struggles vainly to drain an apparently moderate-sized drinking horn; the level of the liquid in it when he has taken three enormous draughts is much the same as it was before. Then he fails in a feat of strength, being unable to pick up even the giant's cat – a game, the giant says, which the little boys play there. Thor goes on to compound his ignominy by losing a wrestling match with an old woman, the giant's foster-mother.

When the god and his companions are thoroughly humbled, the giant reveals that their failure has been only apparent. He had put them under a spell, so that they had been competing not with beings but with hallucinations. When Thor had tried to kill the giant on his way there, his victim had defended himself by placing mountains in the way. Thor's three strokes had produced three deep valleys. The end of the drinking horn in the contest had been placed in the sea itself, and Thor had succeeded in lowering the level to the extent of giving rise to the tidal ebb. The cat was in fact the World Serpent, the coils of which are stretched around the world. And the old woman was old age itself, which in the end has everybody beaten.

Part of an 11th-century Swedish woven tapestry shows three figures taken to be (left to right) Odin (with one eye), Thor (carrying a hammer) and Freya.

Just like Heracles, Thor never rests at home for long, and at once he is off on a new venture. His lifelong ambition is to destroy that same World Serpent which had him fooled in the form of the giant's cat, and he fishes for it with another giant and at one point has it hooked. But the sight of the terrible face of the monster frightens the giant, who cuts the line, and Thor's eternal enemy escapes again into the depths.

In another tale in which Thor is made to look faintly ridiculous, his all-important hammer is stolen by the giants against whom it is the gods' protection. Loki is sent to Giantland to find it, and the giant-king, admitting the theft, demands a ransom of the goddess Freya as a wife. The hammer, he says, is hidden deep in the earth.

43

Freya, on hearing this suggestion, is outraged. Clearly they cannot persuade her to go as bride to a giant, and in desperation the gods persuade Thor to take her place. Accompanied by Loki as a maidservant, he goes to Giantland dressed as a bride. In spite of the monstrous appetite and thirst which he displays at the wedding feast, Thor fools the giants for long enough to get the hammer within his grasp, whereupon he fells the giant-king with it.

So the tales go on. Clearly the elemental god of the thunder had become the giant-killer of fairytale, and in his later period Thor belongs (much more than the aristocratic Odin) to the ordinary people of the rural areas. But behind this simple folk-tale image we can still make out that potent force which the Germanic tribes sought to evoke in the roar of their battle-cries.

Thor's hammer: a 10th-century example in silver from Fossi. As the influence of Christianity grew, this artistic tradition was adapted to the new symbol, the crucifix.

~ Odin ~

Odin is the chief of the northern gods. Every mythology has its father-figure, and for the people of Scandinavia, Iceland and the Germanic lands in the period before their acceptance of Christianity this was Odin – or, as he was known in the German form, Woden. All-Father, they called him, father of all the gods. Surprisingly, however, the Romans did not equate Odin/Woden with their own father-god, Jupiter, but instead with Mercury, and so, as mentioned in connection with Gwydion, the Roman midweek, *Mercurii dies*, was translated by the Germans as Woden's-day (Wednesday). Because of our own Anglo-Saxon ancestry this, like Thor's-day, is another effect of the old religion of Europe which is still with us.

Like Mercury, Odin or Woden was something of a magician. He specialized in supervising, rather than participating in, the feuds of a basically aristocratic society. Like Mercury, too, his distinguishing role was that of the leader of souls: he guided the souls of the dead to their destination. In the Roman version this was an individual, personal matter. But in the north it took a group form, and we find Odin filling a role common in folk-lore and superstition elsewhere. He is the leader of the Wild Hunt, a rampaging, roaring company which rides across the night sky, the explanation, in other words, of the nocturnal storm. This tells us something about his possible roots. The word 'wode', from which 'Woden' probably comes, means 'fury' or 'frenzy' – up to the time of Shakespeare it was still a word in English: 'wood', meaning 'mad'. In that capacity, as the embodiment of fury, Woden was invoked by the Germanic peoples before battle. But the same personage appears in Hindu mythology as Vata, the Lord of the Wind. And this may be the root of Odin's character,

before the time at which he became elevated to the kingship of the northern pantheon: he was a wind god.

The stories of Odin have survived better than those of his German counterpart, Woden, and we find a large collection of them in the Eddas, the originally Icelandic collections of knowledge about the northern gods. He is recognizably the god of an aristocratic, cultured class, unlike the more down-to-earth Thor, who clearly appealed to the common people. Still very much a magician, a shape-changer (like the British Gwydion), Odin has knowledge of all things. He is accompanied by two crows which fly through the world in the mornings and return to tell him all they have seen or heard. They are called Hugin and Munnin, which means 'thought' and 'memory'. This sort of rhyme is characteristic of the stories about Odin.

Pictured as a knight in armour, with golden helmet, Odin rides his wonderful eight-footed horse Sleipnir ('Slippery') which carries him across the waves of the sea as if they were dry land. Just as Thor's identifying weapon was the great stone hammer, the blunt instrument of a giant, so the more refined Odin has a miraculous spear, made for him by the dwarfs, with the special characteristic of always finding its mark.

Odin holds court in his huge hall, Valhalla, at an endless feast which is the destiny and reward of the brave dead. There he is served by the Valkyries, female warrior-fates who act as attendants in Valhalla but on earth are more akin to the Furies. They mingle in human battles and determine the outcome, who shall die, who shall win, who shall join Odin in Valhalla. Odin is married to the chief of the northern goddesses, Frigg. Yet his amorous adventures with mortal women, like his supremacy over other gods and

46

his holding of a permanent court, remind us again of Zeus. Some of his stories tell of such adventures, but the main theme which supports his biography in the Eddas is his gaining of poetic inspiration. This was not something he possessed by birth, but he acquired it, like Finn in Irish myth, through an episode in his tales.

In a fountain near to the roots of the World Tree, the great ash Yggdrasil, lived a wise water-spirit named Mimir. Knowledge and wisdom were hidden in this fountain, and Odin came and requested to be allowed to drink of this source of truth. But Mimir made a bargain: he might drink if he gave one of his eyes in payment. So keen was he to have this total wisdom that he gave an eye, and is represented therefore as being one-eyed. It seems almost certain that this indicates one source of the kaleidoscopic make-up of this figure, that of the sky-god, of which again Zeus is also an example. We are told that Mimir brings out Odin's eye in the morning and hides it at night, an obvious reference to the rising and setting of the sun. And sky-gods are likely, in the nature of things, to be represented as one-eyed.

A more elaborate version of Odin's winning of wisdom or poetic truth is the story of the hydromel. There had been a war between the main gods, the Aesir, and another family of gods known as the Vanir, which was settled between the two parties by a truce. Both sides spat into a jar as a token of their peace, and out of this mixture a man was made. Later in his story he was killed by the dwarfs, and his blood was mixed with honey and kept in a number of containers. Whoever drank that mead would become a wise man or a poet.

The mead, known as the hydromel, eventually became the property of a giant called Suttung, who hid it inside a mountain. With the help of the giant's brother, Odin bored a small hole through

A French 19th-century portrait of Odin emphasizes his role as father-figure. He is accompanied by his two crows, Hugin and Munnin, and carries his miraculous spear; the wolves are another emblem.

the mountain, changed himself into a snake and slipped through it. He succeeded in drinking the whole of the hydromel, and, true to the nature of a sky-god, flew away in the form of an eagle. When he returned to the land of the gods he spat out the mead, with the result that the gods, under Odin's supervision, control the distribution of poetic ability.

Like several other major gods, Odin went through a form of death and resurrection. Parallels have been drawn between his case and that of Christ but, although the stories reached their final form at a late enough date for there to be the possibility of Christian influence, the theme in general is so old and so widespread that it seems likely that this is another instance of a basic idea. He is described as being sacrificed to himself, a reference both to the primitive custom of the representative of the god being sacrificed to the god, and to the idea of the god giving himself for the sake of men. His sacrifice takes the form of being hung from a tree, specifically Yggdrasil, the World Tree, wounded (like Christ again) by a spear. The tree, which is so closely connected with Odin, is an emblem of the world, in the sense that it binds together the various parts of existence – one root holds the sky, one the land of the gods, one the realm of ogres. There on Yggdrasil Odin hung for nine days.

His rejuvenation is brought about by yet another wisdom-winning episode. Looking down from his place of sacrifice he sees on the ground below some runes – magical formulae, or the cryptic writing of secret knowledge. He manages to lift them, and the knowledge they bring gives him new life.

One of the striking and individual features of this northern mythology is the belief that the gods and the life of their world are not immortal, not an everlasting process without beginning or end. They too will pass away. And the process of their passing gives us the most impressive concept which this body of material provides, the idea of Ragnarök. Originally meaning something like 'the gods' fatality', this Scandinavian word

47

takes the German form *Götterdammerung*, from which we get the well-known English phrase 'the Twilight of the Gods'.

It is a time preceded by great battles and disasters, as the gods become conscious of their errors and warned of their doom. Odin rides out with his terrible troop of the dead from Valhalla, his gold helmet shining, his wonderful spear in his hand, as the ash tree Yggdrasil shakes from its tips to its roots and mountains crash apart in a universal cataclysm. The World Serpent spatters poison to the sky; monsters have broken loose, among them the terrible wolf Fenrir, formerly chained by the gods, which now shakes the earth with its rampage. Odin rides in person to encounter this force of destruction, but the wolf's jaws are so vast that they simply swallow him up. He was the first of the gods, their leader, and is the first to vanish in this last terrible battle. Ragnarök rages on. One by one the gods fall to their monstrous foes. Without the gods there is no protection against the powers of evil and disintegration, and the world burns and crumbles.

Yet it begins again. Odin died symbolically and was renewed, and Ragnarök in turn is just such a route through doom to rejuvenation. The earth spins slowly back into its pre-cataclysmic shape. Mountains rise from the turmoil of the waters. In due course men too re-emerge from the chaos, crawling out from their refuge in the ash tree Yggdrasil. But Odin himself does not return. There are new gods in Asgard now. Only one of the old order is reborn into this new age, the good and beautiful Balder. It is he who now sits in Odin's seat in Valhalla.

A memorial stone from Gotland shows battles, the journey to the Other World (symbolized by the ship at the bottom) and the sacrifice of a warrior to Odin by the traditional method of hanging.

~ *Balder* ~

Balder, son of Odin and Frigg, is distinguished by his beauty and goodness, to such an extent that a light glows around him. To see him is to love him. He generates a mood of goodwill and harmony. The glow (like that said to shine around the Irish hero, Lugh) perhaps indicates a reference to the sun. Clearly Balder is in origin a god of light. The meaning of his name – simply 'Lord' – is the same as that of the Greek god Adonis, with whom he is also connected by some of the features of his story.

Balder became troubled by presentiments of tragedy. He suffered from disturbing dreams. The gods, when told, were deeply concerned, and decided to take what action they could to avoid any possibility of harm to Balder. His mother Frigg, chief among the goddesses, aranged a universal guarantee which, she felt sure, would protect him. She asked every being and object on earth to promise never to harm Balder – fire, water, each type of metal, stones, earth, trees, diseases, animals, birds, poisons, snakes, each category of entity was called on. Gladly they all agreed, so widely loved was Frigg's perfect son.

But knowing what we already do of the process of events in myth, we cannot but suspect that this seeming invulnerability is itself destined to lead to his death. Lleu Llaw Gyffes could not be killed inside a house or out, on horseback or on foot; yet circumstances arose improbably to trap him into a position in which he was not immune. Achilles was immortal – except for his heel. There is always some slight loophole, a factor usually so small that our everyday statistical expectations would rule it out as a risk. Myth seems to say that it is the improbable, the statistically unlikely, that is important.

There is a second deep theme present in this element of Balder's story. Just as it concerns the paradox that the apparently impossible takes place, so it does this by means of the idea of the joining points of categories, the items which are somehow neither this nor that. If something is defined and placed, it belongs to our orderly, comprehensible world. But Lleu Llaw Gyffes dies in a position which is, as it turns out, neither this nor that. And as it happens this is Balder's downfall too.

The gods, confident of Balder's invulnerability, played a game. They got him to stand in the middle of a circle, and threw at him missiles of various sorts – darts, weapons, stones. Nothing, it was proved, could hurt him. There was much laughter and merriment at this.

It is here that the evil element of the northern myths makes itself felt. Amid all this goodness and innocence there existed, right among the gods themselves, the embodiment of malice, in the form of the god Loki. Clearly Loki is in origin a fire demon. His name connects him with Lucifer, and we may see in him one form taken by the idea of diabolic forces, a representation of the devil himself. The wolf Fenrir, which breaks loose at Ragnarök and brings about the gods' destruction, is his son. He is, like the devil in some other cosmic systems, himself one of the gods. In the stories Loki is a stirrer-up of trouble, as was the Greek goddess of strife, Eris, when for instance she threw down at the wedding feast of Achilles' parents the apple labelled 'To the fairest'; and as was the Irish character Bricriu, when he invited CuChulainn and the men of Ulster to a feast with the sole purpose of setting them against each other.

Loki is motivated now by envy, and his bitterness against Balder's good fortune leads to an event which is the prelude to the cataclysm of

The malicious god, Loki. Statue by H. E. Freund in Copenhagen.

seems to be a narrator's explanation which disguises the true point. We may guess from what we know of the mistletoe's importance in other lore that its significance here as well is that it fails to conform to the defining qualifications which give us our categories. It is neither a bush nor a tree, since those have their roots in the earth. Yet it is nothing else either. It escapes defining restrictions, and hence exists between two spheres. Consequently if Frigg had set about extracting the promises item by item – trees, bushes, and so on – the mistletoe would inevitably have been left out. The fascination with the rare examples of things existing between two worlds gives us, in myth and legend, many instances of such a theme. We are protected almost everywhere by the orderliness which we have imposed on the continuum of the world through our framework of concepts and categories. It is at the seams of this structure, if anywhere, that the otherworld, the primal chaos, can break through. Midnight, neither one day nor another, is the witching hour. New Year's Eve, or, in an older calendar, the eve of the start of winter (now our Hallowe'en), or that of May-day, the start of summer, provide similar joints in time, and similar beliefs and customs. Convention does not apply to them. You may kiss people, for instance, as you may under the mistletoe, whom convention might otherwise exclude. Ghosts walk. Such times belong to them rather than to us.

Hence, it seems likely, the perennial fascination with the mistletoe, the reason for its being important in lore and custom, and for the central role it played in the Celtic religion of the Druids. And hence it was the mistletoe which was destined to kill Balder.

Loki, having as the old woman learnt this secret, hurried to pick the mistletoe and take it to the gathering. There he found a blind god, Höd, who was taking no part in the fun. He could not see where Balder was, he explained, and besides, he had no weapon. Loki, giving him the mistletoe twig, guided his hand. It is a powerful expression

Ragnarök. He hears the laughter and cheerfulness as the gods prove the success of their scheme to protect Balder, and comes to Frigg in disguise as an old woman to ask what is going on. Frigg explains: nothing will hurt Balder, since she has extracted an oath from all things to do him no harm. All things? asks the old woman. Well, all things except one small piece of vegetation, the goddess replies. It is called the mistletoe, and grows west of Valhalla. She did not bother to extract an oath from that. It looked too young.

Frigg's saying that the reason was the tender age, presumably the innocence, of the mistletoe

The ambiguous mistletoe provides the weapon with which evil, in the shape of Loki, overcomes good, represented by Balder.

of the feeling that behind the blindness, the randomness, of circumstance, lies some malignant guiding force which finds the one weak spot, as Paris's arrow did, guided to strike Achilles' heel by the hand of the god Apollo. Balder falls, slain by that simple dart.

The gods are horror-stricken. They know that Loki's evil is behind this deed, but cannot punish him there, since they are in a sacred place. They hold a stately funeral for Balder, but their main concern is to retrieve him from death. While the funeral pyre is still alight Odin's son, Hermod, rides on Odin's miraculous horse to the land of death. We have seen this theme before, too, the descent to the underworld and the eventual return, and Hermod is in the company of Heracles, Theseus, Odysseus and others, in making this terrible journey.

Reaching the hall of death itself he asks the presiding goddess, Hel, to let Balder go. She agrees (as, in Greek myth, Orpheus was allowed to take back his wife Eurydice) on one condition. It is that all the world should weep for Balder. If the lamentation is truly universal, if Hel can be convinced that there is nobody and nothing who does not wish his return, she will let him go. But if there is a single dry eye, he must stay below.

This general weeping too connects the northern god with the eastern-European one, Adonis, who also died of a wound and was reborn, his worshippers enacting this through general lamentation. An eastern-European origin of elements of the story of Balder might well be suspected from these close parallels, and both myths have been compared to the story of Christ, wounded, lamented, dead, but resurrected. We have seen already that parts of the theme (as in the story of Demeter and Persephone) are considerably older than the Christian era, and it seems an appropriate way of expressing the dual ideas of seasonal death and renewal and of the hope of rebirth after death.

In Balder's case the mission was not immediately successful, for the malice of Loki was still at work. Hermod came back with the news of the condition, the gods sent out a general request, and the world wept. Stones wept, as did trees, metals, men and animals, and the earth itself. Since the image seems to represent the Scandinavian thaw, as the frost drips off the natural and the constructed world, we might well expect the rebirth of Balder and the spring. But if so, then spring is delayed. There was one giantess, living in a cave, who refused to weep. They begged her to weep for Balder, but she replied that she owed Balder nothing. Let Hel keep what is hers, she said. It was, of course, Loki in disguise.

Loki does not go unpunished, just as Balder is not doomed to stay below for ever. As Ragnarök approaches the gods make a belated requital for his death. Loki changes shape to escape them, becoming a salmon, but Thor catches him in a stream and they carry him to the security of a cave. There they bind him with the entrails of one of his sons, since no normal bonds would hold him. A poisonous snake drips venom on to his face, and his wife, remaining loyal to him, catches the drops in a basin before they strike him. When the basin becomes full she has to turn away to empty it, and the poison hits his skin. The fire demon Loki stirs then: volcanoes spout, and we feel the earth shake.

For a view of the confrontation of good and bad there are few sequences in myth or legend to equal the story of Balder. Northern myth is hard-headed and realistic, not admitting easy outcomes. But Loki is permanently imprisoned in the end; and after Ragnarök Balder does come back, reborn into the new order of the gods of a new earth.

The world weeps for Balder: a Scandinavian mythological explanation of a natural event, the thaw which precedes the spring.

Classical and Biblical Times

by James Chambers

IT WAS THE ancient Greeks who introduced the concept of heroism to the world. Their first heroes were the superhuman and mythical descendants of the gods, whose glorious exploits were recorded by their epic poets and who represented the Greek ideal of everything that a man should be: brave, wise, incorruptible and preferably beautiful. From this tradition, heroism became generic to the Greek ethos. As the civilizations evolved and the city states began to emerge, the pursuit of honour was regarded as a duty: the greater a man's prowess, the more he was expected to achieve. But beyond this, the men and women who were venerated as the successors to the children of the gods were those whose exceptional abilities and aspirations set them apart from other mortals and whose conduct in the course of great events exemplified the heroic ideal. They did not have to be perfect: heroism allowed for the lesser frailties of the flesh. And they did not have to be successful: heroism always involved courageous suffering and it could encompass failure so long as it was glorious. But they had to be lucky: although nature could endow them with heroic qualities, only fortune could provide the opportunities to fulfil them.

It is not surprising therefore that the epic histories of the Classical Age, which gave the western world its civilization, and the Bible, which gave it its religion, are crowded with men and women whose lives fulfilled the Greek ideal of heroism. It would be difficult to make a list that was complete and those who have been chosen here are not just outstanding examples, they are the giants of a heroic world.

The exploits of classical heroes and heroines have been an inspiration to the literature of every western civilization that came after them. Although her purpose was to preserve the liberty of her kingdom and restore her ancestral empire, the legend of Cleopatra is retold as one of the world's greatest love stories. Pericles guided the first democracy and gave the world the golden age of Athens, Leonidas sacrificed his life at Thermopylae to save Europe from the Persian empire, and both are remembered as unsurpassed examples of sublime nobility.

Others, who earned their reputations as conquerors, may have been too ruthless and ambitious to fulfil all the twentieth-century ideals of heroism, but from among them Alexander the Great, who united Greece and destroyed the Persian empire, Hannibal, whose vow of vengeance brought him to the gates of Rome, and Julius Caesar, who stabilized the crumbling Roman republic and conquered Gaul, are still numbered among the greatest military commanders in history. And there were those who were seen by their Roman contemporaries as no more than dangerous rebels, and whose undoubted heroism was only recognized by their followers and subsequent historians: Boadicea, Queen of the Iceni, and Spartacus, the gladiator slave, who both challenged overwhelming odds in the name of liberty and justice.

In one respect the Biblical heroes were different. To a varying degree, the classical heroes were all tragic heroes. Cleopatra, Hannibal, Spartacus and Boadicea saw their dreams destroyed; Leonidas was betrayed; Caesar was murdered; and even the achievements of Alexander and Pericles did not long outlast them. But the Biblical heroes were triumphant heroes. Each played his part in the progressive rise of Israel or the spread of Christianity. Joshua led the Hebrew tribes to conquer a homeland; David bequeathed them a empire and a dynasty; and when Christianity emerged in Israel, it was Saint Paul who brought it to the Gentiles and through his courage and resolve laid the foundations of a world-wide religion.

James Chambers

~ *Joshua* ~

Over 3,000 years ago the children of Israel fled from slavery in Egypt and, led by Moses, travelled through the Sinai desert to the oasis of Kadesh-barnea on the southern edge of Canaan. In the Book of Numbers the story is told of how Moses then chose twelve scouts, one from each of the tribes, and sent them to reconnoitre this promised land. When the scouts returned after forty days they reported that they had seen powerful kingdoms with rich cities and flourishing farms; and of all the scouts only Caleb of the tribe of Judah and Joshua of the tribe of Ephraim believed that the Israelites could conquer them. So the despairing tribes remained in the desert and slowly wandered round the south of the

Dead Sea to the eastern bank of the river Jordan. There, at a solemn ceremony in the tabernacle, the still-confident Joshua was nominated by the dying Moses as his successor and invested by the elders of Israel with the absolute authority of a wartime dictator.

The kingdoms of Canaan were divided and weakened by the personal rivalries of their monarchs, but the Israelite nomads were untrained and primitively armed and Joshua knew that, even if he fought those kingdoms one at a time, his novices had neither the equipment nor the experience to capture their fortified cities or defeat their armoured warriors and iron chariots in open country. His initial plan therefore was to

Before attacking Jericho, Joshua sent two spies to assess the situation; in this early Byzantine manuscript roll illustration, they report that the people of the city are terrified and can be conquered with ease.

gain control of the fertile valley beyond the Jordan, from which, if attacked, he could withdraw to the safety of the eastern bank; and then to infiltrate the barren and sparsely populated hills between the river and the coastal plain, where his men would be more mobile than their armoured enemies and the Canaanite chariots would be useless.

The first objective was to establish a bridge-head west of the Jordan at the vital oasis of Jericho. The river was in flood, but upstream the waters had brought down the high clay cliffs, temporarily damming it. Near the mouth at the Dead Sea the Israelites crossed in safety, celebrated the Passover and after building a monument of twelve stones, symbolizing the twelve tribes, advanced five miles to the oasis. Jericho is the oldest walled city in the world, but 100 years before the Israelite invasion it was utterly destroyed in an earthquake and, by the time Joshua reached it, the extensive ruins supported no more than a large settlement. Using a tactic that was later to be employed by Alexander and Pompey, Joshua lulled the defenders into complacency by marching his army round the crumbled walls once every day for six days without making an attack; then on the seventh day he rushed the weakest point in the makeshift ramparts and Jericho was taken.

The capture of Jericho. Early 5th-century mosaic from S. Maria Maggiore, Rome.

Before he advanced into the hills Joshua received ambassadors from the city of Gibeon, the capital of a beleaguered confederacy of recently settled towns, ruled by elders instead of kings; to strengthen their defences against the surrounding kingdoms, the ambassadors offered to make an alliance with the new immigrants. According to the Book of Joshua, they tricked him into acceptance by wearing travel-worn clothes and pretending that their city was far away, whereas in fact it lay in the hills which Joshua intended to conquer, and when he discovered their deception, he condemned them to become 'hewers of wood and drawers of water'. But it is more likely that he welcomed the alliance, for it was as much to his advantage as it was to theirs, and when the Gibeonites were later threatened he raced to their rescue.

From Jericho into the hills the shortest route was dominated and effectively barred by the impregnable walls of Jerusalem, but further to the north there was a longer route which wound past the 1,000-year-old ruined city of Ai and, although Ai was not deserted, Joshua's scouts reported that it contained so few people that he could take it with 2,000–3,000 men. By the time his vanguard reached it, however, Ai had been garrisoned by a detachment from the nearby city of Bethel and the assault was repelled. At once Joshua returned with his whole army. By night he hid two forces of picked men in the hills and hollow ground on the north and south-west of the fortified ruin and with the rest he attacked at dawn from the north-east. After a brief engagement Joshua's soldiers broke and fled into a narrow gorge. Confident after its first successful defence, the garrison gave chase, but the Israelite force which had been hiding in the south moved in to occupy its abandoned strong point and then, while Joshua's soldiers halted and turned, advanced behind it into the gorge. The garrison was trapped and, when the rest of its army marched out of Bethel to join the fight, it was ambushed by the second force which Joshua had hidden in the northern hills. Ai was captured and, having secured the pass and destroyed the Bethelite army, Joshua returned to his base camp at Gilgal near Jericho.

When Ai fell King Adoni-zedek of Jerusalem became apprehensive. He had not been worried by the Israelites' settlement of the exposed western bank of the Jordan, where his armoured warriors could have slaughtered them if they dared to defy him, but the alliance with Gibeon had given Joshua a fortified city and the capture of Ai had established communications between the allies; the heart of Canaan was divided and from either flank the Israelites and the Gibeonites now threatened to overrun the southern highlands. Joining forces with the Amorite kings of Hebron, Jarmuth, Lachish and Eglon, Adoni-zedek led their armies north and laid siege to Gibeon. But Gibeonite messengers reached Gilgal; under cover of darkness, Joshua led the Israelites into the hills and next day launched a surprise attack on the rear of the besieging army. The ranks of the Amorite soldiers were broken by the momentum of the charge and when their kings failed to rally them they fled down the boulder-strewn pass of Beth-horon with the Israelites at their heels. In the last dark hours of the following morning the Amorite army reached the valley of Ajalon in utter confusion; the soldiers were slaughtered and the five kings, who were found hiding in a cave, were executed.

Joshua was a master of surprise and deception, but his greatest talent as a commander was his capacity to recognize and exploit an advantage. Although the Israelites were exhausted by their night march and their victory at Gibeon, he had pursued the Amorite army to destruction, thus eliminating the soldiers who might otherwise have prevented him from entering the southern highlands as King Adoni-zedek had feared. When his men were rested, he marched past the fortress of Jerusalem, spread out his units and at last began to capture the southern towns and cities, where there were so few soldiers left to defend the walls that it was now possible for the Israelites to scale them.

But news soon came that the powerful King Jabin of Hazor, who had formed an alliance with all the northern Canaanite kings, was assembling an enormous army with hundreds of chariots at the Waters of Merom. If this army ever reached the south, the Israelites could not hope to hold their newly captured towns or stand their ground against its chariots in the valleys. In the last and most desperate gamble of his career, Joshua mustered all the men in Israel and force-marched them north through the hills. The camp site at the Waters of Merom was ideally situated between the northern kingdoms and commanded the passes that led into the south, but the narrowness of the gorge made it impossible to deploy a large army or manoeuvre chariots. When Joshua attacked suddenly from the southern hills, King Jabin's startled soldiers were pushed back through the chaos of their camp and cut to pieces in the northern passes. As he had done in the south, Joshua had destroyed the northern army at the one moment when it was vulnerable, and the Israelites' foothold in Canaan was secure.

It was not until long after Joshua's death that the children of Israel finally conquered all the lands that were to become the inheritance of the twelve tribes. By the time the history of the invasion and settlement of Canaan came to be written, the story of Joshua had become a legend and the truth had been obscured by cherished fables: battles had either been exaggerated, to explain the massive ruins of Jericho and Ai, or invented; 'impossible' achievements had been attributed to miraculous intervention and the deeds of forgotten men had been ascribed to known heroes. But although the subsequent researches and excavations of historians and archaeologists have disproved the more fantastic stories, they have also verified others. In the thirteenth century BC there really was an extraordinary soldier called Joshua who disciplined and trained the ill-equipped nomad tribes of Israel, leading them to victory over the armoured warriors, iron chariots and walled cities of the Canaanites, and from this incomplete story emerge the first certain records of a great Biblical hero.

~ David ~

In the middle of the eleventh century BC the Philistines, who lived along the Mediterranean coast on the west of Canaan, invaded the lands of their eastern neighbours, the Israelites. Contrary to their modern reputation, the Philistines were a civilized people: their cities were splendid and heavily fortified, their craftsmen were highly skilled in the forging of armour and weapons, and their soldiers, who had fought as valued mercenaries in the armies of Egypt, were experienced and formidable. To meet the threat, the rustic tribes of Israel united under their first king, Saul, and held off the invaders in the mountains until one day the massed armies of the two nations faced each other across the valley of Elah.

Neither side was prepared to make the first move, and so risk losing the advantage of high ground. For over a month they watched and waited and every day the giant Philistine champion Goliath came forward to offer single combat, safe in the knowledge that there was not a man in Israel who could match him. From the nearby town of Bethlehem, a boy called David arrived in the Israelite camp with food for his brothers. He was a renowned poet and musician and he had already been introduced to the court, where Saul had been so pleased with him that he had made him his armour-bearer; but he was thought to be too young for battle and since then he had returned to look after his father's sheep while his elder brothers served with the army. Hearing about Goliath's challenge, David persuaded Saul that he could defeat the giant with cunning. Armed with only a sling, he taunted Goliath into advancing within range, then stunned him with the first well-aimed stone and, before he could recover, ran forward to slay him with his own sword. As the Philistines looked on in horrified disbelief, the Israelites charged and drove them back through their camp in disorder.

After the victory David was rewarded with a commission in the royal guard and during the campaigns that followed he rose to become the most popular and successful commander in the Israelite army. But although Saul welcomed him into his family, and David became the husband of Saul's daughter Michal and the close friend of his son Jonathan, the moody king's admiration was tainted with envy. Saul had heard the people sing his commander's praises and, afraid that they might choose David to succeed or even replace him, Saul planned his murder. Warned by Jonathan and helped by Michal, David fled.

David attacks Goliath. A mosaic from St Gereou, Cologne.

By pretending that he was on a secret mission for the king, he obtained shelter at the sanctuary of Nob, where the priests gave him Goliath's sword, which had been brought to them after the battle in Elah, and from there he crossed the border to find refuge among the Philistines in the city of Gath. But King Achish of Gath suspected the man who had killed his champion and defeated his soldiers, and, after escaping execution only by feigning madness, David returned to his homeland and the hills of southern Judah, where with a few hundred faithful friends and fellow fugitives he lived for several years as a bandit.

Using the mountain caves as strongholds, David maintained his outlaws by offering 'protection' to rich farmers in return for food and clothing. While he was preparing to wipe out the farm of one uncooperative rich herdsman called Nabal, he was bought off by Nabal's wife Abigail with a wagon train of supplies; and when Nabal died a few days later of a drunken heart attack, David saw it as a sign from heaven and married

Abigail. But he also led his outlaws into the valleys to defend the towns against Philistine raiders and, like Robin Hood, provided protection and aid for the poor and the oppressed. As a result, he became a popular hero of the tribe of Judah, which was the largest in Israel, and Saul grew increasingly afraid that David intended to overthrow him. But David was as patient and shrewd in politics as he was cunning in battle, and, although he certainly believed that he would one day rule Israel, it did not suit his purpose to divide the tribes in civil war or destroy his reputation by shedding the blood of an anointed king.

However, if he and his outlaws remained in Judah it was inevitable that Saul's army would capture them in the end and David once again sought refuge among the Philistines. This time, since it seemed obvious that David was Saul's enemy, King Achish welcomed him and appointed him governor of Ziklag; and so, for sixteen months, the bandit poet who was to become the greatest king of Israel lived in a Philistine town and governed a Philistine province. Fortunately, when the Philistines next attacked Israel, their commanders refused to fight beside David and his mercenaries. While the Philistine advance continued, David attacked the nomad Amalekite raiders, recovering the cattle which they had taken from Ziklag in his absence and capturing their other stolen herds, which he then sent to Judah to be judiciously distributed among the people who had supported him.

Soon after his return to Ziklag, David received the news of an overwhelming Philistine victory: the Israelite army had been routed on Mount Gilboa, Saul and Jonathan were dead, Saul's commander, Abner, had withdrawn east of the river Jordan and the whole of north-western Israel was in the hands of the Philistines. At once David returned to Hebron, with the approval of the Philistines, to be anointed king of Judah by the people whose loyalty he had so carefully cultivated. But in the north Abner had anointed Saul's ineffectual son Ishbosheth king of Israel and while the Philistines consolidated their victory the tribes were divided. After an initial skirmish, in which Abner killed the brother of David's commander Joab, the fighting was sporadic and inconclusive and, while David waited for the Israelites to lose faith in Ishbosheth, he negotiated treaties with their neighbours. Eventually, as he had hoped, Abner arranged to meet him secretly and offered him the allegiance of the discontented northern tribes. But on his way home, Abner was murdered by Joab. To a nation in which blood feuds were traditional the murder was no more than acceptable vengeance for the death of a brother; nevertheless, although David condemned it publicly, the apparent treachery cast doubts on his integrity and soon afterwards, when Ishbosheth was assassinated by two officers who brought his head to David in the hope of a reward, David was quick to restore his reputation by executing them for treason. Leaderless and surrounded by enemies, the northern tribes sent their elders to Hebron and, at the age of thirty, David was anointed king of all Israel.

Having united the tribes, David's first objective was to create a neutral capital which would be acceptable to all of them. For this the ideal city was the Jebusite stronghold of Jerusalem, which lay between the lands of Israel and Judah. It was so heavily fortified that Joshua had not tried to take it during his invasion and since then it had remained an alien community among the Israelites. But by climbing through a drain David's soldiers bypassed the walls and surprised the defenders, and with hardly a fight Jerusalem was captured. David built himself a palace, using craftsmen from Tyre, and, to establish the new capital as a religious centre, he brought the Ark of the Covenant from the shrine at Kiriath-jearim and installed it in a tent on Mount Zion.

After the fall of Jerusalem David's soldiers drove the Philistines out of Israel and in the years that followed he conquered an empire. By the end of his reign he ruled all the lands from beyond Damascus in the north to the Gulf of

A medieval manuscript illustration of King David as composer of the Psalms.

David (top right) sees Bathsheba at her bath. By William Blake, 1757–1827.

Aqaba in the south and, except for the reduced Philistine kingdoms in the Gaza strip, from the Mediterranean coast to the Arabian desert. To unite his house with the blood of his subject peoples, David filled his palace with wives and concubines from all the tribes of Israel and the conquered kingdoms. Yet the wealth of his harem was not enough for him. One hot summer night, while Joab and the army were invading the eastern kingdom of Ammon, David was walking on the roof of his palace when he saw a beautiful woman washing herself in a nearby house. She was Bathsheba, the grand-daughter of his leading councillor Ahitophel and the wife of Uriah, a Hittite who was serving with Joab's army. David sent for her, they became lovers and a few weeks later Bathsheba announced that she was pregnant. To avoid a scandal David ordered Joab to send Uriah home with dispatches, so that he might spend the night with his wife and it would be assumed that the child was his. But after he had reported to David, Uriah, refusing to enjoy the comforts of his house while his fellow soldiers lived in a camp, slept with the guards at the palace gate. When even a good dinner failed to persuade him to spend a night with his wife, David sent him back to the army with a sealed letter for Joab which instructed the general to assign Uriah to the most dangerous area of the next battlefield. Soon afterwards news came that the Israelite army had failed in a reckless assault on the walls of Rabbah and that in the forefront of the fighting Uriah the Hittite had fallen. After the period of mourning Bathsheba married David. The prophet Nathan admonished them for their disgraceful treachery and when their child died it was seen as a punishment from God, but as David comforted Bathsheba she conceived again and the second son, Solomon, lived.

David did not establish any order of precedence in his enormous family and he never named his heir. As a result there was constant rivalry and intrigue amongst his wives and sons, and in the last years of David's reign his conquering armies were engaged at home in the protection of his throne. When his son Absalom resorted to open revolt, he found widespread support among the elders who resented the sudden transition from tribal confederacy to centralized monarchy. In the face of the rebellion David abandoned Jerusalem and moved his court to the military headquarters on the eastern border. But in open battle the ill-organized rebels were defeated by Joab's veterans and, in spite of David's orders to the contrary, Joab ensured that Absalom died. Before David could return to his capital a second rebellion was raised in Israel to throw off the rule of a royal house from Judah, but that too was suppressed and thereafter the attentions of the northern tribes were diverted by famine and a campaign against the Philistines.

David took part in the last campaign, but he was too weak to defend himself and, after he had narrowly escaped death, his anxious officers persuaded him to retire from active service with the army. He was tired and he was old – and yet he still did not name his heir. As he lay dying, his eldest son Adonijah assembled his followers, who now included Joab, and gave a banquet to celebrate his imminent succession, but Nathan brought Bathsheba to David's bedside and reminded the king that he had privately promised his throne to her son Solomon. While Adonijah celebrated, David abdicated in favour of Solomon, who was then escorted by the royal guard and David's mercenaries to the sacred spring of Gihon to be anointed king. Seeing that his rival had the support of the army, Adonijah capitulated.

Soon after his abdication, having reigned for forty years, David died. Under his rule the people of Israel had enjoyed the greatest power and prominence that they have ever known and in time, when even their independence was lost, he and his age became the symbols of their aspirations. As a conqueror, statesman, poet and adulterer, he had exemplified all the achievements, virtues and human weaknesses of the Greek and Roman heroes who were to live long after him. He created a united nation, contributed to its literature, endowed it with a capital and an empire and bequeathed it a dynasty which was to last for over 400 years.

∾ *Leonidas* ∾

In the spring of 480 BC, Xerxes, King of Persia and master of the mightiest empire in the world, set out to conquer Greece with an enormous army of over 200,000 men and a fleet of more than 650 triremes. News of his approach was met with panic among the divided Greek states, many of whom had already sent ambassadors to offer him their allegiance. Everywhere princes and politicians warned their demoralized peoples that the sole alternative to surrender was certain destruction. Only Athens and Sparta seemed ready to defend themselves, and even within these states there were those who welcomed the invasion as a means to fulfil their own ambitions, aware that the Persians had already granted estates within their empire to ostracized Athenian tyrants, and that a deposed king of Sparta, Demaratus, was riding with the Persian

Partially reconstructed statue of Leonidas, found at Sparta.

prevent the Persians from entering central Greece by blockading the narrow mountain pass at Thermopylae and the parallel channel between the mainland and the island of Euboea, where the limited space would deny the enemy the advantage of superior numbers. The Athenians, who had a new battle fleet of over 200 triremes, could block the mouth of the channel at Artemisium, but, since all Athenian soldiers would be needed to fight on the decks, the responsibility for holding the pass fell entirely to the Spartans. Unfortunately, although Leonidas felt sure that the central Greek states would rally round the Spartan army, which boasted the finest soldiers in Greece, the constitution denied him the authority to order mobilization, which lay instead with his councillors, the representatives of the people. They supported a more cautious strategy but one which nevertheless depended on the support of the Athenian fleet. They therefore agreed in principle with Themistocles, knowing that as it was then the month-long festival of Carneia, during which the Spartan soldiers never took to the field, it would probably be too late, when the time came, to execute his plan. In the meantime, as a gesture of good faith, they were prepared to send a token vanguard of 300 men, which Leonidas volunteered to lead.

This was to be the first time that Leonidas had ever commanded an army, and he must have suspected that it was likely to be the last: when selecting his vanguard, he chose only those men who had living sons to continue their family lines. By contrast with the liberal and progressive Athenians, the Spartans were conservative and ascetic. While serfs, known as helots, laboured in their fields and tradesmen served their cities, the Spartan citizens, who were forbidden by law to own gold and silver or to engage in commerce, devoted their lives to military service. Their training began when they were ten years old and at twenty they became soldiers and joined one of the military mess clubs to which all citizens belonged, but it was not until they had undergone another ten years of service that they were

army as military adviser. Greek historians later described how the oracle at Delphi had enigmatically predicted that Athens could be saved only by wooden walls and Sparta by the loss of a king. Whether the story is true or not, it was fortunate for the faint-hearted Greeks and for the future of western civilization that Athens had a leader, Themistocles, with a plan which relied on the wooden walls of ships and Sparta a king, Leonidas, who would be prepared to make the sacrifice.

At a council of war, Themistocles proposed an audacious plan which appealed particularly to Leonidas, who had only recently become one of the joint kings through the death of his two older, childless brothers. Themistocles' aim was to granted the right to vote in the assembly and were recognized as full members of that élite corps which the Athenian historian Thucydides described as an army of officers.

With 300 of these peerless veterans, 600–700 helots to act as their servants and 3,000 soldiers from Peloponnesian Arcadia, most of whom were no more than untrained peasants, Leonidas marched north. On the way he collected 700 experienced volunteers from the gallantly independent little town of Thespiae and a token contingent of 400 anti-Persian extremists from uncommitted Thebes. When he reached Thermopylae, the garrison of the fortress at Trachis agreed to stand with him and, while the Spartans raided farms to collect supplies for themselves and deny them to the enemy, the local Phocians, Malians and even the Locrians, who had already sent their submission to Xerxes, each provided him with a contingent of 1,000 men. At the most, his ill-assorted army was 8,000 strong.

The road through the pass at Thermopylae ran from west to east with the Malian gulf to the north and the cliffs and craggy foothills of Mount Callidromus to the south. Today the hot sulphurous springs which gave the pass its name have silted the gulf with several miles of salt flats, but in 480 BC the pass between the mountains and the sea was no more than twenty yards at its widest point. Here, where the cliffs were so sheer that enemy soldiers with bows and javelins could not climb above him, Leonidas repaired an old Phocian wall and set up his line of defence. The Persians would be prevented from landing soldiers in his rear by the Greek fleet at Artemisium beyond the mouth of the gulf; and the only land route which ran round behind him lay through a deep, narrow gorge, dangerously vulnerable to an ambush and dominated at its entrance by the fortress of Trachis. Leonidas reinforced this fortress with his 1,000 Locrians, but from the garrison he learned of a second route, a goat track which ran through the mountains into a hidden valley and then divided with one track winding down to the eastern end

of the pass behind the Greek line. To guard this, he detached his 1,000 Phocians and stationed them in the valley; they might not be enough to block the track for long, but the Persians were unlikely to find it, and they were all that he could afford.

On 14 August, Xerxes and his vanguard camped on the plains north-west of Thermopylae. Many of his ships had been destroyed or damaged by the early autumn gales, but he still had the strength to outnumber the Greek fleet and, rather than waste men in an assault on the pass, he preferred to wait until he could outflank it from the sea. While his damaged ships were being repaired, he ordered another 200 to sail round Euboea and come up the channel from the south to trap the Greek fleet at Artemisium. However, as the rest of his army began to arrive, he realized that he could not wait; the Spartans had laid waste the countryside so effectively that he was already short of supplies, and on the morning of 18 August he decided to attack.

As the Persian soldiers entered the pass, 300 men, wearing the red plumes and tunics of the illustrious Spartan army and proudly chanting their famous battle hymns, advanced in front of the wall to meet them. The Persians could not use their archers because of the twisting path and, although their light wicker shields and short javelins gave their infantry great mobility in open country, at close quarters they were pathetically ineffective against the long spears, huge heavy shields and bronze armour of the Greeks. Rank after rank and wave after wave they crumbled until, towards the end of the day, Xerxes sent in his crack troops, his 10,000 household guards, known as the Immortals. But even these failed to break the line and, before they could be destroyed like the others, he called off the attack.

Next morning, hoping that the little Greek army was by now exhausted, Xerxes tried again. He had promised prizes if the pass was taken and threatened death to anyone who turned back, but, while the Persians in the front ranks perished and those who fled were cut down by their own reserves, the Greek contingents took it in turn to stand in the front line, and the pass held. During the day Xerxes learned that most of the ships which he had sent round Euboea had been wrecked by a south-east wind and the remainder had been intercepted by an Athenian squadron; and later he saw the victorious Greek ships racing up the channel to join the rest of the fleet at Artemisium, which had been making hit-and-run attacks against his anchored ships. Frustrated and despondent, he withdrew his shattered soldiers from the pass and returned to his tent.

It was at this moment of defeat that a local Greek from Malis called Ephialtes came to Xerxes, 'in the hope of a rich reward', offering to lead his soldiers along the goat track that ran round the back of the pass; and as dusk fell the Immortals set out to follow him into the mountains. The unwary Phocians realized that the Persians were coming only when they heard the tramp of their feet in the fallen leaves. Surprised and frightened, they forgot their allies in the pass and fell back along the southern track that led into their own homeland.

During the night, Leonidas received warning of this outflanking move from Greek deserters from the Persian lines, and at dawn scouts came in with reports that the Immortals were attacking the Phocians. Calling together his allied commanders, Leonidas declared that he intended to stand his ground. Once Xerxes' soldiers were through the pass, there would no longer be any need for the Persian ships to engage at a disadvantage in the narrow channel; then, while their soldiers occupied central Greece, they could use their superior speed to sail south through the open sea, and the one real chance of crippling the invaders would be lost. There were still enough Greeks in Thermopylae to hold both the pass and the mouth of the mountain track for at least another day – and one more day was all they needed to give their fleet time to attack. But only the Thespians and the Thebans volunteered to remain with the Spartans; all the other commanders insisted that the pass was untenable, and Leonidas could do nothing but let them go. Without them a stand was impossible, but he knew that a total withdrawal would have been seen by the uncommitted Greek states as an admission of impotence, confirming the pessimism of their leaders and destroying all hope of resistance. If the fleet could hold its own at Artemisium and if the soldiers in the pass could sell their lives as dearly as possible, there was still a chance that the success and the sacrifice might set an example that would rally the rest of Greece. So while their allies marched away to their eternal shame, Leonidas and his little band of volunteers, less than 1,400 strong, quietly prepared to die. As they were arming, a man from the fortress of Trachis arrived and gloomily recounted how he had seen the Persian archers shoot such enormous volleys that they blocked out the sun. 'Our friend brings good news,' said one of the Spartans, 'we shall fight in the shade.'

In the middle of the morning Xerxes marched his column into the pass. The Spartans were drawn up in front of the wall with the Thespians on a small mound between the wall and the mouth of the mountain track and the Thebans further to the rear. Leonidas led the Spartans' charge, driving so deep into the advancing Persian column that they reached the ranks of the princes and killed two of the Persian king's brothers. So dense was the crush that Persians were pushed into the sea and all the Spartan spears were broken against the bodies of their enemies. Eventually and inevitably, Leonidas was killed. The Spartans formed round him and, carrying his body with them, hacked their way back to the wall. By the time they reached it, the Immortals had arrived, the pass beyond the Thespian position was blocked and the Thebans had surrendered. Still carrying the body of their king, the Spartans joined the Thespians on their mound, in hopeless defiance of the enormous Persian army that now surrounded them. There was no longer any need for the Persians to engage

65

at close quarters; in the open ground they could at last use their archers, and with arrows and javelins they showered the slowly contracting dome of shields until the last man fell.

That evening, after a creditable but inconclusive engagement, the Greek fleet withdrew from Artemisium, and in the following weeks central Greece was overrun and Athens destroyed. But Leonidas's stand at Thermopylae had shamed and inspired the Greeks into resistance. In September the Persian fleet was defeated at Salamis and Xerxes returned to Asia with the survivors. Next year, while Greek ships under the other Spartan king, Leotychidas, destroyed the remnants of the Persian fleet on the Asian coast at Mycale, Xerxes' occupying army was routed at Plataea, and freedom was restored to central Greece.

The defence of Thermopylae became a legend. Those Spartans who had failed to support their king argued unconvincingly that they had not expected the Persians to reach the pass so soon, and the soldiers who had abandoned it claimed that Leonidas had sent them away. The truth was recorded by the historian Herodotus and implied by the poet Simonides in his famous epitaph:

> Go tell the Spartans, passer-by,
> That here, their will obeyed, we lie.

Since then the strategically vital pass at Thermopylae has been the scene of several battles, but none so famous as the first, when Leonidas and a few free men set the example that was to save the seeds of western civilization. During the next fifty years in Athens those seeds were to flower into an unparalleled golden age in which the Athenians were to prove for ever the immeasurable value of liberty, but it was Leonidas, King of Sparta, who had taught the world to pay its price.

∼ *Pericles* ∼

In the middle of the fifth century BC, the free citizens of Athens crowned their city with the glorious architecture of the Acropolis; Sophocles and Euripides wrote plays for them, Socrates taught their sons, and they lived in a confident and aggressive democracy where, more than in any other society before or since, every man enthusiastically played his part in the conduct of his government. It was the most crowded era of intellectual and artistic achievement in history. Yet its greatest hero was not an artist or a philosopher, but Pericles, the supreme statesman whose dauntless faith in his own ideals was to give the world 'The Golden Age of Athens'.

Pericles was born into one of the most influential and aristocratic Athenian families around 490 BC. His father, Xanthippus, commanded an Athenian squadron at Mycale and after the Persian defeat played a leading part in organizing the confederacy of Delos, a defensive alliance of Aegean states and islands under the leadership of Athens. His mother, Agariste, was the niece of Cleisthenes, creator of the Athenian democracy. Shortly before Pericles was born, Agariste dreamt that she gave birth to a lion. Pericles was educated for a career in public life by the most distinguished scholars in Athens, and when the great philosopher Anaxagoras arrived in Athens, Pericles became his pupil and friend for life. Anaxagoras was the first man to

INAX. IGORA

Pericles' tutor, the philosopher Anaxagoras, as pictured by an Italian Renaissance artist.

Anaxagoras taught him to maintain a public image of serene dignity, which Pericles' opponents interpreted as haughty reserve. He spoke seldom in the assembly and only on matters of great importance, and was never seen walking in any street except the one which led to the marketplace and the council chamber. Throughout his career he refused all social invitations except one, a wedding feast given by his great-uncle, which he left immediately after dinner when the drinking began. But Pericles' public discretion contrasted with his private life, which was the scandal and the envy of Athens. His marriage disintegrated after the birth of his second child, and for the rest of his life he lived openly and happily with a beautiful, intelligent and talented courtesan called Aspasia, one of a group of foreign women chosen as children for their beauty and educated to become the intellectual companions of their clients. Amongst those who visited her 'house' were most of the leading men in Athens, including Socrates, who even brought his pupils and their wives to hear her talk.

After the expulsion of the last tyrant in 510 BC, Cleisthenes 'took the people into partnership' and, by the time Pericles entered public life, Athens was already a nominal democracy. Decisions were made by an assembly of all the adult male citizens, while the representative council of five hundred was no more than an executive authority. To ensure that absolute power would never again be consolidated in the hands of one man, the system of ostracism had been introduced, whereby, on the vote of at least 6,000 citizens, an influential politician could be banished for ten years without disgrace or loss of property. Nevertheless, only members of the higher classes could hold office in the government or the judiciary, only rich men had the leisure to engage in politics, and the aristocratic council of the Areopagus, which, like the House of Lords in England, was the supreme court of Athens, still retained the right to veto the resolutions of the assembly.

As a radical, Pericles joined the progressive

determine the true cause of an eclipse, he despised superstition and, contrary to the traditions of the time, he taught Pericles to accept that there was a rational explanation for everything.

Although imposing and handsome, Pericles was so self-conscious about his disproportionately high cranium that in his portraits he was always represented wearing a helmet, and he was by nature so emotional and shy that

The courtesan Aspasia, Pericles' Milesian mistress who was renowned for her political wisdom.

young aristocrats, led by Ephialtes, who were determined to build the Athenian democracy into a power that would rival Sparta. But the government of Athens was dominated by the conservative Cimon, who had engineered the ostracism of Themistocles, the leader who had joined with Leonidas against the Persians. Cimon kept on good terms with the reactionary Spartans, who were natural allies in his attempts to arrest the development of Athenian democracy, and in 464 BC he led 4,000 of his followers into the Peloponnese to help the Spartans suppress a rebellion among the helots. In his absence Ephialtes and Pericles seized the chance to win over the assembly with a programme of constitutional reform. On his return, after being dismissed by the ungrateful Spartans, Cimon was ostracized for supporting

them in the first place. The council of the Areopagus was deprived of its legislative veto and all judicial authority, except in matters of religion and certain appeals, and the conservative minority was left powerless. When Ephialtes was murdered by a fanatic, it only served to promote Pericles, under whose charismatic and uncontested guidance the reforms continued. Social qualifications for high office in the judiciary were abolished and, so that even the poorest citizens could afford the time to play their part in the courts, council and army, payment was provided for state service. Ability was now the sole criterion for advancement and, influenced only by the oratory of their statesmen, the real rulers of Athens were the assembled citizens.

The new foreign policy of the Athenian democrats was dangerously expansive. From the resources of the Delian confederacy they provided a fleet to assist the Egyptians' rebellion against their Persian masters and in support of local democrats they spread their influence across central Greece by force of arms. Even after they had been defeated at Tanagra in 457 BC, when they dared to attack a Spartan army, their success continued. But in 454 BC, at the zenith of Athenian power, the fleet in Egypt was captured and, having for some time resented the expense of Athenian ambition, the islands of the southeast Aegean withdrew from the confederacy of Delos. In the emergency the treasury of the confederacy was moved from Delos to Athens and Cimon, who had been recalled from exile, was empowered to negotiate a five-year truce with Sparta. When the truce had been signed, Cimon led a fleet to Cyprus to hold off the Persians, while Pericles sent squadrons to the islands. Athenian garrisons were installed, colonies of poor Athenian citizens were granted estates, puppet democracies were established and the once-willing members of a free alliance became the subject states of an Athenian empire.

After several victories, Cimon died in Cyprus and a lasting peace was negotiated with Persia, but in central Greece the subject states, fearing the fate of the Aegean islands, rebelled and before they could be subdued the truce with Sparta came to an end and a Spartan army advanced on Athens. Pericles had no alternative but to sue for peace. Although Athens commanded the sea, she was no match on the mainland for the military might of Sparta. In 446 BC a thirty-year truce was signed and Athens relinquished all her dominions in central Greece. The eastern Mediterranean was at last at peace, but the truce was no more than an agreement to maintain the balance of power; and since the Spartans had no capital and no trade, while the Athenians continued to colonize the coasts of the Aegean and the Black Sea and their commerce stretched as far as Carthage, it was a balance which could not be expected to last for ever.

Athens was mistress of an empire: her colonies contributed to her prosperity and throughout the Aegean her subject states provided safe harbours for the navy on which her survival depended. But Pericles believed that those states received more than they gave: they grew rich in an expanding economy and they were protected by a fleet for which they paid far less than it would have cost them to maintain fleets of their own. As a man who had been educated in the heroic tradition, he saw no conflict between this necessary but responsible imperialism and his democratic ideals. The Athenians who carried the burdens deserved the privileges and, to ensure that the government of their cosmopolitan capital would remain in the hands of men who were proud of its achievements, Pericles persuaded the assembly to limit Athenian citizenship to men who were descended from Athenians on both sides of their families. For these men, with the profits from their commerce and the residue of the tributes from subject states, he set out to create a city and a society that would be not only the greatest in Greece but an example to posterity.

Under the direction of his friend the sculptor Phidias, architects adorned Athens and Piraeus with magnificent temples and public buildings, of which the first and the most beautiful was the Parthenon. In the theatres the plays of Sophocles and Euripides were performed and, so that the poorest citizens could attend, Pericles created a fund to compensate them for loss of earnings, just as he had established payment for state service. While the craftsmen of Athens acquired such taste and skill that their work was sold throughout the civilized Mediterranean, the intellectual life of the city reached such a vital pitch that from all over the Greek world men like Herodotus and Hippocrates, the 'fathers' of history and medicine, flocked to take part in it. Superstition and fatalism were discredited and from the rival schools of philosophy there emerged a new rationalism and a faith in the potential of man, reflected in the works of the artists and the open-minded curiosity of the scientists. Yet there were men who clung to the old traditions and Pericles still had enemies. Thucydides, who had succeeded his father-in-law Cimon as leader of the conservatives, accused him of corruption for spending the tributes that had been paid for defence on the decoration of Athens, but the assembly was so incensed that it ostracized him and thereafter, realizing that Pericles was unassailable, the conservatives attacked his friends instead. Even Aspasia was charged with impiety, until the case was thrown out when Pericles, with tears in his eyes, defended her himself.

Inevitably, the Golden Age and the empire which made it possible aroused the envy and resentment of the rest of Greece. When the Athenians supported rebellions in Corinthian colonies and barred the Megarans from the use of all ports in their empire, Corinth and Megara appealed to Sparta and in 432 BC Sparta declared war. At first it seemed to some Athenians that they might save their city by offering to relinquish their empire, but Pericles persuaded them to fight: 'It may have been wrong to take it,' he said with disarming candour, 'but it would be dangerous to let it go.' On his advice the Athenians abandoned the countryside to their enemies and retired behind the impregnable walls which Pericles had built between Athens and Piraeus, where they intended to wait until their superior fleet had blockaded the Peloponnese into starvation. But in the summer heat of a city crowded with refugees a plague broke out, and in the autumn of 429 BC, after burying a third of the population including his sister and both his sons, Pericles also died of it.

After the death of Pericles, Athenian strategy was paralyzed by political rivalries and weakened by reckless raids and, before the Peloponnesian war was over, the Athenian empire had been destroyed. Yet its achievements were as immortal as Pericles knew that they would be: as he had told the Athenians, 'The brilliance of today is the

The south-east corner of the Parthenon, one of the extraordinary legacies of Pericles' rule.

reputation of tomorrow.' From hardly more than a generation of Athenians, western civilization inherited a political ideal and the foundations of its philosophy, architecture, drama and science. What the western world owes to Athens, Athens owed to Pericles. 'We are the school of Greece,' he said, 'we have left behind us imperishable monuments.'

~ Alexander the Great ~

In 356 BC, beyond the civilized states of central Greece, in the still half-savage kingdom of Macedonia, the fierce, mystical Queen Olympias was delivered of her first-born, Alexander. Her husband, the illustrious King Philip II, was seldom at home; while he continued his campaigns, caroused with his officers and slept in the arms of other women, Olympias, a possessive and indulgent mother, consoled herself with the depraved occult rituals of her ancient religion. Philip was far more cultured and civilized than his Macedonian nobles, however, and he saw to it that his son received the finest education that the world could offer. He created a special school for him with the sons of some of his commanders and allies and at the age of thirteen Alexander became the pupil of the great Athenian poet and philosopher Aristotle, whom he was to love thereafter as a second father.

Alexander was astonishingly gifted. Of average height, strikingly handsome, with huge eyes, fine features and blond curling hair, he played the lyre so well that his father teased him about it; his scholarly passion for history, literature and science was insatiable, and from it he developed an intense and permanent love for the culture of central Greece. Alexander had inherited his father's pride and his mother's fiery temper, but he was also warm-hearted and unreproachful. He admired his father as a soldier and he was always deeply devoted to his mother, yet his parents' marriage and morals left their mark on him; in later life his temperance and respect for women, so uncharacteristic of his fellow soldiers, were to give rise to jaundiced and spurious slander.

Under Aristotle's guidance, Alexander developed all the intellectual and moral virtues which the Athenians believed to be the hallmarks of the ideal man, and combined them with the dignity and responsibility of his noble birth. Princes were expected to be proud and ambitious, but before Alexander the Greek world had never seen one who was strong enough to show compassion or remorse. Yet among those ideal virtues there was no place for modesty; to Alexander, as to Aristotle, there was nothing shameful in the pursuit of glory. Even before he became the pupil of Aristotle he had already demonstrated his own yearning for prestige. Once, when he was twelve, he was taken to inspect a fine but expensive black colt called Bucephalas. The colt seemed nervous and, when all the grooms failed to mount him, Alexander announced that he would do it. Hoping to teach him a lesson, Philip agreed to let him try on condition that he bought the colt if he failed. But Alexander had noticed that the colt was shying from the grooms' shadows as they went behind his head; and turning him to face the sun, he calmed him, mounted and galloped away, returning with Bucephalas prancing obediently beneath him. 'My son,' said Philip, 'you must find a kingdom for yourself; Macedonia is not large enough to hold you.' From that day on, Bucephalas was Alexander's principal charger and in time his name was to become as immortal as that of his master.

In 336 BC Philip was murdered and so at the age of twenty Alexander inherited his crown. By threats and by force of arms, Philip had united all the Greek states except Sparta in the League of Corinth, which he had intended to lead against the still-threatening Persian Empire, but on his death they eagerly repudiated their agreements. When Alexander occupied Thessaly, however, they began to change their minds and by the end of the following year, after the destruction of rebellious Thebes, he was the undisputed master

of a reconstituted league.

Alexander was now in a position to fulfil his father's ambitions in Persia and in the spring of 334 BC he crossed the Hellespont with the Macedonian and Greek mercenary army which Philip had armed and organized into the most advanced fighting force in the world. He had over 5,000 cavalry and 30,000 infantry, including his 9,000-strong Macedonian phalanx. His corps commanders and administrators, who included his closest childhood friends, Ptolemy, Hephaistion, Nearchus and Cleitus the Black, were known as the 'Companions' and his eight squadrons of noble Macedonian cavalry were called the 'Companion cavalry'. Apart from soldiers, there were scientists, surveyors and geographers, and as the expedition progressed they were joined by historians, philosophers and artists: the great adventure was not just an invasion, it was a journey of exploration and a mission to disseminate the civilization of Greece.

When Alexander reached the river Granicus, 20,000 Persian cavalry were waiting on the opposite bank with 20,000 Greek mercenary infantry behind them. Although their position was strong, Alexander ordered an attack, but decided it was going to be too dangerous to risk Bucephalas. As the Macedonians fought their way up from the river the Persians began to fall back and Mithradates, the son-in-law of the Persian king Darius III, brought men round from the right to reinforce them. Cutting through the throng, Alexander reached Mithradates and killed him; as he did so, a Persian officer struck the plume from his helmet with a battle-axe, but, as the Persian raised his arm to strike the second blow that would surely have killed him, Cleitus the Black severed it with his sword. The Persian cavalry broke and fled, and Alexander's horsemen fell on the Greek mercenaries, slaughter-

The young Alexander, riding a tamed Bucephalas, is greeted by his parents, King Philip and Queen Olympias. From a 15th-century Tournai tapestry of the life of Alexander.

ing all but 2,000. The victory had cost him no more than 25 Companion cavalry, 60 light cavalry and 30 infantry, but, as he had feared, in the final carnage his substitute horse was killed beneath him.

Alexander then advanced along the coast to destroy the Persian harbours; the Greek towns rose in his support and when the others were taken he turned inland to capture the ancient city of Gordium. Here, in the temple, he was shown the complicated Gordian Knot which according to legend could only be untied by the man who was to rule Asia. But the legend did not say how it was to be untied and, drawing his sword, Alexander cut through it with a single stroke.

In the following spring he advanced into Syria to meet the main Persian army, said to be 150,000 strong, under the command of King Darius himself. On the way, a heavy fever forced him to halt, and while his doctor was preparing a potion he received a letter warning that the doctor had been bribed by Darius to poison him. Alexander did not believe it and, when the doctor brought the potion, Alexander handed him the letter and drank while he read it.

Misinterpreting Alexander's delay as reticence, Darius moved north to meet him at Issus. At first he surprised Alexander by appearing in his rear, but when Alexander turned back Darius drew up his army on a narrow plain where there was no room to deploy his superior numbers. Once again the Greek army broke the Persian left, and Darius fled from the field, leaving his camp, his mother, his wife and daughters to be captured by his enemies. Alexander let the royal family know that Darius was safe; next day, when he visited them, they knelt in gratitude in front of his companion, Hephaistion, who was the taller, and were overcome with frightened embarrassment when they realized their mistake, but Alexander reassured them, 'He too is Alexander.' In the Persian king's tent the Greek soldiers found a magnificent jewelled casket which Darius had used for carrying his priceless trinkets; thereafter

Alexander used it for carrying one of his own treasures: a copy of Homer's *Iliad*.

Detail from a Pompeiian mosaic of the battle of Issus, showing Alexander.

After founding the city of Alexandretta, Alexander marched down the Palestinian coast capturing the Phoenician ports and denying the Persian fleet the last of its harbours. Most of the towns surrendered or fell easily, but Tyre was destroyed only after eight months of siege. Towards the end of 332 BC he reached Egypt and was welcomed as a liberator. Here he reorganized the government, laid out plans for the great city of Alexandria on the Nile delta and made a pilgrimage to the temple of Amon at the oasis of Siwa, where the priests saluted him as the son of God. Meanwhile Darius had assembled a new army in Babylon, including hundreds of chariots with vicious scythe blades on their wheels. In the spring of 331 BC Alexander left Egypt and advanced into Mesopotamia to meet him. This time, at Gaugamela, Darius had chosen the ground carefully for his own advantage, but when some of the Companions advised Alexander to attack by night he answered, 'Alexander does not steal his victories'. Once again, the Persian army was annihilated, and Darius fled to his summer capital at Ecbatana (Hamadan), but before Alexander could reach him he was murdered by his commander Bessus.

In 330 BC Alexander set out to acquire the eastern territories of the Persian empire and during the next two and a half years he defeated Bessus and conquered all the lands now known as Khorasan, Turkmenistan, Uzbekistan and

Afghanistan. One of the last rulers to be defeated, Oxyartes, only surrendered after Alexander had captured the mountain fortress which contained his beautiful daughter Roxane, and shortly afterwards, when Alexander married Roxane, they became allies.

Alexander's aim was to rule, not to destroy. By now there were Persian commanders and thousands of Persian soldiers who fought willingly in his army, and everywhere he founded cities, all called Alexandria, many of which were to grow into great commercial centres under new names. His Persian subjects were treated as equals with the Greeks and he pleased them by wearing eastern clothes, but he began to imitate the arrogance of the Persian kings, making the Greeks prostrate themselves in front of him at court receptions according to the Persian custom, until the Macedonians were exempted from the humiliation when they protested that he was not a god. Seduced by Persian splendour and his own success, he had developed a swollen vanity that was to be punctured only by tragedy. At a banquet in Samarkand, in which everyone including Alexander had drunk more than usual, Alexander allowed his flatterers to imply that all his achievements had been due to his genius alone and he revealed an unworthy contempt for his uncivilized Macedonians. Angered by this, Cleitus the Black shouted that it was the Macedonians who had conquered his empire and that he, a Macedonian, had once saved his life. Alexander rose in a rage and Ptolemy dragged Cleitus out of the tent, but Cleitus fought free and as he turned back Alexander grabbed a spear and ran him through. Cleitus fell dead and Alexander's fury vanished in horror. He put the spear against a tent pole and tried to run on to it, but his guards held him back, and sobbing with shame and grief he was taken to his tent where he remained for three days in unrelieved anguish. He was never so proud again.

In the summer of 327 BC Alexander invaded India, conquering the valley of the river Indus. On the banks of its tributary the Jhelum, then known as the Hydaspes, he met the army of Porus, raja of the Punjab, the finest soldier ever to face Alexander. It was a long, hard battle: the Macedonian horses were terrified by the Indian elephants, but in the end Alexander's concentration on his enemy's left forced Porus to weaken his right and when the Greek light cavalry swung round it to charge the Indian rear the battle was over. Porus was brought before Alexander and asked how he thought he should be treated. 'Like a king,' he said, and so he was. His kingdom was returned to him and he became an ally of Alexander's, adding his elephants to the conqueror's army.

Soon after the battle, tired old Bucephalas died. He had travelled with his master for over 2,500 miles; he had carried him in battle and learned to kneel so that Alexander could mount in full armour; and he was so dearly loved that once, when he had been stolen, he was returned after Alexander had threatened to depopulate the whole district. On the spot where he died Alexander founded the city of Bucephala, the only city to have been named after a horse.

Leaving some of his army on the Hydaspes to organize the construction of a river fleet for the conquest of Sind on the lower Indus, Alexander marched east with Porus. But after the fall of Sangala they halted. Alexander's soldiers had had enough and they refused to advance any further. It seemed to them that the campaigns would never end – even the Persians were already 1,000 miles from home – and when he realized that he would not change their minds, Alexander agreed to return to Babylon.

Towards the end of 326 BC, the long journey home began. Part of the army, led by Nearchus, was to return by sea, the rest, under Alexander, by land. Forced by impassable mountains to turn north into the desert, Alexander led his men through the uncharted wilderness for sixty days, during which time exhaustion, intense heat and lack of food and water threatened to defeat the conqueror who had never lost a battle against mortal enemies. Fortunately, news of his ordeal reached some of his commanders in central Persia, who set out to meet him with a huge train of supplies and found him just in time. During the seven days of celebration that followed, a cavalry patrol along the coast met five ragged, emaciated men and at first did not recognize one of them as Nearchus. Back at the camp Nearchus reported that the fleet was safe but that, without supplies, the crews had been on the point of mutiny by the time he landed them; and as he told the story of his own terrible journey, Alexander held his hand and cried.

In his absence Alexander's new empire had been weakened by corruption and much of the next year was spent suppressing it. After the hardships of the long campaigns and the terrible journey home, it was a period of justifiably magnificent festivals, but it was marred by sadness. In Ecbatana Hephaistion died of a fever and Alexander was inconsolable. Towards the end of 324 BC, still heartbroken, he returned to Babylon and on the way he began to plan a new expedition towards the west. But in the following summer he too was seized by a sudden fever. Each day he grew weaker and when the Macedonian soldiers insisted on being allowed to see him he could do no more than nod recognition as they filed past his bed. On 13 June 323 BC, at the age of thirty-two years and eight months, Alexander the Great died.

The new empire did not long outlast its conqueror. Proud princes and generals who had served as Alexander's captains would take orders from no other man, and soon they were fighting among themselves. Few of the plans which he had made for a flourishing economy among equal peoples were fulfilled. Yet there was one achievement which could not be erased: Alexander had brought the Middle East within the boundaries of the civilized world, the culture of Greece had been permanently planted in its kingdoms and a new epoch had begun. 'I have not come to destroy nations,' he said, 'I have come that those who are subdued by my arms have nought to complain of my victories.'

✍ Hannibal ✍

In 239 BC, a nine-year-old Carthaginian boy stood alone before the altar of his gods and, solemnly placing his hands on the sacrificial offering, swore eternal enmity against the people of Rome. Since the destruction of Tyre by Alexander the Great, the Phoenician settlement at Carthage on the north coast of Africa had become the richest port in the Mediterranean and mistress of a commercial empire, but in the middle of the third century BC that empire began to be eroded by the rapid and ruthless expansion of the Roman republic. By 239 BC the Carthaginians had been driven out of Sicily and most of Sardinia and it was to replace these losses and establish a base from which they could one day be avenged that the most powerful and one of the richest men in Carthage, Hamilcar Barca, had decided to conquer Spain. So great was his determination to crush the Romans that much of the expedition had been organized at his own expense and when Hannibal, the eldest of his three sons, to whom he referred as his lion's brood, had begged to be allowed to accompany him, he had not only agreed, but, in the hope that the boy might grow up to continue his mission, had taken him to the temple to make his vow.

Hannibal, the Carthaginian general who led an army of mercenaries thousands of miles into the heart of the Roman empire.

During the next nine years, while the Romans colonized northern Spain, Hamilcar built an empire in the south, but after his death in battle he was succeeded by his son-in-law Hasdrubal, who ruled peacefully and made a treaty with the Romans. However, when Hasdrubal was assassinated, the Carthaginian army elected Hamilcar's son Hannibal, then twenty-five, as military commander and governor of Spain. Sooner than he could have hoped, Hannibal had been given the power to fulfil his vow.

Throughout the campaigns and governments of his father and brother-in-law, Hannibal had grown up among soldiers. He had shared their hardships, his courage was already celebrated and in several battles he had distinguished himself as an inventive officer. His Greek tutors had fired him with an admiration for Alexander the Great and instilled him with a heroic sense of honour and justice, but, above all, nature had endowed him with a personal magnetism that had won the devoted loyalty of his men. The Carthaginians were merchants; while Roman soldiers fought for their own power and in defence of their republic, the men who served in the Carthaginian army were mostly mercenaries, who fought for pay and plunder. It was as much a mark of Hannibal's genius as any of his victories or tactical innovations that men like these were prepared to follow him for over 1,000 miles through hostile country on one of the most audacious expeditions in the history of warfare.

Under the terms of Hasdrubal's treaty, the Carthaginians had agreed not to attack the Roman settlements north of the river Ebro, but on the south of the river there was a Spanish port at Saguntum which had made its own treaty with the Romans; since the Romans could use this port to land an army in his rear, Hannibal laid siege to it. The Romans naturally protested and, as Hannibal had hoped, when the town fell, they declared war. Carthage and Spain were further from Rome than Sicily and Sardinia and he knew that, before the Romans could organize an attack, his own plans would have put them on the defensive.

Leaving Spain under the governorship of his brother, who, like his brother-in-law, was called Hasdrubal, Hannibal set out from his base at Cartagena in the spring of 218 BC. With about 50,000 Carthaginian, Spanish and Libyan infantry, 10,000 Numidian cavalry, squadrons of small Berber elephants and trains of mules and ox-drawn wagons, he fought his way north, crossed the Pyrenees and turned east through southern France towards Italy. On the east bank of the river Rhône, the Volgae Gauls were waiting to prevent his crossing, but, while their kinsmen on the west bank made rafts and sold them to the Carthaginians, Hannibal sent 10,000 men to ford upstream under cover of darkness, and at the first charge on their flank the defenders fled. By the time two Roman legions landed at Marseilles, Hannibal had crossed the Rhône and

A French engraving of the passage of Hannibal's elephants across the Rhône, using rafts made by the Gauls.

disappeared northwards. Failing to find him, the Roman commander, Publius Cornelius Scipio, returned to Pisa after sending his legions on under his brother Gnaius to attack Spain. It was now October and the snow was beginning to fall in the mountains; if Hannibal intended to invade Italy, he would have to wait until the spring thaw and meanwhile his army would be weakened by a winter among the hostile Gauls.

But Hannibal crossed the Alps in November. For two terrible weeks, raided by mountain tribesmen and misled by treacherous guides, his soldiers struggled south through uncharted passes. They scrambled along icy ledges, dug their way through snowdrifts and when the boulders that blocked the gorges were too big for their elephants to shift, they heated them with fires and then cooled them quickly with iced vinegar until they split. When they reached the undefended foothills of northern Italy they were exhausted and starving, and the losses had been heavy, but, with the plunder of Rome within their reach, their morale was unshaken. After a brief rest, Hannibal captured the city of the Taurini, persuaded some of the local Gauls to join him and then, to retain his advantage of surprise, marched swiftly towards the river Po.

With two legions from Pisa, Publius Scipio joined forces with the two legions of his fellow consul, Tiberius Sempronius, on the south of the Po. Between them they had 40,000 men and, in spite of Scipio's protestations, Sempronius insisted that they had the strength to attack. When Hannibal pitched camp four miles away on the left bank of the river Trebia, Sempronius advanced to engage him. It was to be the first of Hannibal's great victories. While the Roman wings were driven into the river by elephants and Numidian cavalry, their centre was trapped between the Carthaginian front and 2,000 picked men who had been hiding in the bed of a stream under the command of Hannibal's young

brother, Maro. The Romans abandoned northern Italy and, having killed 20,000 of his enemies with minimal losses to his own side, Hannibal retired to winter quarters.

In the spring of 217 BC, reinforced by northern tribes, Hannibal crossed the Apennines, laid waste northern Etruria and then turned east towards Lake Trasemene. From Arretium, Gaius Flaminius set out after him with 30,000 men. There was another Roman army marching across from the east coast and there was a chance that they could trap the Carthaginians between them. But Flaminius advanced too quickly. As he marched along the shore of Lake Trasemene, the Carthaginian army, hidden by the hills and the morning mist, ambushed his column, killing 15,000 Romans, including Flaminius, and capturing nearly all the others. Hannibal's second great victory was the only battle in history in which the commander of a large army used his entire force to lay an ambush and also in which practically the whole enemy strength was eliminated.

The road to Rome lay open and the roads that ran south from it were crowded with refugees. But Hannibal was in no position to attack. The city walls had recently been repaired and on the long journey from Spain Hannibal had been unable to carry heavy siege engines. He could not take the city by storm and, as long as the confederation of Italian states remained intact, he could not risk the prolonged siege that would give them time to assemble an army in his rear. Instead, hoping that a campaign of systematic devastation would drive some of the confederated states to join him, he recrossed the Apennines and marched south into Apulia, laying waste the countryside.

In the state of emergency the Romans elected a dictator, Quintus Fabius Maximus, whose cautious strategy of 'masterly inactivity' against the Carthaginian genius was to earn him the surname 'Cunctator' (the delayer). Fabius believed that, with Roman command of the sea denying the invaders reinforcements and sup-

plies, it was only a matter of time before Hannibal's invincible soldiers became hungry, ill-equipped and dispirited. In the spring of 216 BC his assessment was confirmed when Hannibal's first act was to capture the important Roman supply depot at Cannae, but by then his six-month term as dictator was over and the new consuls, Lucius Aemilius Paulus and Gaius Terentius Varro, were impatient. With the largest army that Rome had ever put into the field, which, allowing for the exaggerations of contemporary historians, was still over 50,000 strong, they marched east to engage the Carthaginians at Cannae. It was to be the third and greatest of Hannibal's victories: only 14,000 Romans escaped from the battlefield and only 10,000 were taken prisoner.

At last some of the southern Italian cities declared for Hannibal and, although an assault on Rome was still impossible, its eventual surrender seemed inevitable. But in the next year Fabius was elected consul and thereafter the Romans continued his patient policies. As years passed in desperate but determined austerity, they built up new legions, sent some of them to Spain and used others to attack the cities that had joined Hannibal, but they never engaged him in open battle. In this way, they denied Hannibal his only advantage: his genius on the battlefield.

In Spain Publius Scipio and his brother Gnaius prevented Hasdrubal from reinforcing his brother, and after they were both killed in battle Publius's talented son began the systematic suppression of the Carthaginian provinces. In 207 BC, however, Hasdrubal eluded him and set out with his army for Italy. But after crossing the Alps, he was intercepted and defeated, and his severed head was flung contemptuously into Hannibal's camp by a Roman cavalry patrol. In 203 BC, fourteen years after he had entered Italy, Hannibal learned that the young Publius Scipio had landed an army in North Africa and was advancing towards Carthage. Thwarted by his own strategy, he returned to defend his capital.

In October 202 BC, the armies of Scipio and

Hannibal met on the battlefield of Zama. They were about equal in numbers, but Hannibal was dangerously weak in cavalry; moreover, the Romans had learnt from their mistakes in previous encounters with the Carthaginians. By the end of the battle, some 20,000 of Hannibal's soldiers had been killed, another 20,000 taken prisoner, and Scipio had earned the surname 'Africanus'. On Hannibal's advice Carthage surrendered. Instead of destroying it, the Romans, who had been nearly bankrupted by their magnificent war effort, allowed the citizens to continue trading and imposed an indemnity of 10,000 talents of silver to be paid in annual instalments for fifty years.

For the next six years Hannibal ruled in Carthage and restored the economy so effectively that the apprehensive Romans demanded his arrest for conspiracy. He escaped to Syria, where he incited the king to make war on the Romans, but when that ended in defeat, knowing that his surrender would be one of the terms of peace, he escaped again and eventually found his last refuge in Bithynia. In 183 BC the Bithynian king agreed to hand him over to the Romans and, with his house surrounded by soldiers, Hannibal took poison and died.

On the basis of the lessons that they had learned from Hannibal, the Romans reorganized and retrained their legions into the army with which Pompey and Caesar were to conquer an enormous empire. Their stubborn tenacity had destroyed his dreams, but he had led an army into the heart of their country, maintained it there unsupported for fourteen years, and brought it safely home again. The failure of his purpose had denied him the title of conqueror, but his achievement had earned him a place beside his hero Alexander as one of the very few men in history who can truly be described as a military genius.

～ *Spartacus* ～

One of the abhorrent domestic benefits of Roman imperialism was an inexhaustible supply of slaves. In the cities family servants, particularly educated Greeks, were often valued members of their households, but the easily replaceable prisoners who laboured in gangs on the country estates were on the whole treated no better than the animals and, in spite of their enormous numbers, the Romans did not even regard them as a threat to internal security: when Asian slaves rebelled in Sicily, they were so disorganized that they were soon suppressed.

In 73 BC, however, seventy-four gladiators, who had been trained to a peak of excellence in the art of killing each other for their masters' entertainment, broke into the armoury of their training camp in Capua, stole all the weapons and fled to take refuge on the summit of Mount Vesuvius. When thousands of slaves from the neighbouring estates escaped to join the revolt, the praetor Caius Claudius Glaber marched south with a legion and confidently began to surround Vesuvius. But these rebels were not the wretched and servile products of eastern slave markets, they were Thracian, Gallic and Teutonic prisoners of war, organized and instructed by formidable gladiators and led by an instinctive military commander – a Thracian gladiator called Spartacus, who had once served as an unwilling conscript in the Roman army and had been enslaved for desertion. One by one the Roman units were cut to pieces and by the end of the year the whole of southern Italy was under the control of an army of slaves.

In the following spring the consuls Lucius Gellius Publicola and Gnaius Lentulus Clodianus took the field with two legions each. The rebel army, which had been swollen to nearly 100,000 strong by the slave population of southern Italy, was divided into two corps, one commanded by Spartacus and the other by a Gallic gladiator called Crixus. Crixus was carried away by the temptations of easy plunder; exposing themselves to the inevitable attack of a Roman army, his men roamed aimlessly from town to town until they were isolated and annihilated by Gellius at Monte Gargano. But Spartacus was not interested in plunder or vengeance; his only objective was the freedom of his followers and, knowing that they could not survive in Italy for ever, he decided to lead them north to the Alps, where they could split up and escape over the mountains to their homes. As they marched north with more slaves joining them every day, Gellius followed and Lentulus raced past to intercept them. The destruction of Crixus had been no more than the Romans had expected and what followed was as terrifying as it was incredible. In Picenum Spartacus halted his slaves, fell on the following legions of Gellius and then turned to attack the army of Lentulus a few days later. Both the consuls were crushingly defeated and half their soldiers were killed.

The last army that stood between the slaves and freedom was the army of Caius Cassius, pro-consul of Cisalpine Gaul, and when that too was defeated the roads through the mountains lay open. But by then their own success had convinced the slaves that, once they scattered, the humiliated Romans would track them down relentlessly. Believing that so long as they remained united they could always defeat a Roman army, they decided instead to return to the south and take over Sicily for themselves with the support of the Sicilian slaves and eastern

Bronze sculpture of a *retiarius* (a gladiator who fought with trident and net).

pirates. It was a suicidal ambition: the slaves could never hope to hold the island against a republic that was capable of conquering Spain and most of the Middle East. Nevertheless, although his own chance of freedom was as good as it would ever be, Spartacus would not desert them and he led them south again.

The Romans were the masters of the Mediterranean, but their homeland seemed to be as vulnerable as it had been in the days of Hannibal and, already demoralized by political unrest and the first violent tremors of civil war, they began to blame their self-seeking leaders and demanded that soldiers be recalled from the outposts of the empire. When the rebels reached Rhegium, in the toe of Italy, Roman ships prevented them from crossing into Sicily and the praetor Marcus Licinius Crassus came up behind them with no less than eight legions. Hoping to contain the rebels until they starved, Crassus built a wall from coast to coast across the peninsula, but in spite of the size of his army it was ridiculous to imagine that he could hold all thirty-seven miles of the wall at once. Spartacus broke through and headed east to escape out of Italy from the port of Brundisium, in the heel. Before he reached it, however, it was occupied by Marcus Lucullus, who had sailed across with an army from the Black Sea. There was now no alternative but to return to the Alps. Yet the slaves were still so confident that two dissident groups, led by the Gallic gladiators Castus and Cannicus, began to make bandit raids as Crixus had done, and Spartacus lost valuable men extricating them from Roman ambushes until they were finally cut to pieces by Crassus.

Spartacus's army no longer had numerical superiority and at last the full military might of the Roman republic was closing in on him. Lucullus was behind him, Crassus was somewhere on his left flank and ahead of him Gnaeus Pompeius (Pompey), who had just returned in glory from Spain, was marching south from Rome. There was little left to do but hide in the mountains, but the slaves were eager to attack Crassus before Pompey arrived and once again Spartacus gave in to them. He knew that their chance of victory was slight, yet so now was any

hope of freedom, and a glorious death was better than slavery or torture. Before the battle he rode out in front of his army and killed his horse so that he would have no means of escape. 'If I am victorious,' he said, 'I shall easily get another, and if vanquished I shall not need one.' By the time Pompey reached him, Crassus had already defeated the rebels and the body of Spartacus had been found in the middle of the field, covered in wounds on a pile of slaughtered Romans.

Along the roadside from Rome to Capua, 6,000 prisoners were crucified in hideous vengeance. A catastrophe had been averted and when the two victorious commanders returned the jubilant citizens elected them consuls. To the Romans, Spartacus was the dangerous bandit who had threatened their republic with re-volution when it was already weakened by political rivalries, and it was not until their empire had fallen that he was remembered as a hero. All he had ever wanted was freedom and to that end he had defied the most powerful nation in the world, dominated southern Italy as Hannibal had done and defeated three Roman armies in open battle. It had taken more than a dozen legions to destroy him and his downfall had been due at least in part to the aimless indecision of the desperate fugitives whom he refused to desert.

~ *Julius Caesar* ~

Gaius Julius Caesar was born 100 years before the birth of Christ, on the twelfth day of the month which was later renamed July in his honour. His father was a politician who served as praetor and pro-consul of Asia and his aunt Julia was married to Gaius Marius, leader of the

progressive popular party in Rome. Educated under the careful supervision of his mother Aurelia, Caesar was brought up in the radical atmosphere of Marius's entourage and at the age of sixteen he married Cornelia, the daughter of his uncle's chief supporter, Lucius Cornelius

Julius Caesar.

and, when some of the patrician senators persuaded Sulla to relent, he warned them that the boy had many Mariuses in him. Before Sulla could reverse his decision, Caesar discreetly sailed east to serve on the staff of the pro-consul of Asia. In 79 BC, however, Sulla inexplicably resigned and Caesar came home. But fearing that he would be implicated in the foolhardy *coup d'état* which was being planned by Marcus Aemilius Lepidus, a consul who had deserted Sulla for the popular party, he sailed east again, ostensibly to study rhetoric in Rhodes. On the way he was captured by pirates. He was well treated and when he was released after forty days on payment of an enormous ransom, he promised laughingly that he would return to crucify the lot of them – which he did shortly afterwards with the help of a fleet from Miletus.

On his return to Rome Caesar was elected military tribune and his long political career began. The *coup d'état* had failed and its supporters had fled to Spain, which since the ascendancy of Sulla had become an independent province controlled by the followers of Marius. But Spain was reconquered by Pompey, who had been a commander in Sulla's army, and in 70 BC, after the destruction of the slave rebellion under Spartacus, the grateful Roman people, in defiance of the senate and supported by the armies, elected the conquering rivals Pompey and Crassus as consuls. Order was restored and the Romans were at last able to turn their attention to the east, where pirates and the armies of King Mithradates of Pontus were threatening the economy of the republic and the security of its Asian empire. Four years later the senate, encouraged by Caesar, gave Pompey a fleet and an army and granted him dangerously absolute authority over Asia.

The crumbling constitution of the Roman republic was no longer capable of coping with the consequences of an empire. Military command made men rich, and, as Pompey and Crassus had demonstrated, power now lay, not with the political parties, but with the men who com-

Cinna. But by the end of 82 BC all semblance of democracy in the Roman republic had disappeared, the traditional constitution had been abolished, Marius, Cinna and Caesar's father were dead and the conservative consul Lucius Cornelius Sulla had been made dictator for life.

Sulla had been the first consul to lead his soldiers through the gates of Rome and with their help he began to eliminate his opponents. Even the young Julius Caesar was sentenced to death for refusing to disassociate himself from the popular party by divorcing the daughter of Cinna

manded the loyalty of the legions. But during Pompey's absence Caesar rose rapidly in office and revived the popular party. He was tall, lean and imposing, and his skill as an orator forced even Cicero to admit that he was second to none. He built up an enormous body of support among the common people and earned the ardent admiration of the rich and simple-minded Crassus, who paid for some of the public festivals that Caesar had organized. After the death of Cornelia he married Pompeia, but so careful was he of his public image that he divorced her five years later for being innocently implicated in the trial of a heretic, since Caesar's wife should be beyond suspicion. By 61 BC he had risen so high in public esteem that he was appointed pro-consul of Spain.

When Caesar returned from his year in Spain, Pompey, who had expanded the Asian empire and destroyed its enemies, was attempting to obtain an extension of his authority, but the senate was apprehensive, and in a master-stroke of political diplomacy Caesar reconciled Pompey and Crassus, who had both been thwarted by the conservative party to which they had once belonged, and offered to put the support of his popular party behind them in return for their support of his candidacy for consul. As a result, in 59 BC, Caesar was elected consul, Pompey was re-appointed pro-consul of Asia and Crassus was put in charge of the republican revenues. During his year of office Caesar forced through the senate all the laws which Pompey and Crassus had supported, including the recognition of Ptolemy XII as King of Egypt, and increased his popularity still further by dividing state-owned lands into small farms for the poor. On his retirement, when he was appointed pro-consul of Gaul for five years, he married Calpurnia, the daughter of Lucius Piso, who succeeded him as consul, strengthening the less reliable half of his alliance by marrying his daughter Julia to Pompey. With Crassus's wealth, Pompey's army and Caesar's mob behind it, the authority of the triumvirate was unassailable. In 56 BC, with

minimal opposition from the senate, Pompey moved to the pro-consulship of Spain and Africa, Crassus replaced him in Asia, and Caesar's term of office in Gaul was extended for a further five years.

As pro-consul of Gaul, Caesar had at last been given command of an army. Thus, at the age of forty-two, an age by which most successful Roman generals had already become conquerors, he began his extraordinary military career. Every summer he campaigned north of the Alps, returning each winter to Cisalpine Gaul, where he could keep in touch with developments in Rome. The Mediterranean coast between Italy and Spain was already a Roman province, but beyond it the rich lands between the Atlantic and the Rhine supported an enormous population of disparate peoples whose migrations and internal conflicts were a growing threat to the security of the European empire. The Germanic Suevi had crossed the Rhine in support of the Gallic Arverni and Sequani, defeated the Aedui, who were Roman allies, and settled in Alsace, where their preparations to annex the lands of their neighbours had induced 300,000 Helvetii to migrate towards Provence. In 58 BC Caesar crossed the Alps with four legions, halted the Helvetii and marched into Alsace, where he routed the Suevi and drove the survivors back across the Rhine.

Encouraged by his success and convinced that there would be no lasting peace without Roman rule, Caesar then began the systematic conquest of Gaul. By the end of 56 BC he was in control of the Atlantic coast, and in 54 BC he led a reconnaissance in force into the island of Britain. Renewed opposition in Gaul in 52 BC threatened to reverse everything that Caesar had achieved, but on an open battlefield near Dijon the Gallic army, led by the young Arvernian chief Vercingetorix, was broken by the discipline of the Roman legions. By the end of 50 BC Gaul was a peaceful Roman province, paying an annual tribute of forty million sesterces, and Julius Caesar, who had conquered nearly 300 tribes and

One of Caesar's coins, showing the Gallic arms and a captive Gaul.

captured 800 towns and villages, was a rich man.

During Caesar's last years in Gaul the triumvirate disintegrated: Crassus was killed and, after the death of Julia, Pompey returned to the conservatives. In 50 BC Caesar's supporters, who included Marcus Antonius (Mark Antony), persuaded the senators to rule that both Pompey and Caesar should resign as pro-consuls, pending the consular elections in the following year, but the conservatives defied them and it looked as though Pompey was about to become a second Sulla. On 7 January Caesar was dismissed as pro-consul of Gaul and Mark Antony fled to join him. On 11 January, with no alternative but to abandon his own ambitions and surrender Rome to a reactionary dictator, Caesar crossed the river Rubicon, which was the southern boundary of the provinces in which he had been legally entitled to command an army, and advanced on Rome at the head of a legion.

The opposition knew that the masses would welcome their hero, but it had seriously underestimated the loyalty of his army: during the campaigns in Gaul, Caesar had inspired such devotion that, according to Plutarch, men who on previous campaigns had been no more than average became invincible when his honour was at stake. As Caesar marched south, the soldiers who met him capitulated and the people in the towns turned out to cheer. By the time he reached Rome most of the conservatives had absconded, but, to the surprise of those who remained, he was both lenient with his opponents and moderate in the means which he took to restore order. A few days later, Pompey, who had once boasted that he had only to stamp his foot to fill Italy with soldiers, sailed east from Brundisium with two legions.

Before he set out after him, Caesar marched west with the army from Gaul and destroyed Pompey's Spanish army at Ilerda. Then, returning through Rome, where he was elected consul for 48 BC, he sailed across the Adriatic. At Pharsalus in Thessaly the two greatest conquerors in the Roman world met on an open battlefield. With reinforcements from the garrisons of his former dominions, Pompey had assembled 45,000 infantry, 7,000 cavalry and many thousands of light auxiliaries, and against them Caesar had brought no more than 22,000 infantry and a mere 1,000 cavalry. Nevertheless it was Caesar who attacked, and at the end of the day 15,000 of Pompey's soldiers had been killed and 24,000 taken prisoner, a victory which, it was said, had cost Caesar only 30 centurions and 200 men. The prisoners, who included Marcus Junius Brutus, were all pardoned and formed into new legions which were sent to Asia; and as Caesar surveyed the battlefield on which Roman had slaughtered Roman, he said sadly, 'They drove me to it.'

Pompey fled to Egypt, where he was murdered by a friend of the young king, Ptolemy XIII, and when Caesar reached Alexandria he was presented with his head; but instead of rejoicing at the death of an enemy, he wept for the loss of a friend. His stay in Alexandria was prolonged by his infatuation with the king's sister and consort, Cleopatra, and he became dangerously embroiled in their violent rivalries, which ended with the death of the king. In the following summer, however, he learned that Pharnases, the son of Mithradates, had invaded Pontus. Regretfully he left Cleopatra and marched into Asia Minor, where he defeated Pharnases so quickly that the victory was recorded at his triumph with the simple caption, 'I came, I saw, I conquered.'

At the end of 47 BC, Caesar returned to Rome. But the civil war was not yet over: the conservative republicans had assembled an army in Africa and Pompey's sons were beginning to assemble another in Spain; and before he could embark to meet them Caesar's own army mutinied. Caesar had always addressed his men as 'Fellow soldiers', but this time, accepting their resignation, he addressed them simply as 'Citizens'. With this one humiliating word, the mutiny was quelled. Early in 46 BC the African army was defeated at Thapsus and eleven months later Caesar won his last victory over Pompey's sons at Munda. In less than a year he was dead.

After his appointment as dictator and consul for ten years in 46 BC, Caesar's authority was as unconstitutional as Sulla's had been, but he did not behave as though he intended it to remain that way. During his brief visits to Rome between the campaigns of the civil war and in the few months that were left to him, he completely reorganized the machinery of Roman government, centralizing the administration of the empire and giving greater autonomy to the Italian provinces. He increased the membership of the senate, outnumbering the reactionary patricians by providing for the appointment of provincial representatives and distinguished soldiers, and he established a daily publication of its proceedings. He revised the Roman calendar into the one which has survived to this day and expanded the qualifications for Roman citizenship. Nor did he forget the plight of the people who had brought him to power: an enormous programme of public building was instigated to create employment, he passed laws protecting tradesmen from the unfair competition of slave labour, he founded colonies throughout the empire and, when he had distributed all the remaining state land to the needy, he bought more with his own money and distributed that.

At the beginning of 44 BC Caesar was preparing for an expedition against the Parthians, who were still threatening the Asian empire, and he had discussed the possibility of using the title of king in Asia, as Alexander had done, to help him in his negotiations with hereditary monarchs. But there was no reason to suppose that he would have used the title on his return: when a man in the crowd once hailed him as king, he answered, 'I am not king, but Caesar'; when his statue was erected with an inscription describing him as a demigod, he ordered it erased; and when Mark Antony crowned him at the festival of the Lupercal, he took off the crown and noticed that the crowd did not cheer until he did so. Nevertheless he was a dictator, appointed in the emergency of a civil war, and like many modern dictators he had remained in office after the war to establish a stable government. In the circumstances it was only prudent to retain his authority at least until his return from Asia, but there were a few ardent republicans like Brutus who believed that he should have resigned immediately after the battle of Munda, and there were many patricians who feared his radical reforms and ambitious men who envied him. Since Caesar had dismissed his bodyguards, it was not difficult for these opponents to plan his assassination. On 15 March, the day when the senate was to confirm him as king in Asia, they stabbed him to death beneath Pompey's statue.

After the murder of Caesar the Roman republic collapsed into the long and bloody civil war which was to destroy it for ever. When it was over, Caesar's great-nephew Octavian became the first Roman emperor, Augustus, and Caesar, the hero of the Roman masses, became 'The Divine Julius', the first deified hero of the Roman Empire. As recognition of his achievements, it was an honour no Roman more justly deserved. In a combination of prodigious military and

'The Murder of Caesar', by Pilotry.

political careers, he had stabilized the Roman republic, planted the classical culture in western Europe as firmly as Alexander had planted it in western Asia, won fifty-six battles, one for every year of his life, and even found time to write more than a dozen books. He was not just the greatest soldier and statesman in the Roman world, he was one of history's most versatile, prolific and accomplished men.

∾ Cleopatra ∾

After the death of Alexander the Great, his companion Ptolemy became King of Egypt and for the next 300 years Ptolemy's descendants ruled in Alexandria; but their empire decayed and only the last of the dynasty, Cleopatra VII, inherited the adventurous courage of the Macedonian conquerors. When she came to the throne in 51 BC, Alexandria was a far more splendid city than Rome and her kingdom was still the richest in the world, but her father had only retained its throne with Roman support; since then, the Romans had garrisoned its capital and dictated the policies of its government and it seemed no more than a matter of time before they annexed it to their empire. Nevertheless, rather than accept the inevitable or destroy Egypt by opposing it, Cleopatra set out to turn the merger into a partnership and, by seducing the masters of Rome, to restore the empire of the Ptolemies and make herself mistress of the Mediterranean.

Cleopatra was a cool, shrewd, cultured Greek. An exceptional scholar, a versatile linguist and a cunning diplomat, she enjoyed the company of politicians and philosophers, and she wrote treatises on such varied topics as cosmetics, coins and weights and measures. Yet she was also vivacious, sensuous and totally uninhibited and, although her hollow, chiselled face was hardly handsome, her body was beautiful and she moved with the provocative poise of a dancer. Unlike her predecessors and contrary to the propaganda of her enemies, she was popular with her Egyptian subjects. She was the first of her family to learn their language and to play a part in the ceremonies of their religion and, although there had been many rebellions against the Ptolemies in the past, in her reign there were none; when she was threatened, the Egyptians were even prepared to fight for her.

When Ptolemy XII died, Cleopatra and her half-brother, Ptolemy XIII, were married and succeeded jointly to the throne. Ptolemy, who was only ten years old, was manipulated by his regency councillors, but they were often thwarted by the assertive independence of the nineteen-year-old Cleopatra, and so they accused her of pro-Roman sympathies and persuaded the Alexandrians to depose her. By the time Julius Caesar arrived in search of Pompey, Egypt was on the brink of civil war: Cleopatra had raised an army in Ascalon and Ptolemy was waiting for her with the Egyptian army on the eastern border.

Although he found Pompey dead, Caesar decided to remain in Alexandria to collect the debt incurred by Ptolemy XII in return for Roman support, money which Caesar needed to continue his campaigns against Pompey's supporters. Despite riots protesting against his interference, he established himself in the palace and, setting himself up as arbitrator in the royal quarrel, he summoned the young king. On hearing this, Cleopatra decided that she too would plead her case in person. After reaching Alexandria in an inconspicuous merchant ship, she persuaded a Sicilian merchant called Apollodorus to smuggle her past the guards in a roll of bedding. On the morning after she landed Ptolemy went to Caesar's quarters and found to his horror that the sister who he thought was 200 miles away had not only landed safely in Alexandria, but had spent the night in Caesar's bed.

Cleopatra was twenty-one and Caesar was fifty-two; she fascinated and charmed him and, however much he had intended to be an impartial arbitrator, he became instead her devoted partisan. In spite of the opposition, he persuaded the council to re-establish her on the throne and when he learned from his barber that they had secretly recalled their army, he turned the palace into a fort and summoned reinforcements from Syria. Under constant attack from the angry Alexandrians, the Egyptian army and the Roman garrison which had once supported Pompey, Caesar's soldiers held the palace, burned the Egyptian fleet and captured the lighthouse of Pharos which effectively controlled the harbour. When the relieving legions crossed the eastern border, Caesar slipped through the lines to join them; on 27 March 47 BC the Egyptian army and the Roman garrison were routed and in their flight Ptolemy XIII was drowned in the Nile. Without intending to, Caesar had conquered Egypt, but he did not annex it to the Roman empire. In accordance with the tradition of the Ptolemies, he married his mistress to her younger half-brother, Ptolemy XIV, and installed them together on the throne.

When Caesar returned to Rome Cleopatra followed him and brought with her the thirteen-year-old Ptolemy XIV and her infant son Caesarion, who she claimed was Caesar's. Caesar housed them on his own estate beyond the Tiber and in his new temple dedicated to Venus he erected a statue of Cleopatra beside the goddess.

But Caesar's supporters resented her and his opponents believed that if he was given the title of king he would marry her and set himself up as emperor in the east. When he was murdered she was friendless and, fearing that his adopted son Octavian would regard Caesarion as a rival, she returned to Egypt.

After the defeat of the republican assassins at Philippi, the victors established a second triumvirate: Lepidus became pro-consul of Africa, Octavian ruled the west from Rome and Mark Antony ruled the east. By then Cleopatra had arranged the death of her half-brother and was ruling with her son Caesarion as Ptolemy xv. In her own interest she had nearly sent her fleet to support the triumvirs, but in 41 BC Antony summoned her to Tarsus to answer the unlikely charge that she had given financial support to the republicans. After a haughty delay, she came. As Antony sat waiting on a throne in the forum, a barge with purple sails and silver oars cruised into the harbour to the sound of harps and flutes. On the decks stood serving maids disguised as sea nymphs and in the gold-encrusted poop sat Cleopatra dressed as Venus. The crowds swarmed down to the docks, leaving Antony and his guards alone in the forum. That night Antony dined on board the barge and later he returned with Cleopatra to spend the winter in Alexandria. Like his generals, he was seduced by her luxurious splendour and, like Caesar, he was infatuated by her charm and her ancient lineage, but in the following spring, when the news came that the Parthians had invaded the Roman provinces in Asia Minor, he rejoined his army. Cleopatra did not see him again for over three years and, although she bore him twins, her influence seemed to have been shortlived.

Smuggled past the guards in a roll of bedding, the determined Cleopatra presents herself to Caesar, then fifty-two.

Antony's stay in Asia Minor was brief: learning that his wife Fulvia had led an unsuccessful rebellion against Octavian, he returned apprehensively to Italy, renewed the uneasy alliance and, since Fulvia had meanwhile died in exile, agreed to marry Octavian's beautiful sister Octavia. For the next year he lived quietly but restlessly in Athens under Octavia's respectable influence. But in 37 BC, when he decided to lead a punitive invasion of Parthia and needed money to pay for it, he sent Octavia back to Rome, rejoined his army and for the second time summoned Cleopatra to meet him in Antioch. At last Cleopatra was in a position to dictate her own terms. She had needed Caesar to regain her throne and at first she had needed Antony to retain her independence, but this time Antony needed her. In a ceremony which was legal in the east in spite of his Roman marriage to Octavia, he married Cleopatra; he recognized her twins, Alexander and Cleopatra, as his children; and he restored the empire of the Ptolemies. Although some of the territories were not just client kingdoms but Roman provinces, he appointed Cleopatra queen of Cilicia, Crete, Cyprus and all the lands in Judaea, Arabia and Phoenicia which had once belonged to her ancestors. In return Cleopatra gave him money and promised to build a fleet.

By the beginning of 35 BC it looked as though Cleopatra's faith in Antony had been misplaced. The invasion of Parthia was a disaster and in a long and terrible winter retreat Antony lost nearly a third of his army. In 34 BC, however, he restored his reputation by conquering Armenia and on returning to Alexandria he held a magnificent triumph in which he proclaimed an eastern empire with Cleopatra's children as rulers of the various kingdoms and Cleopatra at its head as 'Queen of Kings'.

By now Cleopatra's influence over Antony was absolute and she had persuaded him that he was ready to challenge Octavian. To Octavian, her expansionist ambitions had been obvious for some time, but, in spite of Antony's irresponsible disposition of Roman provinces and his contemptuous divorce of Octavia in 32 BC, there were still many senators who supported him. To persuade them that Antony's loyalty lay with the Queen of Egypt and not with the Roman republic, Octavian produced a document which he represented as Antony's will, in which Antony named Cleopatra's children as his sole heirs and expressed the wish to be buried beside her in Alexandria. Convinced, the senate declared war on Cleopatra. While Octavian mustered his legions, Antony and Cleopatra assembled an army from all the eastern kingdoms, where the rulers were eager to throw off the tyranny of Rome. As they prepared, both sides knew that this was to be no mere struggle for power like the civil war between Caesar and Pompey, this was to be a decisive confrontation between east and west, and the prize was the future dominion of the civilized world.

At the end of September 32 BC Antony and Cleopatra stationed 100,000 infantry, 12,000 cavalry and 500 ships on the west coast of Greece. But in the following spring Octavian's brilliant admiral, Marcus Vipsanius Agrippa, captured most of their naval bases in the Peloponnese, cut off their supply routes to Egypt and distracted their attention while Octavian safely transported 80,000 infantry and 12,000 cavalry into northern Greece. By the end of the summer their army and fleet were concentrated at Actium on the south of the Ambracian Gulf, where Octavian had built a fortified camp on the northern side and Agrippa had blockaded the mouth. Antony's men were short of supplies, weak with malaria and their allies were beginning to leave them. Octavian refused to be drawn into open battle and, since he could not withdraw by land without abandoning his fleet, Antony decided to break the blockade. In the centre Cleopatra's squadron smashed through, but on the wings Antony's ships were held and, abandoning his flagship, he escaped to join her. Leaving the rest of their fleet and their army to surrender, they sailed back to Egypt.

In the following year, as Octavian's army

Cleopatra, the asp at her breast, by Michelangelo, 1475–1564.

approached Alexandria, Antony, who was stationed with his fleet in the harbour, sent several ambassadors offering to capitulate in return for his freedom and eventually to kill himself if Cleopatra were spared, but Octavian ignored them. At the same time, unknown to Antony, Cleopatra sent her submission and, when Octavian ignored that too, she locked herself in her mausoleum with all her treasure and threatened to destroy it and herself unless Octavian granted an honourable peace. After a last attempt at a stand, Antony's fleet and cavalry surrendered while his infantry fled and, hearing that Cleopatra was dead, he stabbed himself. When news came that the report had been false, he asked to be taken to the mausoleum where he was hauled into the barricaded upper chamber and died in Cleopatra's arms. Octavian allowed her to come out for Antony's burial, but it was obvious that he would accept nothing less than a humiliating total surrender. And so, dressed in her royal robes, with the deadly bite of the asp which was the symbolic minister of the Egyptian sun god, Amon-Ra, Cleopatra committed suicide. Octavian captured the fabulous treasure of the Ptolemies and ascended their throne, Caesarion and Antony's eldest son by Fulvia were executed and the children of Antony and Cleopatra were sent to Rome where they were brought up by the saintly Octavia.

The victorious Romans had feared and hated Cleopatra and their historians represented her as an evil, scheming and wanton opportunist, but she was a responsible, courageous, single-minded and far-sighted queen, and she was too proud to be promiscuous. She probably slept with only two men in her life, and she did it not for love but, like everything that she did, for the freedom of her kingdom and the restoration of her ancestral empire. For hundreds of years afterwards, the Egyptians revered her memory and throughout the Greek-speaking world of the eastern Mediterranean the last of the Ptolemies became as legendary as the conqueror who had created their empire.

~ St Paul ~

The capital of the Roman province of Cilicia in Asia Minor was the flourishing, cosmopolitan city of Tarsus, made rich by the commerce of its harbour, which stood on one of the most important trade routes in the ancient world, famous for its university, which rivalled even the university of Athens, and, having survived the influences of Greece and Rome, grown decadent through its hedonistic, oriental way of life. Into this luxurious, depraved and idolatrous society, some time during the childhood of Jesus Christ, a Jewish boy was born who, through his conversion, conviction and courage, was to change the moral and spiritual life of the western world for ever.

His Hebrew name was Saul. Like several leading members of the Jewish community in Tarsus, his parents were Roman citizens, but they remained devout Pharisees, loyal to the religion and traditions of their people, and their son was educated, not by Greeks in the schools and university of the city, but by rabbis in the synagogue. Nevertheless, Saul learned to understand something of the Gentile society, for which his contempt was to turn to compassion, and to speak the Greek language, in which he would one day preach the Gospel.

When he was about eighteen, Saul was sent to Jerusalem to study under the great Rabbinical teacher, Gamaliel. The Pharisees believed in resurrection and retribution after death; for them, spiritual peace on earth and subsequent salvation could only be achieved through obedience to all the Law which Moses had received from God. It was a doctrine which the devout and earnest young Saul interpreted rigidly and during his years in Jerusalem, as he strove for absolute and meticulous fulfilment of its demands, he became increasingly frustrated by his own human imperfection. So zealous was his faith that he was horrified by the growing new sect of Nazarenes, who proclaimed blasphemously that their crucified and risen Jesus was the Messiah and the son of God, and whose concept of the father as a God of forgiveness repudiated the discipline to which Saul had submitted his life. The more he studied the creed of the heretics, in order to confound it, the more he became convinced that they should be exterminated. When he was about thirty, after the Nazarene Stephen had been stoned to death in Jerusalem, Saul was granted a commission to pursue and arrest the other heretics who had fled to Damascus. But on the way he changed his mind. In one literal blinding flash, the doctrines of the Nazarenes fused with the prophesies and promises of the Hebrew scriptures. Suddenly Saul believed that Jesus of Nazareth was indeed the Messiah, and the doubts and fears of a fallible man were dispelled by the certainty of redemption through the death and resurrection of the son of God: salvation was no longer a prize to be won, it was a gift to be cherished. For the rest of his life, Saul was to find his elusive spiritual peace in the paradox of liberty in the love of God and suffering in the service of his son.

In Damascus Saul was welcomed by the disciple Ananias and, after spending some time alone in the desert, he returned to the city and began to preach. But to the Jews who had once seen him as their champion, the equally zealous new convert was now a dangerous traitor. When he learned that outraged Jews were planning to murder him, he escaped to Jerusalem, where the disciples were sceptical until reassured by Barnabas who had heard him preach; and when, as at Antioch, his ardent evangelism aroused

Saul's conversion on the road to Damascus. A woodcut from William Caxton's *Golden Legend*, 1493.

open hostility, the disciples escorted him discreetly to the port of Caesarea and sent him home by sea to Tarsus. For the next ten years Saul lived and worked as an isolated missionary in Cilicia and Syria.

Meanwhile, among Greeks as well as Jews, the Nazarene sect gained so many converts in the city of Antioch that Barnabas was sent from Jerusalem to organize their church; and soon afterwards he went to Tarsus to fetch Saul. It was in Antioch that the Nazarenes first proudly accepted their Greek name, Christians, and it was there that Saul and Barnabas decided that the time had come to take their gospel to the rest of the Gentile world. The ancient, fatalistic polytheism of Rome was already declining and throughout the empire men were turning towards the cults of the east and searching for a new benign god who would share their suffering and promise salvation. It was a search for which Saul saw Christianity as the answer and, as both a Jew and a Roman citizen who spoke the common Greek language of the eastern Mediterranean, he

Law were the same as the ethics of Christianity, it also incorporated customs such as circumcision, and it was both unreasonable and fruitless to expect that people who had not been educated in the Jewish faith should observe them. Soon afterwards Paul set out on his second journey, which took him to Europe. At Philippi in Macedonia he stayed with a Jewish cloth dealer

The remains of the main street in Ephesus, where Paul preached successfully against the heathen cult of Diana.

saw himself as the ideal man to introduce it. Adopting the Latin form of his name, Paul, he devoted the rest of his life to the task.

In AD 44 Paul embarked with Barnabas on his first great missionary journey. From Cyprus, where they converted the Roman pro-consul, they sailed north to the mainland and, after three dangerous but encouraging years in Asia Minor, they returned to Antioch. In the summer of AD 49 they attended a conference in Jerusalem and, against ardent opposition, Paul persuaded the disciples to exempt gentile converts from some of the traditional Hebrew duties demanded by the Law of Moses. Although the ethics of the

called Lydia, who with her household became the first European convert to Christianity. In Athens he failed to convince the rational Athenians, to whom he preached at the Areopagus, but in Corinth he established an enormous church among the poor and he remained there for eighteen months before returning again to Antioch.

In AD 57, after his third journey, in which he confounded the cult of Diana at Ephesus, Paul came back from Corinth to Jerusalem with money that had been collected in the rich city for the poorer Christians in Judaea. But there were still some Christians who opposed his liberal attitude to gentile circumcision and many Jews were outraged by rumours that he had encouraged Jews in other Roman provinces to abandon the Law of Moses. To appease them, some of the disciples suggested that Paul should go to the Temple and observe seven days of ritual purification. While he was there, however, he was recognized by a group of Asian Jews, who stirred up a mob, claiming that Paul had profaned the Temple by bringing Greeks into it, and he was saved from death only by the intervention of Roman soldiers. Believing him to be an outlaw, the soldiers were preparing to examine him under torture when Paul warned them that he was a Roman citizen. Unharmed, he was led before a council of rabbis, where he so satisfied

the Pharisees among them with his defence that the council broke up in an argument between the Pharisees and the Sadducees. But during the night Paul's nephew warned the captain of the guard that forty Jews were planning to assassinate Paul next day when he was brought back to the council, and the captain, already embarrassed by his brutal treatment of a Roman citizen, sent him under armed escort to the proconsul, Felix, at Caesarea.

To please the Jews, and in the hope that Paul might raise a bribe, Felix kept him in 'protective custody' for two years, until relieved in office by Festus. But when Festus ordered that Paul should be returned to Jerusalem for trial, Paul knew that he could not hope for mercy and, falling back on his rights as a Roman citizen, he appealed to Nero, who was then emperor. After a dangerous journey, in which his ship was blown

'Paul before Felix', by William Hogarth, 1697–1764.

by a hurricane from Crete to Malta, Paul reached Rome and rented a house, where he remained for two years under guard until his trial, writing letters and receiving visitors from the Christian community which had already been established in the imperial capital.

The rest of the story remains a mystery. Paul was tried at least once. Perhaps, after acquittal in a first trial, he returned to Macedonia and he may even have fulfilled his ambition to visit Spain. All that seems certain is that in the end and in Rome he died the death of a martyr.

Among the disciples, Saint Paul was the most deeply committed to Christ's concept of a universal church and the brotherhood of man. Against the opposition of Jews, Romans and even fellow Christians, and constantly hampered by his own physical frailty, he interpreted the Christian religion to the gentiles. He was stoned, tortured and imprisoned for it, and he died for it. But with the doctrines of a new Judaean cult he laid the foundations of a world religion. Since then, whenever men have sought to reform or revitalize that religion, they have returned to the teachings of Saint Paul, and to this day he remains the greatest of all the Christian missionaries.

~ *Boadicea* ~

Although Julius Caesar led the first Roman expedition into Britain in 54 BC, it was not until the reign of the emperor Claudius, nearly 100 years later, that the island began to be conquered. In the meantime, a steady flow of intrepid Roman pioneers had settled in southern England, made friends with the local tribes and grown rich in the export of cattle, grain, gold and silver. When Claudius's legions landed, therefore, some of the smaller southern tribes welcomed them and joined in the easy suppression of their belligerent neighbours. But Roman rule turned out to be harsh. In the wake of the conquering armies came a new breed of settlers, unscrupulous opportunists who seized land and contemptuously cheated the simple tribesmen; and the administration of the new Roman province was totally corrupt. In accordance with a tradition that was older than the empire, the procurator, who levied the imperial revenues, always helped himself to more than was due to his emperor, and it was accepted as inevitable that the retired legionaries who served as his officers and the slaves who acted as his secretaries should follow his example.

Defeated by the legions, dispossessed by the immigrants and regularly robbed by the revenue officers, the British languished in helpless resentment. In the south, the Romans exacted brutal reprisals on the starving tribesmen who had raided their settlements; in the west, merciless legions began the systematic extermination of the Druids, who had been encouraging and co-ordinating resistance; and in Essex, while settlers drove the Trinovantes out of their homes, revenue officers added insult to injury by compelling them to pay for the construction of a temple at Camulodunum (Colchester), dedicated to Claudius, their conqueror. But in Norfolk and Suffolk, under the rule of King Prasutagus and his wife Queen Boadicea, the rich Iceni remained comparatively free. Prasutagus had saved them from the exploitations of the settlers and the ravages of an occupying army by submitting to a treaty with Claudius whereby he became, like Herod of Judaea, a 'client king'.

In AD 60, while the bulk of the Roman army was in Wales where the new governor, Caius Suetonius Paulinus, was preparing for his final assault against the Druids' last stronghold on the island of Anglesey, King Prasutagus died. He had no son and, in the hope that his two daughters might continue to rule the Iceni under the regency of their mother Boadicea, he had bequeathed his kingdom jointly to his daughters and the Roman emperor. The procurator of Britain, Gaius Decianus, knew that in the end the new emperor, Nero, would take everything, but for the time being he sent some of his officers from London to survey the land, make an inventory and bring back half the king's jewels and livestock, particularly the beautiful horses for which the Iceni were famous. Unlike her southern neighbours, Queen Boadicea was not accustomed to Roman contempt and when the procurator's officers burst into her village, she threatened them and commanded them to leave.

Boadicea in her chariot, a statue by Thomas Thorneycroft, 1815–1885, in London; Boadicea's army took Londinium, then already an important commercial centre, inflicting hideous deaths on those citizens who had not been evacuated.

But to the Roman bullies she was no more than an angry savage and they had their own entertaining way of dealing with that. Boadicea was stripped naked and flogged, and her two daughters were raped by every Roman in turn. When the procurator heard about the incident, he simply declared that by obstructing his officers the queen had forfeited her rights and he sent more men to collect the rest of her property and confiscate the property of the tribe's leading families as well.

While the Roman army was in Wales, the few Druids who had survived in hiding had been desperately attempting to provoke a rebellion in the east, and in the outraged Queen of the Iceni they had found both a symbol and a leader. The Iceni swore vengeance, and the discontented Trinovantes pledged their support. From the scattered villages of East Anglia the British warriors assembled behind the chariot of Queen Boadicea and, with the desperate courage of men who have nothing left to lose, swarmed south towards the hated settlement at Camulodunum.

There were few soldiers in Camulodunum, which had not even been fortified with a defensive wall, and the procurator could only spare 200 men from London to reinforce it, but the local British had persuaded the settlers that Boadicea was still far away, and so when her warriors burst in on them they were taken by complete surprise. Some tried to use the foundations of the temple as a fort, but the British burned them out with piles of blazing brushwood; and by the end of the day every man, woman and child had been slaughtered.

When news of the rebellion reached Wales, the governor, Paulinus, sent orders to the IX Hispana to intercept the rebels and, leaving his infantry to follow as fast as possible, set out with his cavalry at full speed for London. The IX legion was too widely deployed throughout central England to concentrate quickly; with only 2,000 legionaries and 500 auxiliary cavalry, the commander, Petilius Cerealis, marched towards Camulodunum. But somewhere along the road Boadicea was waiting in ambush, and only Cerealis and a few of his cavalry escaped.

On reaching London, Paulinus realized that, without his infantry, who could not be expected to arrive in time, the town was indefensible, and he ordered an evacuation. Nevertheless, there were still several thousand people in London when Boadicea attacked. The British tribesmen had sworn to their gods that they would take no prisoners and the defenceless citizens were hideously tortured to death. The horrifying mutilations and agonies that were inflicted on the women were later described by Roman historians to titillate their decadent readers, but the equally appalling sufferings of the men were thought to be too horrible to record.

With her steadily growing army, Boadicea advanced up Watling Street from London to Verulamium, near St Albans, which was not only a Roman town but also the old capital of the Catuvellauni, allies of the Romans who, led by King Cymbeline, had once conquered the Trinovantes. Like London, it was partially evacuated before she arrived and the casualties can not have been as high as the hysterical Roman historians suggested; nevertheless, in the ruins of Camulodunum, London and Verulamium together, more than 30,000 people were killed.

By now Boadicea's horde was over 100,000 strong, but she had already made her fatal mistake. After the sack of Camulodunum, while Paulinus was returning from Wales, her undisciplined warriors had wasted two weeks celebrating their victory and raiding Roman farms before attacking London. If she had marched on London at once and then continued along Watling Street, she would have been in control of central England before Paulinus could concentrate his soldiers in sufficient numbers to hold her, and she could have destroyed his units one by one, as she had done with the cohorts of the IX Hispana. But by the time she reached Verulamium, Paulinus had assembled the XIV Legion and most of the XX.

Boadicea's warriors fought half naked with slings, spears and long clumsy swords. In close combat against disciplined, experienced and well-drilled Roman legionaries, protected by strong armour and shields, and armed with javelins and efficient short swords, they were at a considerable disadvantage. But at least some of them were extremely mobile. With a con-

A Roman floor mosaic from Verulamium.

servatism that was evident even then, the British were the only western nation still using chariots on the battlefield. They were not the heavy battle chariots that had once been used for charging infantry, and, contrary to the popular myth, they did not have scythe blades on their wheels like the chariots of the Persians. They were lighter, faster and much more stable, and were used for carrying warriors from one part of the battlefield to another. Once they reached their enemies, the warriors would jump down to engage them on foot, while the drivers would turn and stand ready for a hasty retreat. In spite of the weight of their numbers, the British warriors' only chance of victory over a Roman army drawn up in battle formation lay in careful manoeuvring and the use of their mobility at the right moment to outflank

it. But the destruction of London and their success in an ambush over the IX Hispana had made them over-confident, and they streamed north-west along Watling Street with long wagon trains filled with their families, who had come to witness their triumph.

In southern Northamptonshire, Paulinus was waiting with about 8,000 legionaries and 4,000–5,000 auxiliaries including cavalry. He was an experienced soldier and he had chosen his ground with the principal purpose of protecting his flank. With a forest behind them and wooded hills on either side, his soldiers were drawn up at the narrow end of a valley which grew wider and wider ahead of them until it opened into a plain. On reaching that plain, the British drew up their wagons in a semicircle round the mouth of the valley to make a grandstand for the battle. Then, contemptuous of their tiny enemy, they made a massed charge, screaming and blowing their horns. When they were within range and crowded together by the narrowing funnel of the valley, the Romans advanced behind a volley of javelins. Without the space to wield their weapons and with their front ranks falling against the shields and short swords of the Romans, the British fell back until, when the valley widened and the Roman cavalry came round from the rear to attack their flanks, they broke and fled. But their escape was barred by their own crescent of wagons. Those who reached the wagons first could not outrun the cavalry and those who came behind had legionaries on their heels. In one short battle the rebellion was broken, nearly half the British warriors were killed, and, knowing that she could not evade the victors for long, the proud Queen of the Iceni poisoned herself.

Paulinus pushed on into East Anglia, burned the granaries and so devastated the farm lands that the ensuing famine lasted for years. Fresh legions were brought in from Germany and in the name of Mars Ultor, the god of vengeance, the oppression and attrition were more terrible than ever. But in time the rule of the Romans relaxed and under the liberal governor Agricola,

101

who had served as an officer in Paulinus's army, the British became contented Roman subjects. It had been inevitable that Boadicea's rising would fail in the end and, as the British generations that followed her became Romanized, the spirit of rebellion died, but for a few weeks in AD 61 she had seriously threatened the 'north-west frontier' of the Roman empire.

The Age of Chivalry

by JOHN GILLINGHAM

ROLAND, ALFRED, HEREWARD, Saladin, Bruce, Henry V, Joan of Arc, Columbus, More: all but one of them European Christians; all but one of them male; four of them sovereign princes; four English, two French, a Scot, a Genoese, a Kurd. This looks suspiciously like the unbalanced kind of list of heroes and one heroine which could be compiled only by someone who is a white, Anglo-Saxon, male monarchist. It must be admitted that this deduction is three parts correct. But a list of heroes and heroines is not just a matter of individual taste. My own private preference would be for nine anti-heroines but it is of the essence of a hero or heroine that he or she should be a public figure. If no man is a hero to his valet this is because the relationship between them is a private one. However much a valet might admire his master's qualities, what he knows is the man as he is behind the scenes, whereas the hero lives in the public arena, at centre stage. He may see his master in a favourable light, but it cannot be a heroic one. A description of King Alfred's private life written by someone close to the king has proved so disconcerting to those who regard him as a great English hero that they either omit it altogether or dismiss it as a forgery. But Alfred is a particularly interesting case. What we know about his public personality is very largely precisely what he wanted us to know. As a king he was able to exercise some degree of control over the media of the day and, to judge from the surviving evidence, he seems to have done this remarkably effectively. If we think of him as Alfred the Great it is partly because he tells us that that is what he was. This problem of the self-made hero applies to all the other ruling princes in this list as well: Saladin, Bruce and Henry V. To some extent it also applies to the type of hero illustrated here by Roland: the man who deliberately chooses a course of action which he knows the song-writers – the image-makers of the day – will love. None the less if these men demonstrated an awareness of the value of propaganda and an ability to manipulate it, this worked only because their public was *already* receptive to the values which they were claiming to embody. All heroes represent in some way the public values of a society, whether it is the society of their own day or – in the case of people like Joan of Arc who only later achieve truly heroic status – the values of the society which erects statues in their honour.

Thus the fact that it is not easy to find a medieval heroine tells us a good deal about the status of women at that time. Generally speaking those who did become public figures did so not in their own right but by virtue of their husband's position – and to be swept along in her husband's wake is not the proper behaviour expected of a heroine. It might have been possible to cast Eleanor of Aquitaine in a heroic role: the wife who rebelled against her husband, the queen against the king. But however attractive this might seem to some twentieth-century feminists, there is certainly no evidence to show that twelfth-century women looked upon her as the embodiment of their aspirations, perhaps because this rebel queen was not fighting for the rights of her sex but for the traditional independence of her duchy, Aquitaine. On the other hand it was not easy for a woman to reject marriage – except by entering a nunnery and becoming the 'bride of Christ'. There is a brave, even a heroic ring about Heloise's declaration to Abelard: 'God knows I never sought anything in you except yourself; I wanted you, not your property. I looked for no marriage-tie, no marriage portion. The word wife may sound more sacred or more binding but sweeter for me will always be the name of mistress.' None the less she married Abelard and then, at his command, entered a nunnery. There was perhaps a heroic firmness of purpose about Queen Elizabeth I's refusal to marry, but sovereigns have certain advantages when it comes to getting their own way and there was very little that was heroic about her political caution and her passion for saving money – even at the expense of the sailors who fought against the Spanish Armada. This great scarcity of heroines only serves to emphasize just how extraordinary Joan of Arc was. In her case there are plenty of signs that her brand of heroism won the admiration of many contemporaries, though this was a development which the establishment of the day was anxious to play down.

Most heroes and heroines, however, precisely because they stand for public values of the day, are members of an establishment – even if, as in the case of Hereward, it is an establishment which is in the process of being destroyed. Most of them distinguished themselves in war. In part this is because the society of the time was dominated by a military aristocracy. Making courtly war was the characteristic activity of the medieval noble: thus Roland, Saladin and Henry V. But in part it is also because many heroes are created out of crisis; their function is to embody the way of life of the threatened society and to defend its values. Thus Alfred and Hereward, representing Englishness, under threat from Vikings and Normans; thus Robert Bruce and Joan of Arc, representing Scotland and France, both under threat from the English. These were the military threats of conquest and occupation and had to be countered by military means. To be heroic in these circumstances it was necessary to fight, to lead and inspire the resistance. If ever there was a figure who, by virtue of her sex and social status, most emphatically did not belong to the establishment, it was Joan of Arc, but in these circumstances she too adopted the way of life, as well as the dress, of the warrior-class, and the 'sign' by which she proved her worth was the raising of the siege of Orléans – a very soldierly sign indeed. On the other hand the two who on this list represent the peaceful professions – Christopher Columbus and Thomas More – were equally members of the establishment. To describe Columbus, as he often is, as a weaver's son, is misleading. His father was a member of the guild of weavers at Genoa, but this did not make him a manual worker. In 1479, long before he was a famous man, Columbus was able to marry the grand-daughter of one of the noble companions of Prince Henry the Navigator.

Some 'potential heroes' I discarded because they have no discoverable basis in fact. Thus King Arthur, St George and Robin Hood had to go, while Roland and Hereward could stay – though only just. Others went because although they were heroes once they have now been completely forgotten. In his prologue to the 1481 printed edition of *The History of Godefrey of Bologne and of the Conquest of Iherusalem*, William Caxton names Godfrey de Bouillon as one of the great heroes of the age. One of the leaders of the First Crusade and the first ruler of the Crusader kingdom of Jerusalem, he remained a hero for as long as going on crusade to Jerusalem remained a genuine social ideal. But as the idea of recapturing Jerusalem became more remote, so the figure of Godfrey de Bouillon receded into the distance and today he is forgotten by all except serious historians. If an occasional crusader still possesses heroic stature – Richard the Lionheart for example – it is no longer because the name of Jerusalem exerts a powerful pull (Richard, after all, failed to recapture the Holy City) but because he is remembered as a king who shared with his soldiers the dangers of hand to hand combat. The Lionheart's image is that conjured up by an Elizabethan playwright:

> O, still, methinks, I see King Richard stand
> In his gilt armour stain'd with Pagan's blood,
> Upon a galley's prow, like war's fierce God.

In other words Richard became and remained a hero because he came close to the ideal of a brave, fighting knight – the ideal summed up in the figure of Roland in the *Chanson de Roland*. We should do well to remember that Richard was brought up in a part of the world – south-western France – where Roland's shrines were to be found and where his reputation was particularly cultivated. For this reason I have included Roland but left Richard out. On the other hand even today the name of Jerusalem exerts a powerful pull in the Middle East and for this reason I have included Richard's great opponent, Saladin: the honorary Christian gentleman of medieval romance who is still revered in the Muslim world as the liberator of Jerusalem.

Different as these Nine Worthies are, what they all have in common is contemporary fame and enduring reputation. Both their life and after-life has been spent in the glare of the public stage. Some of them, like Roland, Joan of Arc and Thomas More, also died in it. Indeed Thomas More, a man who – unlike Roland – did not much want to die a hero's death, felt that, in the end, he could not avoid it. However much he wanted to withdraw into private life he was, in fact, a public figure and for this reason he had heroism forced upon him – a salutary warning perhaps to all those who wish to take their quiet principles into the noisy arena.

John Gillingham

~ *Roland* ~

Charlemagne was the greatest conqueror in the history of early medieval Europe. In his remarkable career (King of the Franks from 768 to 814 and Emperor from 800) he suffered few setbacks. One of them occurred in the summer of 778. He laid siege to the city of Saragossa but failed to take it. Then, on 15 August, while they were withdrawing across the Pyrenees, his forces were badly mauled in a Basque ambush. Among the Frankish dead was a certain 'Duke Roland'. This is almost all we know for certain about the events of that day since contemporary Frankish writers preferred to draw a discreet veil over what happened. Yet despite their tactful silence the memory of that defeat lived on. One writer indeed justified his omission of a casualty list by saying that the names of the dead were still fresh in all men's minds. And clearly he was right; their names lived on in song. But as time passed and the songs took on a life of their own, some new heroes were brought in to fight at Roland's side while the names of some of those who had been his real companions slipped away and were forgotten. Who today has heard of Ekkehard the Seneschal and Anselm, the Count of the Palace? Even more strikingly, the enemy also changes. In place of the Christian Basques come the infidel Saracens; the engagement at Roncesvalles becomes an episode in a Holy War. But one name

A Carolingian army in battle. From the 12th-century Chronicle of Otto.

The statue of Roland. Relief from Verona Cathedral.

throughout remained at the centre of the stage and, more than 300 years later, when an anonymous poet composed a new song on the old theme, it was known simply as the *Chanson de Roland*. To the Song of Roland we must now turn.

After seven years of war in Spain, Charlemagne's great army was on its way back, following the road which led northward from Pamplona to the Pass at Roncesvalles. When at last, still high in the mountains, the soldiers caught their first distant glimpse of France, they wept tears of joy, thinking of the dear friends and wives whom they would soon see. They were home already in their imaginations. Perhaps they also wept tears of relief, for the valley road through the Pyrenees had been a forbidding one, dark with the ever-present threat of ambush; with a long, successful and profitable war behind it, the army's waggon train was piled high with the plunder taken from the rich Mediterranean civilization of Muslim Spain. But now they and their booty were both secure. Behind them, still at Roncesvalles, the rearguard watched over the last stages of the main army's withdrawal. In command here was Count Roland, Charlemagne's nephew and his most famous soldier. With Roland were his companion at arms, the brave but unheroically sensible Oliver, Turpin, the warlike archbishop of Reims and a whole galaxy of outstanding French knights. A trap had been set for Roland which was about to snap shut, and in it all of them would die.

Between Roland and his step-father Ganelon there was an old hatred which a recent incident had fanned into new life. Ambassadors from the court of the Muslim king, Marsile, had come to Charlemagne's headquarters. The Arabs, it appeared, were ready to concede defeat; if Charlemagne would agree to withdraw, Marsile in his turn would agree to become a Christian and hold his kingdom as Charlemagne's vassal. At a meeting of the French council Roland had argued that they should fight on until the Arabs were forced to surrender unconditionally, but Ganelon and the wiser counsellors persuaded Charlemagne to negotiate. The next item on the agenda was to decide whom to send as an envoy to Marsile – a ticklish problem since the Arab king had hanged two earlier envoys. Roland and several others offered to go, but in Charlemagne's eyes they were too valuable to lose. Eventually, at Roland's suggestion, the choice fell upon Ganelon. Ganelon, understandably, was angered and humiliated. He swore to revenge himself on his step-son. The net which was now closing in at Roncesvalles was the result of a mutually satisfactory arrangement made by Ganelon and the Muslim leaders who looked upon Roland as their most dangerous enemy.

Oliver was the first to sense the significance of some nearby trumpet calls. 'I think', he said, 'that today we shall be fighting with Saracens.' Roland's reply was characteristic: 'By God, I hope you're right. Every man should be ready to die for his lord, so let's strike some mighty blows. There'll be no songs sung about our cowardice.' While Roland looked forward to the chance of winning yet more renown, Oliver spurred his horse to higher ground where he could spy out the enemy. When he saw their huge array and knew that the rearguard was hopelessly out-numbered, he urged his men to stand firm, but at the same time asked Roland to sound his horn, Olifant – the agreed signal which would bring Charlemagne hastening to their aid. But Roland would have none of it. 'In fair France my name would suffer scorn.' Twice more Oliver besought his friend and twice more Roland refused. 'Now God forbid that any man should say he saw me go blowing of horns for fear of a pagan foe. Never shall my kindred be put to such reproach.'

Spoke Oliver: 'Herein I see no blame:
I have beheld the Saracens of Spain;
They cover all the mountains and the vales,
They spread across the hillsides and the plains:
Great is the might these foreigners display,

And ours appears a very small array.'
'I thirst the more,' said Roland, 'for the fray.'

As the Arabs closed in, Archbishop Turpin just had time to preach a sermon, reminding the French of their duty to their king and religion and promising them a seat in paradise should they fall. Then, with the war cry 'Montjoie!', they urged their horses forward and battle was joined. On the Muslim side, King Marsile's nephew had been granted the honour of being the first to exchange blows with Roland. It did him little good. Roland's lance shattered his shield and hauberk, pierced his breast and drove his backbone right through his body to come out the other side in the shape of a bow: so at least the poet says. That day all the French performed mighty deeds of knightly prowess, but Roland outshone them all.

Count Roland through the field goes riding
With Durendal, fine sword, he cuts and slashes.
The toll he takes of Saracens is frightful.
Would you had seen him, dead man on dead man
    piling,
Seen the bright blood about his pathway lying.
Bloody his hauberk and both his arms with fighting,
His good horse bloody from crest to withers likewise.

But though Roland, Oliver and Turpin slew more than 4,000 between them, and though they beat off four attacks, their own losses were heavy. Eventually just sixty French knights were left. Now, at last, Roland decided he would sound his horn, but first he had to face the full blast of Oliver's anger. 'When I asked you, out of sheer pride you refused. Had you done it then, Charles [Charlemagne] would have been here already, but now it's too late. Your reckless prowess has destroyed us all.' The archbishop hurried over to separate the quarrelling friends:

A 19th-century impression of Roland, surrounded by French dead as he sounds his horn, Olifant.

It will not save us to sound the horn, that's true;
Nevertheless, 'twere better so to do.
Let the king come; his vengeance will be rude.
The French will find our bodies and give us burial
   due,
We'll not be food for dogs and pigs and wolves.

Then Roland set Olifant to his lips and blew a long, echoing blast. Thirty leagues away Charlemagne heard the sound and, though Ganelon tried to make light of it, the king knew what it meant. He ordered his army to retrace its steps with all possible speed. But by now Roland was already dying. Such was the determination with which he had blown the horn that his temples had burst and his life was slowly ebbing away. Not that this could prevent him carrying on the fight. Nor did Oliver stop when he received his mortal wound – a spear thrust in his back. Instead he went on striking out right and left, though as his eyes glazed over he became a danger to friend as well as to foe. Even Roland had his helmet split by a blow from Oliver's sword.

Count Roland, at the blow, looks up at him
And asks him in a gentle, tender voice,
'Lord comrade, did you mean to strike that blow?
For this is Roland, he who ever loved you.'

The dying Oliver asked pardon and so at the end the two friends were reconciled. Finally all the French except Roland lay dead or dying beneath the blows of their enemies. He alone they had not managed to kill when the far-off clarion call of trumpets proclaimed Charlemagne's return and told them it was time to flee. But by now what brains Roland had were seeping out of his ears and so, after a vain attempt to break Durendal by smashing it against a stone, he lay down on the grass and turned his face towards Spain. Those who found his body were to know that he had died victorious.

Later that day, after Charlemagne had spoken with the angel Gabriel and stayed the sun in its course, so that there was still time for a second battle, the main French army caught and defeated King Marsile's force. Finally Charlemagne beat a second Arab army under King Baligant. The French king had avenged, as a good lord should, the deaths of those who had served in the rearguard. Then once more the French headed for home, taking back with them the bodies of the fallen. Roland, Oliver and Turpin were buried in the church at Blaye on the northern shore of the Gironde, while the horn Olifant was deposited at the shrine of Saint-Seurin in Bordeaux. Ganelon was punished for his treachery by being tied to four stallions and torn to pieces.

Down subsequent centuries Roland remained a legendary hero. To compare a knight with Roland was to award him the highest praise. To modern readers of the Song of Roland this has always seemed a strange and inappropriate verdict. Was not the valiant and prudent Oliver the true hero? But when Oliver reproached him for wanting to sound the horn only when it was too late, Roland replied – and it is worth noticing what he said – 'I've struck good blows today.' It was this which he had sworn to do earlier when Oliver had begged him to sound the horn. Now he had fulfilled this vow and had given a good account of himself as a formidable fighting man – and it was precisely because he was a fighting man, as he reminded Oliver, that Charlemagne loved and trusted him. Only now that no one could possibly point a finger at him and accuse him of cowardice, thus shaming him and his family for ever, now that his honour was secure, was Roland ready to send to Charlemagne for help. In Roland's world reputation is all, the songs that men will sing of you after your death. Other matters, the safety of your life and that of your companions too, are secondary. And what better way is there to die than in the fight against overwhelming odds? However brave men might be in the manner of their lives, even in the manner of their facing death, it is the songs which come after which make them heroes. It was Roland, not Oliver, who understood this and who chose to live and die by these heroic standards.

~ *Alfred the Great* ~

In January 878, when the Twelfth Night festivities were scarcely over, an army of Danes under Guthrum's leadership launched a surprise attack on King Alfred's palace at Chippenham. Taken unawares by this midwinter blow, the king and his family fled to the Isle of Athelney in Somerset. Today the land thereabouts is well-drained and the 'isle' a mere hummock rising a few feet above the surrounding countryside. But in 878 the River Parrett ran through a desolate fenland of marsh and swamp, particularly impenetrable in winter and spring when the flood-level was high. Only in summer was this region suitable for settlement – thus the name Somerset. Here the King of Wessex found a safe refuge. If, as has been plausibly conjectured, Guthrum's sudden swoop at a time when the army of Wessex was disbanded had been intended to capture the king himself, then Alfred was lucky to be alive. The fate of kings who fell into Danish hands was not a pleasant one. Kings Aella of Northumbria and Edmund of East Anglia had both undoubtedly been killed, possibly sacrificed to Odin in the ritual of the blood-eagle, in which the victim's ribs and lungs were ripped out so that his mutilated corpse was marked with the shape of the spread-eagle. Up to a point,

Three Anglo-Saxon kings: (left to right) Alfred, Edgar and Aethelred.

then, Guthrum's strike had failed. None the less Alfred's precipitate flight could well have confirmed contemporary pessimists in their conviction that the outlook was a gloomy one.

By this date only Wessex stood between the Danes and their conquest of the whole of Christian England. The kingdoms of Northumbria, East Anglia and Mercia had already fallen to the armies of Halfdan and Guthrum, and it seemed as though Wessex would soon follow. Its resources must have been stretched to breaking point by the fighting which had been going on ever since a raiding party of Danes first landed on the Dorset coast in the reign of King Beorhtric (786–802). Throughout this time the strength of the Danes lay neither in the weight of their numbers nor in the savagery and expertise of the individual Viking warrior. The Viking, in fact, was no fiercer than an Englishman. The only difference between them was that English soldiers, being Christians, would sometimes spare churches and monasteries, whereas the Danes, being pagan, saw no reason why buildings full of rich treasures should escape their attention. To the bulk of the population, when their lands were ravaged, their crops destroyed, their cattle driven off, their women raped or enslaved, it can have made little difference whether the raiders who did this were Englishmen or Danes. But nearly all the history of the age was written by churchmen, and to them there was a world of difference. They wrote about the Vikings as though they were a different breed of men: inhuman, ruthless and bloodthirsty beyond belief. This mistaken view has lasted well, and even today film-makers still do their best to keep it alive. Nor did the Danes come in overwhelming numbers. In fact only their biggest armies were more than a few hundred strong. A law promulgated by Ine, a seventh-century king of Wessex, gives a good idea of what an Anglo-Saxon understood by the word 'army'. It runs: 'We call up to seven men "thieves"; from seven to thirty-five a "band"; more than that it is an "army".'

What was it then which made the Danish threat so serious? In the first place they held the initiative: as the attackers, they always had the advantage of knowing where they would strike next. This was particularly true of their initial landings. Once ashore the smoke of plundered and burning houses usually gave some warning of their approach, but sea-raiders came from out of the blue – and when they left there were no tracks for an avenging army to follow. In the second phase of Danish attacks after 855 when, for the first time, they wintered in England instead of going home after the summer season, they retained the advantage by keeping their forces concentrated, by building or seizing a fortified camp and using it as the base from which the whole army operated. Once they had begun to settle down and take over farms and estates they lost this advantage. For this reason the normal strategy adopted by their leaders was to delay this stage until they had destroyed the political fabric of the country they were invading – until, that is to say, they had killed or driven out kings and a proportion of the aristocracy. This was the strategy which had brought down the other English kingdoms and which now threatened to dispose of Wessex. Certainly this is the impression which is created by the *Anglo-Saxon Chronicle*, the most detailed contemporary account of the events of 878.

The enemy occupied the land of the West Saxons and settled there, and drove a great part of the people across the sea and conquered most of the others; and the people submitted to them, except King Alfred. He journeyed in difficulties through the woods and fen-fastnesses with a small force.

It conjures up a vivid picture of the heroic king standing alone in his resistance to the invader and it is, of course, this picture of the king at Athelney which has entered legend. Here it was that he burned the cakes; here that he saw a vision of St Cuthbert prophesying victory when all seemed lost; and from here that, disguised as a minstrel, he went into the enemy camp and made a careful note of their dispositions. No one doubts that these later legends are simply fictions which serve to heighten the drama of those weeks in early 878. The real problem comes with the *Anglo-Saxon Chronicle*. How truthful is its account? Did, for example, all the people of Wessex except for Alfred and his small force submit to the Danes? Clearly not, since the *Chronicle* itself goes on to say that another Danish army was defeated in Devon – and not by Alfred's small force but by local levies. Moreover a few months later, when Alfred won the decisive battle at Edington, he was helped by levies from Somerset, Wiltshire and Hampshire. In other words the *Anglo-Saxon Chronicle* exaggerated the extent to which Wessex fell under Danish domination in 878 and did so in a way which emphasized the significance of Alfred's stand. The *Chronicle* was clearly giving a version of events which suited the king and it is hard to avoid the suspicion that it was written under his supervision and at his command. This suspicion is confirmed by the *Chronicle*'s entry for the year 853: 'King Aethelwulf sent his son Alfred to Rome. At that time lord Leo was pope in Rome and he consecrated him as king.' This simply cannot be true. In 853 Alfred was a small boy who had three elder brothers. In 853 the chances of Alfred ever obtaining even a share of Aethelwulf's kingdom were remote. Though he may have gone to Rome he cannot have been given a distinction which was withheld from his brothers. But one by one his elder brothers died and in 870, against the odds, Alfred came to be king of Wessex. What then was the point of a *Chronicle* statement, implying that Alfred was set apart from his brothers and especially chosen to be king? In 870 the claims of the sons of his brother Aethelred had been ignored. There were two Danish armies on Wessex soil and it was no time to think of having a child-king. So Alfred came to the throne. But in the 890s, when the *Anglo-Saxon Chronicle* was compiled, Aethelred's sons were grown men. Why should they still be excluded from the kingship? Why

should Alfred's own son be preferred to them? The story that on a pilgrimage to Rome Alfred received this sign of his destiny would strengthen the rights of his line as opposed to that of his brother. This is not mere speculation: Alfred's death in 899 was in fact followed by a succession dispute between his son Edward and Aethelred's son Aethelwold. The dispute had clearly been foreseeable and it is only in a context of this kind that the 853 entry makes any sense. The conclusion we have to draw from all this is that the *Anglo-Saxon Chronicle* is a work of propaganda conceived in Alfred's court. It was then copied out and circulated to various centres of learning throughout the kingdom. It was designed to cultivate the image of a great king who upheld the traditions of his ancestors. A similar concern can be detected in the biography of Alfred written by his Welsh friend and adviser, Bishop Asser. As propaganda these works were supremely successful. The image they projected has remained to this day the conventional picture of Alfred – the only king in English history to be called 'the Great'.

But to say this is not to debunk Alfred, nor to belittle his achievement. Propaganda can be recognized for what it is on those occasions when it distorts the truth. None the less we should also remember that the more closely it resembles the truth the more likely it is to be effective. It is possible that by 878 the Danish assault was running out of steam as more and more Viking warriors settled down to become yeoman farmers and country gentlemen. As a result Guthrum's January attack may have been a gambler's throw, a last desperate attempt to conquer Wessex before his army finally dissolved. But 878 did not mean the end of the struggle. A crisis had been surmounted but there was still much fighting to be done. Even those years free of war were filled with the bustle of preparation for war: towns fortified, ships designed and built, the militia reorganized. Thanks to these measures, when the largest Danish army ever to come to England landed in Kent in 892, Alfred was able to contain it and, though it did considerable damage, it never threatened the very existence of Wessex as Guthrum had done in 878. The survival of Wessex was Alfred's great political and military achievement and if his defence measures worked it was largely because men were persuaded of the value of carrying out his instructions. And how were they persuaded if not by Alfred's intelligent use of the media of the day? What all this means is that, as much as any twentieth-century political leader, Alfred was aware of the need to influence public opinion, of the value of propaganda. This was certainly not an insight unique to Alfred. Like all Germanic kings, he and his ancestors used songs as propaganda. These songs do not survive: in a largely illiterate society the chances of them ever being written down were small. But in one song, the epic of Beowulf, the text of which has miraculously come down to us, there is a description of the system at work. The monster Grendel has been mortally wounded and the hero, Beowulf, returns to the king's hall in triumph: 'Then one of the king's chieftains, a man with a gift for words, whose mind was stored with a host of old legends, composed a new song. Juggling with phrases he told the story of Beowulf's exploit, relating it to the deeds of past heroes.'

There can be no doubt that all kings and chiefs were accustomed to listen, as unblushingly as Beowulf, to recitals of their achievements and noble qualities. It is against this social background that we must set the *Anglo-Saxon Chronicle*. What was special about Alfred was not his use of propaganda but the fact that he chose to set some of his propaganda in a medium which turned out to have a relatively high survival rate: written English prose.

Here is another aspect – and in many ways the most striking one – of Alfred's many-sided genius. When he was about forty years old he made himself learn to read Latin and then he set about implementing a remarkable plan which can best be described in his own words:

I remembered how it was here before the Vikings came. The churches were full of treasure and books, but few men could understand what was in those books because they were not in English. I remembered too how the Greeks had translated the Old Testament out of the Hebrew into their own language; then the Romans had translated it into Latin. Therefore it seemed right to me that we should turn some books – those from which we can gain most – into that language which we can all understand and which many can still read. So, busy though I was with the manifold cares of the kingdom, I began to translate the *Cura Pastoralis* [a manual of instruction for churchmen written by Pope Gregory I]. And I shall send a copy of my work to each diocese in England.

He found the time, indeed, to translate three more books and encourage the translation of others. Just how extraordinary an achievement this was we can estimate only if we remember that he is the only king in more than 300 years of

Alfred's patronage of the arts extended to the making of jewellery; this gold, enamel and rock-crystal jewel, which was found near Athelney in 1693, is inscribed 'Aelfred mec heht gewyrcan' (Alfred ordered me to be made).

English history, including the whole of the ninth, tenth and eleventh centuries, who is known to have been able to read and write.

Alfred had a vision of a well-ordered society in which the rich and powerful were also wise and just, so that the poor had no need to fear oppression. He had no plans for a revolutionary change in the social structure; he 'only' wanted to make men good and, like many other idealists, he believed that this might be done through education. If only the nobles would study wisdom, as he had done, it might be achieved. Asser's account reflects the king's own hopes. He describes the groans of earls and magistrates who were now, despite their grey hairs, forced to learn to read if they wanted to retain their positions. Perhaps Alfred's own strength of personality may have breathed some brief life into the scheme, but even Asser had to admit that the king did not always get the co-operation he looked for. His writings helped to lay the foundations of English prose but men remained much as they have always been. Yet the vision, however unattainable, was an astonishing one and we are particularly fortunate in that Asser's biography allows us to see something of the personality which lay behind it.

Asser portrayed Alfred as an intensely religious man who had gone through a very difficult adolescence and was disturbed to the point of illness by his own capacity for sin. He was tormented by sexual desires which he was afraid to indulge lest he should thereby incur God's displeasure. So he used to get up early in the morning and secretly visit a church or shrine where he could pray for release from this dilemma. What Alfred had in mind was some kind of affliction which would virtually force him to remain chaste but which would not interfere with the duties and other pleasures of a prince.

His prayer was granted, but the illness which came was all too painful and not long afterwards he had to make a second application, this time for a gentler disease. Once again his prayers were heard. This, however, was not the end of the story. In 868, when Alfred was twenty, a marriage was arranged between him and a Mercian noblewoman. It was intended to cement the Mercia–Wessex alliance against the Danes. For Alfred, Asser tells us, it had other consequences.

After his nuptials had been honourably celebrated with all due solemnity and after continued feasting both by day and night, he was suddenly seized – before all the people – with a severe disease unknown to all physicians. And alas! the worst feature of it is that it should have continued incessantly for so many years, even from his twentieth to his fortieth year and longer. If it is, by God's mercy, assuaged for a single day or night, or even for just one hour, the nervous dread of its excruciating pain still remains with him, rendering him – in his own opinion – almost useless for both religious and secular duties.

Most historians gloss over this side of Alfred's character. The one writer to give it due consideration decided that Asser's work must be a later forgery on the grounds that the picture of a 'neurotic invalid' which it presents cannot be reconciled with the historic figure – a courageous soldier, a wise judge and an inspiring leader of men. An alternative view might be that Alfred's tremendous intellectual and military activity gave him desperately needed release from his sexual tensions. However this may be, there is certainly no reason for believing that either a troubled sex life or a series of psychosomatic illnesses is incompatible with greatness in other fields. It might indeed be thought to enhance the heroic stature of an extraordinary man.

~ Hereward the Wake ~

It is no accident that 1066 is the most memorable date in English history. As a direct result of the Norman Conquest, England received not just a new royal family but also a new ruling class, a new culture and a new language. The old English aristocracy was dispossessed and a language barrier was erected to stand between the ordinary people and their new, alien lords. Probably no other conquest in European history had such disastrous consequences for the defeated. Inevitably this was a painful process which was frequently punctuated by riot and rebellion. One such revolt flared up in the Fenlands in 1070. Among its leaders was an English nobleman called Hereward, known from the thirteenth century onwards as Hereward 'the Wake'. During the course of the next twelve months hundreds of new recruits, including Earl Morcar of Northumbria and Bishop Aethelwine of Durham, flocked to join the rebels at their headquarters on the Isle of Ely. What happened then is recounted by the *Anglo-Saxon Chronicle*.

When King William ['the Conqueror'] learnt of this, he ordered out naval and land levies and entirely surrounded the district, built a causeway and made naval patrols to seaward, so that they all surrendered

A 19th-century French version of the death of Hereward.

to him, namely bishop Aethelwine and earl Morcar and all their followers, except Hereward alone and all who were able to escape with him; and he courageously led their escape.

Hereward's escape from Ely in 1071 was also an escape from history into legend. What happened to him in subsequent years we do not know. This is the one and only contemporary reference to his revolt and only legend follows him in his later career. There is, however, an apparently reliable early twelfth-century account of one of his exploits during the 1070 revolt and it is worth a look before turning to the legend.

News came to the monks of Peterborough Abbey that some of their own tenants, namely Hereward and his gang, wanted to plunder the monastery because they had heard it said that the king had appointed as abbot a Norman called Turold. By this time Turold, who was reputedly a very ferocious man, had reached Stamford with retinue of eight score Norman soldiers. Now in the monastery there was a sacristan called Yware and during the night he took what things he could, gospels, church vestments and the like, and on the advice of the monks, he sought out Turold and asked for protection. But that morning, 2 June 1070, the outlaws came in boats, determined to force an entrance into the monastery. The monks resisted until the outlaws set the abbey and town on fire, and burnt down everything except for one house. Then they came in by the Bolhithe Gate and entered the monastery and seized precious crosses, shrines, ornaments and all the gold and silver they could lay their hands on. They returned to their ships and were away by the time that Turold and his soldiers arrived to find everything destroyed and only the abbey church itself left standing. And they said they had done this out of loyalty to the monastery.

Taken together with some entries in Domesday Book which give us the location of some lands which had belonged to a certain Hereward, these two episodes comprise the sum total of our knowledge. The rest is legend and, though that legend may well contain some substratum of truth, it is all so confused and garbled that there is no hope of disentangling fact from fiction. One twelfth-century writer, for example, gives a vivid description of Hereward's death at the hands of his Norman enemies. Ambushed while dining alone he none the less slew fifteen of them, using his shield as a weapon, before he was brought to his knees by spear thrusts in his back; but even then, with a dying effort, he managed to kill the man who had slain him. Is this an essentially accurate account which has been romantically embroidered? An example of this kind of thing would be the legendary story of the sack of Peterborough, where we first of all hear of Abbot Turold's capture by Hereward, his release in return for a ransom of £30,000 and his failure to keep his word, as a result of which Hereward attacks the monastery, only to be persuaded to return the plunder by a midnight vision of St Peter brandishing the great key to heaven's gates. In the case of the sack of Peterborough there is an essential residue of fact. Is this also true of the story of Hereward's death? Or did he, as another twelfth-century version would have it, end his days in peace? We do not know. All we do know is that, 100 years after his death, songs of Hereward's deeds were still being sung in Fenland taverns and 200 years later men still went to visit the ruined wooden building which they called Hereward's Castle. But if there is anything which is less reliable than a pub song, it is a guide at a historical monument. Yet these sources, though no one should ever believe the 'facts' they relate, can at least tell us about something which is just as important – about feelings and attitudes. Take, for example, the story of Hereward's return home as told in a twelfth-century Latin version, the *Gesta Herewardi*.

Hereward had been in exile and while abroad had performed many fantastic deeds. Among the foes with whom he had grappled had been giants and bears endowed with human intelligence. But during his absence William had conquered England and with Hereward's return the mood of the story changes from romantic adventure to a grimmer realism. Worried about what might have happened to his family, he travelled incognito accompanied by only one servant. On reaching his own village he learned that a Norman lord and his men had arrived there the day before and had demanded all the lands belonging to Hereward's family. When two of them had laid rough hands on Hereward's widowed mother, his younger brother had killed them, whereupon he himself had been surrounded and slain. His head now looked down from over the door of his home. Hereward, still concealing his identity, heard the news in silence. Later that night, however, he was roused by the noise of singing and shouting as the Normans celebrated their victory in his own house, and he determined on immediate revenge. First he took down his brother's head, kissed it and wrapped it in a cloth. Then he entered the house and stood quietly in the shadows. He watched as the Normans, by now thoroughly drunk, enjoyed themselves in the arms of some of the women of the village whom they had rounded up. A jester kept them amused by singing insulting songs about the English. At length one of the women, irritated by the jokes, protested: 'If our lord's other son, Hereward, were here, you would soon change your tune.' The Norman lord silenced her: 'That rogue is not likely to show his face on this side of the Alps for a good while yet.' At that moment Hereward leapt into the room. The Normans were too drunk to defend themselves properly. Most of them fell to his sword, while others, attempting to escape, were cut down by the servant whom he had posted at the door. In the morning the village woke to find that his brother's head had been replaced by fourteen Norman ones. As the news of his exploit spread, his countrymen came flocking to join Hereward's revolt. Later on he was persuaded to join forces with that group of rebels, including Edgar Atheling, the last representative of the Anglo-Saxon royal house, who had made their base at Ely. At this time Ely was an island among the fens, difficult of approach and well supplied with fish, waterfowl and fertile soil. It made an ideal

Norman soldiers set fire to a house, driving out a woman and her son. From the Bayeux tapestry.

gathering place for the last defenders of a lost cause. Under a commander of Hereward's calibre it should have been able to hold out indefinitely. William the Conqueror's first attack failed when the bridge which he had built across the marsh collapsed under the weight of his marching troops. Few of those who were plunged into the bog escaped. The author of the *Gesta* says that he himself has seen skeletons, still in rusty armour, which had been retrieved by fishermen many years later. Only one Norman managed to reach the island and he was treated

with great courtesy by Hereward before being released to take back to William a vivid description of the outlaws' life and of their determination to resist.

For his next attack the king hired the services of a sorceress whose spells would undermine the courage of the garrison. Knowing that something was being plotted, but not sure what, Hereward decided to make his way into the Norman camp to find out. This he did disguised as a potter – a common feature of outlaw stories, notably the Robin Hood ballads. On the way he happened to lodge in the house where the witch was staying and overheard her talking (in French, which she supposed a potter would not be able to under-

stand) about her schemes. When William launched his second attack, led by the witch casting spells from a wooden siege tower, Hereward and his men beat it off and set light to the tower. Against the flames the sorceress had no enchantments.

Eventually, however, William found a way of forcing the rebels to surrender. The monks of Ely Abbey heard that their lands outside the island were being confiscated and granted to others. This threat to their property brought them to heel. Secretly they entered into negotiations with William and in return for the restoration of their lands agreed to guide the Normans on to the island. Hereward was out on a raiding party and by the time he learnt what was happening it was too late to prevent it. But while the other leaders surrendered, he and his men escaped to continue their careers as outlaws elsewhere.

In the various disguises and stratagems he adopted – for example, sometimes reversing the shoes on his horses so that pursuers were never sure in which direction he was travelling – Hereward is very much the typical outlaw of legend. But in two ways he was very different from Robin Hood. Firstly, there was a real Hereward; and secondly, even in the legends, Hereward was a hero of the resistance against the Normans – and this Robin Hood never was. The Robin Hood ballads contain plenty of criticism of some members of the ruling class, but one thing which is never held against them is that they were French or Norman. It was only in the nineteenth century that some writers, seeing the parallels between the Robin Hood and Hereward stories, turned Robin into an Anglo-Saxon anti-Norman hero. What the parallels do show is that there was a common stock of good stories and that anyone who attained the status of being a popular hero was likely to have a number of these stories grafted on to his own career.

There were, of course, other resistance heroes in the catastrophic years after 1066. Several legendary tales are told about an Anglo-Saxon noble known as Eadric the Wild who held out for several years in the Welsh Marches. The *Gesta Herewardi* refers in passing to a man called Brumannus who captured a Norman abbot and dumped him in the sea in a sack. At the time Brumannus was clearly a name to conjure with but this one deed is all we know of him now. Doubtless there were other heroes of other protest songs who have now vanished without trace. Even in the case of Hereward, the original songs, sung in the language of the oppressed, no longer survive. We know the contents of some of them only because there were some twelfth-century writers sufficiently interested to turn his story into one of the languages of polite society, French or Latin. Yet despite the problems of language, these are stories which enable us to catch a glimpse of the real Norman Conquest, the violence which lay behind the take-over of town after town, village after village. We can sense the note of wish-fulfilment in the description of Hereward's revenge on the Normans who had stolen his home. We can see why it was that in the first decade after the conquest the Normans preferred to live like an army of occupation, living, eating and sleeping in castles, huddled together for safety. Only when the danger of being murdered in their beds had receded did they split up and go to live on their new estates. Even then they still felt at risk. A law of the time laid down that whenever a dead body was found it was to be assumed to be Norman unless its 'Englishry' could be proved; otherwise the whole local community was to be punished by a fine, since it was taken for granted that anyone who killed a Norman would be protected by a wall of silence. As late as 1137, seventy years after the conquest, a rumour got about of a plot to kill all the Normans in England on the same day and hand the kingdom over to the Scots. In a tense political climate like this, the songs about Hereward could be sung again and again. Doubtless in the course of time many of his deeds became 'improved' out of all recognition, more heroic and more legendary. The harsh realities which could compel a rebel to become a bandit, as in the sack of Peterborough Abbey, paled into insignificance by the side of that one central reality – the Norman oppression – in the light of which everything seemed justified. For this reason, though the legends of Hereward may not be true, they none the less have great importance. In them we can hear that which conventional history rarely records, the voice of the defeated.

~ *Saladin* ~

Perhaps no man in history has ever been so much admired by his enemies as was Saladin. As the great statesman who liberated Jerusalem, one of the holy cities of Islam, and who did much to unify the Arab world, it is hardly surprising that he should be regarded as a Muslim hero. Yet he became a legend in the Christian world just as much as in the Muslim. To understand just how remarkable this was, we have to remember that Christians had very good reason to fear him. He it was who destroyed those Frankish Christian states which had been established overseas (*Outremer*) in Syria and Palestine as a result of the First Crusade. In 1187 Jerusalem, which had been a Christian city since 1099, fell into his hands and the news of its capture sent shockwaves of horror and indignation throughout Europe. In response to this the massive Third Crusade set out to recover Jerusalem but, though it made some headway, it failed to achieve its main objective. Always Saladin and his troops stood between the crusaders and the goal on which their hearts were set. Yet even the crusaders themselves fell under the spell of Saladin's reputation. To Ambroise, the Norman minstrel who accompanied Richard the Lionheart's army, he was, quite simply, 'the brave and generous Saracen'. This view of Saladin became the standard European opinion. Typical of the many anecdotes which were told about his courage, largesse, wisdom, humanity and humility is the following account of his death:

When the great Sultan Saladin, the greatest terror of the Christians, was dying he commanded that there was to be no pomp and ceremony at his burial, but only his shirt made fast to a lance and carried before his dead body in the manner of an ensign, a plain priest going before and crying aloud to the people in this manner. 'Saladin, Conqueror of the East, of all the greatness and riches he had in his life, taketh with him nothing more than his shirt.' A sight worthy of so great a king, mindful of man's fragility and the vanity of worldly honours.

This view of Saladin was not without its problems. He was a pagan, yet was morally good; he was chivalrous and yet not a knight. It was a paradox to which there was only one satisfying solution. Appearances to the contrary, Saladin must have been both a Christian and a knight. So the many stories that Saladin was attracted by the self-evident truths of Christianity but was prevented from becoming a convert by what he saw of Christian practice, gave way to the many more stories which spoke of his actual baptism,

A late 18th-century engraving of Saladin.

though it was usually either a secret or a deathbed conversion. Another set of stories told how he was educated in chivalry and dubbed knight by a Frankish noble. Astonishingly the earliest known version of this story dates back to a time when Saladin was still alive – an indication of the extent to which, even among his enemies, he was a legend in his own lifetime. In a society in which, even more than in our own, a man's status was determined by his birth, it was perhaps inevitable that all this was explained by giving him a mother who was a French noblewoman, the Count of Ponthieu's grand-daughter. For a man of

Kurdish origin, a great exponent of the *jihad*, the Holy War against all who did not acknowledge the authority of Islam, it was an extraordinary transformation. As such it tells us a great deal about the way men thought in twelfth- and thirteenth-century Europe. But what did Saladin do to deserve this fate?

Certainly the manner in which he first caught the attention of the political world gave no hint of his future reputation. In January 1169 he engineered the *coup d'état* which brought his uncle, Shirkuh, to power in Egypt. Two months later Shirkuh died and Saladin took his place as vizier, nominally the lieutenant of the caliph of Cairo but in fact the real ruler of the country. (Contemporary western opinion explained this political arrangement on the grounds that the caliph had so many wives that he was always too tired to be able to rule himself.) At this time Egypt was in total disarray. The economy was flourishing but by the early 1160s internal political difficulties had reached such a pitch of violence and chaos that the country appeared to be a fruit ripe for plucking. It was merely a question of seeing which of its neighbours would reap the harvest: Nur ed-Din, the Muslim ruler of Damascus, Mosul and Aleppo, or Amalric, the Christian king of Jerusalem. By 1168 both Nur ed-Din and Amalric had entered (or invaded) Egypt no less than four times in six years. Shirkuh had been Nur ed-Din's leading general and so the *coup* of January 1169 was a victory for Damascus, but equally clearly it was not the end of the affair. Amalric had negotiated an alliance with the emperor of Constantinople and Saladin was daily expecting the invasion of their joint forces. Guessing what his internal enemies would do when his hands were tied by the external threat, he decided to give them no chance. In July the Byzantine fleet sailed from Constantinople and in August Saladin ordered the massacre of all troops of whose loyalty he was doubtful. When the invasion eventually materialized he was able to cope with it. Within the space of a single year he had shown himself to be a skilful and utterly ruthless politician. After a generation of unrest and confusion he was to give Egypt stability and security.

In 1170 Saladin marched into Arabia and the Yemen, asserting Egyptian hegemony over the Red Sea area and over the trade routes to Asia. Saladin had been brought up in Nur ed-Din's household and he continued to recognize the formal overlordship of his old master until the latter's death in 1174. At once he occupied Damascus, setting aside Nur ed-Din's son and, two years later, marrying his widow. The Latin kingdom of Jerusalem was now caught in a deadly encirclement and Saladin intended to take full advantage of his position. Though he had ousted Nur ed-Din's son he none the less saw himself as the heir to the father's political and religious programme. From him he had learned to appreciate the importance of the *jihad*, the powerful religious force which alone was capable of uniting the divided Muslim world. Like Nur ed-Din, Saladin became the champion of Islamic orthodoxy and unity, the patron and friend of poets and preachers whose eloquence was pressed into the service of the *jihad* – and its leader. The Franks called him Saladin; his real name and title was Al-Malik al-Nasir Salah ed-Din Yusuf, 'the king who brings victory to the faith'. In 1169 Nur ed-Din had commissioned a pulpit for the al-Aqsa mosque in Jerusalem. It was up to Saladin to ensure that the pulpit would be duly installed.

In 1177 and 1179 he led invasions of the kingdom of Jerusalem, but the outcome of these campaigns seems to have convinced him that no decisive victory could be obtained while Aleppo and Mosul remained outside his control. From 1179 to 1185 Jerusalem enjoyed a respite while Saladin concentrated his resources on overcoming his Muslim rivals. This was, of course, a struggle for power, but it was also something more than that. The struggle for the hearts and minds of the Muslim population necessarily involved their religious and moral values and it therefore made good sense for Saladin to use religious and moral, as well as political, diplomatic and military methods in order to win the struggle. He realized that any success he might enjoy would depend in large measure on the moral authority he possessed. Thus in his dealings with friend and foe Saladin showed himself to be remarkably reliable. He hardly ever broke his word – a rare quality in a politician who wielded so much power. He presented himself to the Muslim world as a strict pillar of orthodoxy. In the biography written by Baha ad-Din, a member of his household, Saladin was 'a man of firm faith, one who often had God's name on his lips'. He prayed regularly and in public. 'If the hour of prayer came round when he was travelling he would dismount from his horse and pray. He never omitted the canonic prayer except when he was unconscious in the last three days of his life.' He was a lavish alms-giver, so generous indeed that when he died his treasury contained only 47 drachmas and one piece of gold. Again according to Baha ad-Din, his treasurers used to keep an emergency reserve of cash concealed from him, knowing that if he learned of its existence he would spend it at once. To him money was like the dust on the road.

Because of illness and involvement in the Holy War he did not always manage to keep the fast of Ramadan, but in the last year of his life he was to make up for his earlier omissions. In one respect only did he not succeed in fulfilling the requirements of Islam: he never found the time to go on the pilgrimage to Mecca, though he always intended to, Baha ad-Din assures us. Precisely because he was a pillar of orthodoxy, he could not abide heretics; rather, he had them crucified. Heretics apart, Baha ad-Din portrays him as a prince who was merciful as well as just. 'Every Monday and Thursday he gave an audience and administered justice in public session. He never turned away anyone who had suffered wrong and was seeking a remedy. No one ever implored his help without his stopping, listening to the complaint and examining the case.' For, in a phrase attributed to Abu Bakr,

Muhammad's successor and the first caliph, 'The just prince is God's shadow on earth, and his mercy.' It is clear that during his lifetime Saladin made every effort to conform to the model of the ideal ruler that was described, after his death, by the faithful Baha ad-Din. His sense of his historic role, his conviction that his destiny was to unite Islam, meant that he had to be a pious and good ruler and it was the job of his secretariat to ensure that everyone knew that he was. But it is clear that he was also good at the essential task of man-management. He was a generous patron and a prince who shared the interests of his emirs: 'He was well-versed in the genealogies of the Arabs and in the genealogies of their horses.'

By 1185 he had brought both Aleppo and Mosul under his control. As Saladin's star rose, so the Frankish one sank. King Amalric was succeeded first by a leper and then by a child. When the child died in 1186 his mother was crowned queen and her second husband, Guy of Lusignan, crowned king, but jealousies meant that the kingdom of Jerusalem was hopelessly split into rival factions. Moreover its military resources were stretched to the limit and defeat in just one battle might result in the loss of the whole kingdom, while, with the combined wealth of Egypt, Syria and Mesopotamia at his disposal, Saladin could afford several defeats and still keep on coming. On 3 July 1187 King Guy decided to risk battle; on 4 July his army was annihilated at Hattin. Of those who were taken prisoner Saladin treated some, including Guy himself, generously; others, whom he regarded as his special enemies, particularly the Templars and Hospitallers, he had decapitated.

For the Latin kingdom the consequences of the battle of Hattin were immediately disastrous. Most of its fighting men had been killed or captured. Apart from a few small garrisons there was nothing to stand in the way of Saladin's triumphal progress. On 10 July the great port of Acre fell and in the next few weeks some fifty towns and fortresses capitulated. Because the Franks knew that Saladin would keep his word, they had fewer qualms about agreeing terms of surrender. By September Saladin had captured all of the coastal towns south of Tripoli except for Tyre. In terms of military strategy Tyre should have been his next target, for once the Franks had lost the coast the rest of the Holy Land was bound to fall. Instead Saladin turned inland and laid siege to Jerusalem. As a result his army was able to enter the Holy City on 2 October. The al-Aqsa mosque was restored to Islam on the anniversary of Muhammad's ascent to heaven from Jerusalem. It was a brilliant stroke of propaganda skilfully utilized by Saladin's chancery in the jubilant letters which they circulated throughout the Muslim world. After Mecca and Medina, Jerusalem was the most holy place in Islam and its recovery ensured that Saladin's name would never die.

None the less with the wisdom of hindsight it seems clear that Saladin had made a mistake. After the emotional climax of the entry into Jerusalem it was hard to push his weary army to yet further efforts and he failed to take Tyre. Thus the Christians were left with a beach-head from which they could hope to recover Jerusalem. A crusade was summoned. Reinforcements from the West poured into Tyre. In August 1189 a small army of Franks marched south to lay siege to Acre and for two years all eyes in the Muslim, as well as in the Christian, world were focused on the see-saw struggle for this key city. In April 1191 King Philip of France landed at Acre, to be followed seven weeks later by the king of England, Richard the Lionheart. In July Acre surrendered to the kings. Its fall was a great blow to Saladin's prestige. After Philip returned to France, Richard carried on the war and showed himself to be a better general than Saladin. But though he defeated the Muslims in battle and recovered much of the Palestinian coast, he was unable to take Jerusalem. Eventually a combination of exhaustion and domestic problems forced Richard to call off the Third Crusade in September 1192. In the following spring Saladin died. Despite his recent losses he had managed to hold on to his greatest gain. On each occasion that Richard threatened Jerusalem, Saladin chose, at times going against the advice of his emirs, to remain within the city walls. It was a gesture which made his priorities clear; he might yield some of his conquests but not this one. Yet however dear to Saladin was his reputation as the liberator of Jerusalem, he did not deny access to the city to men of other creeds. The Jewish community was allowed to return to Jerusalem and four Christian priests were allowed to hold services in the Church of the Holy Sepulchre. In contrast, ever since 1099 when the first crusaders had captured the Holy City and massacred the people who lived there, Jews and Muslims alike, the Christians had treated Jerusalem as if it belonged to them alone.

Doubtless the fact that Saladin prized Jerusalem so highly made him a more comprehensible figure to Western Europeans. On the other hand the atmosphere of Holy War hardly seems conducive to the development of mutual sympathy and understanding. Saladin systematically executed Templars and Hospitallers; Richard massacred the prisoners of Acre. To Ambroise, Muslims were 'the pagan cattle, the unbelieving black-faced brood'. What then was special about this one Muslim which made him different from the rest of the 'pagan cattle'? It is probable that the image of Saladin which was carefully cultivated in the Arab world, the image of the just and generous prince, was one which was known to the Franks of the kingdom of Jerusalem. The great bulk of the population of the kingdom was Arabic-speaking and much of it was Muslim. In these circumstances it would be odd if the Arab view of their great opponent remained entirely unknown to the Latins of *Outremer* and, through them, to Western Christians. Moreover through their own ex-

Richard the Lionheart watches the execution of the Muslim garrison after the capture of Acre in 1191.

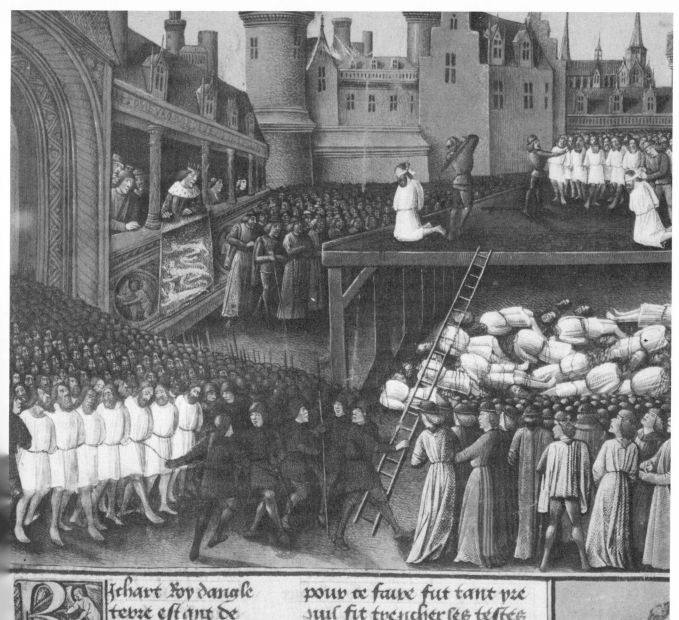

 ichart Roy dangle
terre estant de
monte en ater le
ant apres le dept
du Roy phelippe le
iour estre benu que salhadin
deuoit rendre la braye trow
et ne sauoit fait. Non obstat
quil eust eu de lui et du Roy
phle plusieurs alongemens

pour ce faure fut tant pre
quil fit trencher les testes
a plus de b. ʹꝰ turcs et auts
sarrazins quil tenoit priso
mers et le demourant des
autres mist a rancon. Et
tost apres sesmeust grant
dissenaon entre lui et le duc
dosteriche. Pour quoy Il fit
ietter en fange a boe la bame

perience the Franks knew that Saladin was capable of chivalrous gestures. Once, when besieging a castle, he learned that its seventeen-year-old lord had just been married. Having established in which of the towers the bridal chamber was sited, he then gave orders that it should not be bombarded by his siege-engines. Above all the Franks knew that, however ruthless Saladin could be at times, once he had given his word, he kept it. And as the kingdom of Jerusalem collapsed around them it was to this political honesty that many of them owed their lives. So the stage was set for that astonishing transformation whereby a Muslim statesman of unimpeachable orthodoxy was turned into a Christian knight of French descent.

~ *Robert Bruce* ~

On 10 February 1306 Robert Bruce murdered John Comyn of Badenoch, 'the Red Comyn', in the Greyfriars' Church at Dumfries. With this act of violence and sacrilege Bruce catapulted right to the forefront of the Scottish political stage. Six weeks later he was crowned king at Scone and he remained king until he died (struck down, some said, by leprosy) twenty-three years later. Before 1306 he had been just one of a number of Scottish barons struggling to stay on their feet in an immensely difficult and turbulent arena. It is true that, unlike nearly all the other barons, he could lay claim to the throne, but up till now any efforts which he may have made to prosecute this claim had been, at best, half-hearted. In 1305 and early 1306 Scotland was governed by the king of England – and not just by any king of England but by Edward 1, one of the toughest, ablest, most ruthless, most determined of the Plantagenets. Scotland was still a conquered country, as it had been on and off since 1296. Except in the south-east (by far the wealthiest part of the country), most of the local officials were Scotsmen, but power at the centre was kept firmly in the hands of a triumvirate of foreigners headed by King Edward's nephew, John of Brittany. As for Robert Bruce, he was a man in his early thirties, a rich landowner, with large estates in England – including a house in London and the pleasant suburban manor of Tottenham – as well as in Scotland. He had a younger brother who was doing well at Cambridge. Moreover, on the face of it at least, he had been a committed supporter of King Edward since 1302; certainly he had done his best to help hunt down the great patriot leader William Wallace. When in August 1305 Edward 1 sent Wallace to the scaffold at Smithfield, to be hanged, disembowelled, beheaded and quartered, he must have felt that Scotland was broken at last.

Then Bruce struck. His first biographer, John Barbour, Archdeacon of Aberdeen, tells the story. Robert Bruce and the Red Comyn, indignant at Scotland's servitude, made a pact. Bruce was to take the crown and Comyn, in return for his support, would receive Bruce's lands. But Comyn went to King Edward and betrayed the plot, citing as proof a document sealed with Bruce's seal. The King summoned Bruce to a parliament and, showing him the document, asked him if the seal was his. Bruce replied that he had unfortunately forgotten to bring his seal with him and asked for a night to think it over. While he was at his lodgings, the Earl of Gloucester sent him a messenger with a shilling and a pair of spurs. Bruce took the hint, tipped the messenger the shilling and put the spurs to his horse. On finding Comyn at Dumfries he challenged him with his treachery and in the ensuing quarrel Comyn was killed.

This is the beginning of the legend. It is certain that very little of this can be true. Probably what happened is that Bruce, knowing that he could not succeed if Comyn was against him, arranged to meet him, perhaps to offer some such pact as that described in Barbour. But Comyn would not agree and once he knew of Bruce's plans he was too dangerous to be allowed to live. Robert Bruce was a conventionally devout man but at this crisis not even the proximity of the altar could save Comyn from the immediate consequence of Bruce's violent anger, whether spontaneous or calculated. In the next six weeks the pre-arranged plan was put into operation. The fiery cross was carried through Scotland and Englishmen fled for safety into castles or to the Border. The Bishop of Glasgow, far from excommunicating a murderer whose crime had been committed in his diocese, actually exhorted his flock to fight for his cause as though it were a crusade. The timber intended to repair the bell-tower of his cathedral was used instead to build siege engines. At the end of March Bruce was enthroned in the abbey of Scone. King Edward had removed the Stone of Destiny to Westminster, but he had not as yet taken the whole abbey – though it was characteristic of his thoroughness that he was soon to ask the Pope for permission to move it brick by brick. The speed with which Bruce had been able to move in these

Robert Bruce, who became King of Scotland in 1306, in defiance of Edward I, after murdering his accomplice in a church.

short weeks shows just how grievously the old English king had miscalculated. His vindictive treatment of Wallace had not, after all, taught the Scottish people a lesson. It had merely reinforced their hatred of foreign rule. And in another way too it had strengthened the national cause. In the previous stage of the struggle for Scottish independence many of the most powerful nobles had looked uneasily at the spectacle of Wallace, a man from another class, doing 'their' work for them. Now that he had been so brutally removed, the way was open for a new leader to emerge – and this time an aristocratic leader.

Remarkable as Bruce's success had been in February and March 1306, the odds were still heavily stacked against him. Not only did he have a civil war with the powerful Comyn family on his hands, he still had to face the inevitable English comeback. England was five times wealthier than Scotland and could put correspondingly larger and better equipped armies in the field. Edward appointed Aymer de Valence, Comyn's brother-in-law, as his lieutenant in Scotland and gave him authority – in Barbour's phrase – 'to burn and slay and raise dragon', in other words to hoist the dragon standard of all-out war. In June 1306 at the battle of Methven Bruce was routed and his army scattered. In August he was defeated again, this time by his Scottish enemies. With just a handful of followers Bruce 'took to the heather'. He had lost his kingdom and it was all he could do to save his life. He became a hunted fugitive, travelling westwards by hill tracks and hidden glens, until he came to Dunaverty at the tip of the Mull of Kintyre. From there he got away by boat and vanished. For all we know for certain he may have spent the next four-and-a-half months exclusively in the company of spiders.

The story of the fugitive's return to Scotland, of how he overcame each setback and won the initiative, of how by a mixture of patience and daring he made himself master of nearly all the castles held by the English until at last he was strong enough to meet the challenge of a full-scale invasion led by the king of England in person, is one of the great heroic romances of history, all the more incredible for being true. It must, however, be said that in a sense Robert Bruce had the co-operation of the kings of England, both Edward I and Edward II. Despite the experience of ten years of Scottish resistance, Edward I went on obstinately making the same mistakes. In the summer of 1306 he ordered a policy of judicial terror. Among those whom he hanged were ordinary country folk, knights and the Earl of Atholl. When it was pleaded on Atholl's behalf that he was a distant cousin of the king, Edward merely ordered that he should be hanged from higher gallows, then decapitated

Edward I enters London on his return from the Crusades.

and burned. The Countess of Buchan and Robert's sister Mary were imprisoned for years in cages hung from the walls of Berwick and Roxburgh castles, so that passers-by might stare at them. Many more, whom Edward could not catch, were outlawed and when Bruce returned they had little option but to join him, preferring to risk death in battle rather than be tried by English law. Then, in July 1307, the old king died. He was succeeded by a son who had none of his father's hideously masterful qualities. Edward II was more interested in his friendship with Piers Gaveston than in his quarrel with Robert Bruce. With the immediate threat from England removed, Bruce could afford to ignore the heavily fortified Lowlands and concentrate instead on defeating his enemies in the Highlands. By the end of 1309 he had effectively gained control of the whole of Scotland north of the Forth; from this region he could now recruit armies to carry the war against the English troops stationed in Lothian.

But however inadequate the English high command may have been, they still possessed by far the greater resources. If Bruce was to succeed he could do so only by adopting guerrilla tactics. Somehow he had to capture the castles which were the backbone of English power in south-east Scotland: Perth, Stirling, Edinburgh, Jedburgh, Roxburgh and Berwick, and he had to do it without resorting to drawn-out, full-scale sieges for which he lacked the equipment and which might lead to pitched battles in which he would be heavily outgunned. The only hope was a war of speed, mobility, ambush and scorched earth to win control of the countryside. For the moment the English could keep their castles so long as they dared not venture out or at least found no provisions when they did so. By this method he could try to make the war as expensive as possible for the English to maintain. Inevitably the people who suffered most from this kind of warfare were the country people. Constantly under pressure from both sides at once, any kind of consistent loyalty must have been impossible and they might have been expected to feel nothing more than 'a plague on both your houses'. Yet according to a Cumberland chronicler, 'in all this fighting all or most of the Scots who were with the English were with them insincerely, for their hearts if not their bodies were always with their own people.'

The first of the major castles to fall was Perth. On a dark night in January 1313 a Scottish assault party waded through the ice-cold waters of the moat carrying light weapons and rope ladders. Using grappling-hooks to attach their ladders to the wall, they scrambled over and into the town. Taken completely by surprise, the men of Perth surrendered almost without a fight. The king himself had led the way into the moat and, with the help of his own rope ladder, had been the second man to scale the wall. Here, certainly, we have one of the secrets of Bruce's heroic reputation: like Richard the Lionheart, he was prepared to share the dangers which he asked his soldiers to run. Such courage, moreover, was useful. His men fought better knowing that their king was with them and other leaders were inspired to follow Bruce's example. In February 1314 James Douglas captured Roxburgh by using similar assault tactics and, three weeks later, Thomas Randolph, determined not to be outdone, took Edinburgh itself with a brilliantly organized piece of rock-climbing. Both castles were immediately razed to the ground. This was Bruce's consistent policy. The most effective way of preventing strongholds falling into English hands again was to demolish them – and without strongholds no English force, however large, could hope to dominate Scotland.

Unfortunately Edward Bruce had failed to grasp his brother's strategy. At midsummer 1313 he had come to terms with the commander of Stirling Castle; the castle would be surrendered without a fight if in the next twelve months no English army came within three miles of its walls to do battle for its rescue. It may have seemed an easy way to win a great castle but in reality it was to issue so public a challenge to Edward II's honour that not even that king could fail to pick up the gauntlet. And with a major English army loose in the heart of his realm, would Bruce be able to maintain his policy of avoiding battle? It was a terrible dilemma to be landed with and he left his brother in no doubt about his feelings.

On 17 June 1314 Edward II's army left Berwick. The king's intention was not just to relieve Stirling but to settle Scotland once and for all. He had some 15,000 infantry and 2,000–3,000 cavalry, many of them heavily-armoured knights, the pride of an aristocratic and

Bruce reviews his troops before the battle of Bannockburn.

military society like medieval England. Against him Bruce mustered about 6,000 infantry and 500 light horse at the Torwood, south of Bannockburn on the main road between Falkirk and Stirling. Though outnumbered, the core of the Scottish army consisted of men who had seven years of successful war behind them and they were in good heart. On the other side King Edward neither took decisive charge of events himself nor handed over sole command to an experienced general; the result was muddle. On 23 June the English vanguard sighted a part of the Scottish army and at once charged at them. Sir Henry de Bohun, the foremost English knight, suddenly realized that there in front of him, mounted on a small grey horse, carrying an axe and wearing a crown on his helmet, was the Scottish king. It was the opportunity of a lifetime. Levelling his lance he rode straight at him. At the last moment Bruce pulled out of the way, stood in his stirrups and brought his axe down clean through Bohun's helmet, splitting his

head in two. When he was very properly rebuked for risking his life and the whole cause in this unnecessary fashion, he merely smiled and made a rueful remark about his poor old axe, shattered by the impact of the blow. This indeed was a soldier king. From the Scots' point of view no more morale-boosting start could be imagined.

In several other clashes that day the Scottish spearmen, fighting in close formation, got the better of English cavalry units. None the less the memory of the battle of Falkirk sixteen years before, when a combination of English archers and cavalry had slaughtered Scots in their thousands, was still vivid and Bruce spent a night in doubt before deciding to risk another pitched battle. At daybreak on 24 June he gave the order to attack. The English had feared a night-attack, but this they had not expected. Outmanoeuvred and ineptly led, they fought bravely for a while, but Edward II was not allowed to risk his life and his withdrawal from the field was the signal for general flight.

Robert Bruce reigned for another fifteen years after Bannockburn. In that period his armies went over to the attack, raiding England hard and often. Eventually in 1328 he obtained what he wanted: the formal recognition of Scottish independence by an English government. But however reluctant the English may have been to admit defeat, in the eyes of most people – and above all in the eyes of Scots – God, by giving them the verdict in the trial by battle at Bannockburn, had recognized that the Scots should be free. And no matter what went before and what came after, it is clear that it was the dramatic sequence of events between 1306 and 1314, beginning at the high altar in Dumfries and ending at Bannockburn, that established Robert Bruce as a legendary figure. Undoubtedly he had been driven hard by personal ambition, had fought with fierce violence for himself and his family, but he had fought too for something bigger, and it was this which lent a dignity and heroic grandeur to his own struggle. All this is summed up in the Declaration of Arbroath, the letter sent in 1320 to the Pope in the name of the barons and freeholders of Scotland:

Through God's grace we have been set free from countless evils by our most valiant prince, king and lord, the lord Robert, who, that his people and his heritage might be delivered out of the hands of enemies, bore cheerfully toil and fatigue, hunger and danger, like another Maccabeus or Joshua. We are bound to him for the maintaining of our freedom both by his right and his merits, as to him by whom salvation has been wrought unto our people, and by him, come what may, we mean to stand. Yet if he should give up what he has begun, seeking to make us or our kingdom subject to the king of England or to the English, we would strive at once to drive him out as our enemy and a subverter of his own right and ours, and we would make some other man who was able to defend us our king; for, as long as a hundred of us remain alive, we will never on any conditions be subjected to the lordship of the English. For we fight not for glory, nor riches, nor honours, but for freedom alone, which no good man gives up except with his life.

～ Henry V ～

Shakespeare's Henry V stands for all time as the ideal English hero-king. The images are all Shakespeare's – from the nimble-footed madcap Prince of Wales, plump Jack Falstaff's boon companion, to the mirror of Christian kings, the royal captain on the eve of Agincourt, who

... goes and visits all his host,
Bids them good morrow with a modest smile,
And calls them brothers, friends and countrymen.

But is this the real Henry V? Or was he a tightlipped, calculating king who was later transformed into a symbol of patriotic ardour by the spurious fame of one victory in a battle which he had done his best to avoid?

Inevitably we know less about his youth than we would like and it is possible that Henry misspent his in traditional fashion, but the evidence that he did so is all based on rumour – and later rumour at that, committed to writing at a time when the king was already a figure from

Henry V, by an unknown artist.

the heroic past. What is quite certain is that there was no sudden reformation when the prince became king, no overnight banishment of the fat knight with the great-belly doublet. In fact from an early age Henry became so deeply immersed in the business of war and politics that his first biographer (a chaplain who accompanied him on the Agincourt campaign) could comment that while still a young man he had possessed the maturity of an old one. This is, of course, just the kind of platitude one would expect from an official biographer – but it is no more unreliable than the romantic stereotype of a conversion from wild youth to responsible adulthood.

Henry was made Prince of Wales in 1399, in the month after his father's coronation. He was twelve years old and was soon plunged into the troublesome affairs of his unquiet principality. In 1400 Owain Glyn Dwr raised the standard of revolt, attacking the town of Ruthin with a following which was said to include three wives, two widows and a concubine. For the next six years Prince Henry was educated in the harsh realities of waging war with little money and over difficult terrain. Several English armies floundered forward between mountain and bog only to be driven 'bootless home and weather-beaten back'. Not until the capture of Aberystwyth and Harlech castles in 1408 and 1409 was it clear that the rebels had been brought to their knees by the greater military resources of the English. In these years the sign which dominated his life was not that of the Boar's Head Tavern but that of the Red Dragon of Wales.

From December 1406 onwards, moreover, the prince took an active part in the politics of his father's court. He was assiduous in his attendance at council meetings – and King Henry IV's council was a hard-working body. One privy seal clerk, the poet Thomas Hoccleve, complained that they had to work even on saints' days. Already the chief political issue was the question of France. The tension in the latter part of Henry IV's reign was as nothing to the troubles which beset the court of King Charles VI of France.

Mad on and off since 1396, the unfortunate man suffered from the delusion that he was made of glass and might be shattered by the slightest touch. Life at his court was dominated by the feud between the dukes of Burgundy and Orléans. In 1407 Orléans was assassinated by Burgundian agents. By 1410 the country was in a state of civil war and both sides appealed to England for help. In 1411 an English expeditionary force of 800 lances and 2,000 archers crossed the Channel – the first to do so for nearly thirty years. Unfortunately Henry IV's uncertain health meant that there was no unquestioned authority in England either. The way was open for dispute and the development of court faction. In 1412 the prince and other magnates brought armed retinues to London and rumour spoke of a *coup d'état* in the offing. The situation was saved by a further deterioration in the king's health which made it clear that the masterful prince would not have long to wait. Practical experience of war and politics, in Wales and Westminster, not an instinctive understanding of the life of the common people gained by hard boozing in London pubs, was the training which made Henry V a fine king.

The overriding concern with French affairs from 1410 onwards meant that no new orientation of policy was required when Henry V came to the throne in March 1413. Since the reign of Edward III the English king had also claimed to be king of France, and even were he to renounce this crown there were still older claims to the twelfth-century Angevin Empire which could be revived. However not even in divided France could Henry find a government which would agree to terms such as these and so, thwarted in diplomacy, he turned to war – as perhaps he had intended all along. In September 1415, with an army 9,000 strong, he captured Harfleur, now a suburb of Le Havre but then the main port of the Seine estuary. The town, however, had held out for five weeks and it was not clear what Henry could do next. Simply to return to England would not have been a very impressive start for the kind of enterprise implied by Henry's exorbitant diplomacy. On the other hand, with his force depleted by dysentery and by the detachment of a garrison for Harfleur, he could hardly afford to strike deep into France. So Henry decided to march north-east to Calais (in English hands since 1345), inspecting what he was pleased to call 'his' duchy of Normandy on the way. On 8 October less than 6,000 men left Harfleur taking with them provisions for eight days. At first all went according to plan, but on 13 October as he approached the Somme he was informed that the ford of Blanche Taque had been staked and was being held against him. To cross the river he would have to march upstream, inland, and this he did for five days while a French force, moving along the Somme's north bank, kept watch. For five days the English marched south-eastwards further and further into enemy country, probing the river crossings, but always finding the bridges and causeways broken down before them. Inevitably the army began to lose heart. 'Sad and grieved,' wrote the king's chaplain, 'we expected only that when our victuals were all gone the enemy would lay waste the country before us and strike us with famine until at the head of the river they would use the advantage of their great numbers and superior artillery to overthrow us who were so few, and wearied with much fatigue, and weak from want of food.' Only God could save them now and it was in this mood that Henry sent to the gallows a soldier who had robbed a church.

Luckily, on 19 October, they found two unguarded fords and then set off as quickly as possible in the direction of Calais. But the main French army kept just ahead of them and by 24 October it was clear that battle was unavoidable. During a night of steady rain the subdued English soldiers confessed their sins and tried to snatch some rest within easy earshot of the confident hubbub coming from the French camp. By now the only feasible English policy was to trust in God and keep their bow-strings waxed. According to the chaplain, when Sir Walter Hungerford was heard to wish for another 10,000 English archers, Henry turned and said, 'Thou speakest foolishly, for by the God of heaven, by whose grace I have a firm hope of victory, I would not, even if I could, increase my number by one; for those whom I have are the people of God, whom he thinks me worthy to have at this time. Dost thou not believe the Almighty, with these his humble few, is able to conquer the haughty opposition of the French who pride themselves on their numbers and strength?' Brave but commonplace words and whether or not he persuaded Sir Walter we do not know. The events of the next day (the feast of saints Crispin and Crispinian), the combination of French tactical mistakes and English archery, meant of course that the king's words became heroically memorable – and for the next 200 years, culminating in Shakespeare's *Henry V*, constantly improved in the telling.

There can be no doubt that this was Henry's finest hour, that, in Peter Earle's words, 'after half a millenium his reputation still rests squarely on the day he spent fighting in the middle of a very large cornfield halfway between Boulogne and Arras'. He lived another six years, and spent most of them at war. Many professional soldiers and historians admire the methodical skill displayed in his later years more than they do the risky enterprise which led to Agincourt. They argue that all he won in 1415 were some ransoms and one town and that the real achievement was the steady acquisition of Normandy by conquest in 1417-21. Up to a point they are right, but only up to a point. Pitched battles were rare and frightening occasions. Particularly from the point of view of the commander they were very different from the humdrum routine of day-to-day warfare. In the confusion of battle a moment of panic might decide the issue one way or another and the fortunes of a few hours could undo the patient work of months or years – just as, for the French, Agincourt undermined everything they had done since 1370. Moreover the king who committed his cause to battle was

The battle of Agincourt, 25 October 1415: the cavalry charge, supported by archers and infantry.

also putting himself in jeopardy, since it was always clear that the surest way to win a battle was to capture or kill the opposing commander – just as, in 1403, the battle of Shrewsbury was decided by the death of Hotspur. At Shrewsbury Henry IV, knowing the risks he was running, had dressed some of his household knights in the royal surcoat in order to confuse those who were aiming to kill him. At Agincourt eighteen French knights bound themselves by oath to make a concerted attack on the English king or die in the attempt, but Henry, spurning the ruse adopted by his father, alone wore a crown around his helmet and a surcoat embroidered with the royal

arms. At Agincourt, against enormous odds, Henry V committed his person and his cause to the judgment of God in battle, and he won. The eighteen knights, true to their oath, were killed to a man. But once victory was in sight Henry, after so many risks, would take no more; an apparent threat to his rear led him to give the order to kill all prisoners.

Two immensely important consequences flowed from this victory and made possible the conquests which followed: an enthusiastic parliament voted him all the money he needed, and never again did a French army dare to stand in his way.

The systematic conquest of Normandy began in 1417 with the storming and pillaging of the city of Caen. The massacre of civilians – men, women and children – which this involved spelt out a dire warning. In the whole Normandy campaign, Henry did not have to order another general assault on a town. But French resistance was undermined less by Henry's ruthlessness than by their own civil war. As Burgundian fought Armagnac no major army marched to the relief of beleaguered towns. In January 1419 Rouen itself, the capital of Normandy, surrendered. On 28 August 1419, on the bridge at Montereau, Duke John of Burgundy was assassinated. Taking full advantage of the Burgundian cry for vengeance Henry was able to negotiate the Treaty of Troyes (ratified in May 1420). By its terms the Dauphin was disinherited and in his place Henry v was to rule France, initially as regent for the old and pathetic Charles vi, later as king by virtue of his marriage to Charles vi's daughter Catherine. In December 1420 Henry entered Paris in triumph. Naturally the Dauphin rejected the Treaty of Troyes and so the war continued. Despite an occasional setback, the English forces continued to hold the initiative and in August 1422 they were still pressing slowly forward when Henry v, aged thirty-five, died of dysentery. From the point of view of his posthumous reputation he was perhaps fortunate to die while still at the height of his powers, but from the point of view of the

policies which he had pursued the succession of his baby son Henry vi was to be disastrous. This has made it possible for historians to argue that the aggressive policy itself was disastrous. But this is not how contemporaries saw it and the fact remains that, during his own lifetime and even for some years after it, the English position in northern France remained both tenable and profitable. It is clear that he was a competent and masterful ruler; even while absent in France, he was able to dominate the government of England and bend men and policies to his will. This was what was expected of a king. If Henry v came to be seen in a heroic light it was because to a remarkable degree he consciously and unconsciously lived up to contemporary standards of princely conduct. The magnificent pageants with which the Londoners welcomed the victorious king to their city in 1415 and again in 1421 can tell us a great deal. Through noisy scenes of splendour and revelry the king moved quietly, grave-faced and unassuming. In carefully stage-managed spectacles such as these he publicly conformed to the model of an ideal king – a role which came naturally to this pious, taciturn and self-disciplined man. In pageant and battle Henry v knew how to catch the imagination of his age.

∾ *Joan of Arc* ∾

On 30 May 1431 a farmer's daughter, sentenced to death as a relapsed heretic, was burnt in the Old Market Place at Rouen. By 1910 it was reckoned that there were some 20,000 statues of Joan of Arc in France. It is hardly surprising then that in 1920 the Vatican, yielding to this monumental pressure, decided to recognize her as a saint. The date of Joan's canonization is an

indication of her appeal to the nationalist sentiment so characteristic of the nineteenth and twentieth centuries – the kind of sentiment evoked in the highly-charged prose of Jules Michelet, the most influential French historian of the mid-nineteenth century: 'She loved France so! And France, touched by it, began to love herself. ... Let us always remember, people of

France, that the beloved nation was born in the heart of a woman, of her tenderness and her tears, of the blood she gave for us. . . .' And what myth could be more appropriate to our own times than that of the visionary who took up arms in a just cause, the resistance heroine, the woman fighting in a man's world?

Michelet at least was well aware of the risks inherent in this approach to Joan of Arc: 'What legend is more beautiful than this incontestable story? But one must be careful not to make it into a legend.' The risks were well known in the fifteenth century too. In 1456 the Archbishop of Reims and the bishops of Paris and Coutances prohibited the setting up of 'images and epitaphs' of Joan at Rouen and elsewhere. By this time there was already one legend of Joan in existence – the English one, the story that she was a sorceress who had used the black arts to conjure them out of France – and the French authorities, while determined to scotch this legend, were equally determined to prevent a new one rising, phoenix-like, in its place. They presumably felt that there was some danger of a cult developing – another sign of which might be the existence of several imposters, claiming to be Joan, active in the late 1430s and 1440s. On the whole the authorities succeeded. There was a flourishing local cult of Joan at Orléans and she always remained a famous figure, but not until the nineteenth century did she become, in effect, the national saint, thus fulfilling centuries later the prophecy which Shakespeare put into the Dauphin's mouth:

No longer on Saint Denis will we cry
But Joan la Pucelle shall be France's saint

It is not hard to see why it was that she eventually became a saint; the more interesting question is why, in the fifteenth century, French bishops were anxious to ensure that she did not. What, in other words, was her real historical role? And why did even those who had benefited most from her efforts feel so uneasy about her?

Joan was born about 1412, in the village of

Domrémy on the borders of Lorraine. In May 1428 this young country girl arrived at the castle of Vaucouleurs and told its captain, Robert de Baudricourt, that her lord wanted the Dauphin to be king and that she herself would lead him to his coronation. When Baudricourt asked her who her lord was, she replied, 'The king of heaven.' Naturally the captain ordered her to be given a good spanking and sent back home. But Joan was persistent and in the meanwhile the Dauphin's cause continued to drift downwards. In October 1428 the English, under the Earl of Salisbury, laid siege to Orléans, threatening to cross the Loire and strike at the heartland of the Dauphin's southern French kingdom. Early in 1429 Joan was summoned to Nancy, to the court of Charles, Duke of Lorraine, an old, sick man who had heard the local gossip about her and hoped that she might possess powers of therapeutic healing. Although she was unable to help him, he gave her some money and when she returned to Vaucouleurs Robert de Baudricourt was won over. He dispatched her with an escort to see the Dauphin. She arrived at Chinon on 23 February 1429. Two days later the Dauphin agreed to receive her and, according to her own testimony, 'I recognized him among the others by the advice of my voice which revealed him to me.' For a while she was allowed to speak privately with him and she evidently impressed him deeply but how she did this will always remain a mystery since neither of them ever told anyone what was said. Joan, indeed, at her trial, though ready to give information on oath on many matters, always refused to say anything about this, as she also refused to say anything about the nature of God's revelation to her.

This mystery at the most crucial moment in Joan's career has inevitably caused endless speculation as writer after writer has given free rein to his or her imagination. It is, however, worth saying a little about the widely held theory

The meeting between Joan of Arc and the Dauphin. 15th-century French manuscript.

that she released the Dauphin from tormenting and debilitating doubts about the legitimacy of his birth. This theory is most vividly expressed in Shaw's *Saint Joan*: 'The dauphin is at Chinon, like a rat in a corner, except that he won't fight. We don't even know that he is the dauphin: his mother says he isn't; and she ought to know.' But in fact, right from the moment of his birth in 1403, Charles, third son of the mad King Charles VI and Isabella of Bavaria, despite his mother's extra-marital activities, had always been treated as his father's son. In 1417 after the death of his elder brothers he was accepted as his father's heir. In 1418 he was driven out of Paris by a Burgundian *coup* and forced to set up a separate administration of his own based chiefly at Bourges. When Duke John of Burgundy was murdered next year, the Dauphin, with good reason, was widely held to be responsible. As a result the Treaty of Troyes, drawn up between Henry V and Charles VI in May 1420, declared him to be disinherited – not, it should be noted, on grounds of bastardy but on account of homicide. This did not prevent him being acclaimed king in October 1422 immediately after his father's death. In 1429, so far as 'the Dauphin' was concerned, he was already king. For the next few years, while the Anglo-Burgundian alliance held firm, Charles was forced to fight for survival; an aggressive policy of counter-attack against the English was out of the question. In these circumstances the conventional picture of a timidly apathetic dauphin makes little sense. Knowledgeable later contemporaries portrayed him as an inscrutable and subtle man. To his friends he seemed well-disposed, affable and clever – to his enemies, devious, ingenious and deceitful. There is no reason to believe that the man whom Joan of Arc met was any different. In a difficult political climate he had survived – and that in itself was an achievement.

Though we will never know what Joan said to him, there is good reason to suppose that Charles was likely to lend a sympathetic ear. In common with most men of the time, he was in the habit of consulting astrologers. As early as 1419 his interest in this aspect of the supernatural was noted by a distinguished theologian, Jean Gerson, who warned him against the perils of spiritual seduction by a 'strange woman' who would claim to be able to predict the future and perform wonders. The date of this warning shows that Charles's susceptibility on this score preceded any doubts which the Treaty of Troyes might have sown about his right to the throne of France. Moreover Charles may well have known of Marie of Avignon, a late fourteenth-century prophetess who was said to have foretold the coming of a virgin who would save France. After the interview at Chinon he decided to have Joan's claims investigated by a commission of inquiry. In April 1429 they reported in her favour, declaring her to be a good Christian, possessing the virtues of humility, honesty, simplicity – and virginity. When the commissioners asked her for a sign to prove that she was sent by God, she replied: 'In the name of God I have not come here to make signs, but lead me to Orléans and I will show you.' The commissioners concluded that Joan should be put to the test. In political and military terms it would be hard to imagine a more convenient test than the raising of the siege of Orléans. Charles had nothing to lose. And besides, his court astrologer, Pierre de St Valerin, was in favour of her.

So Charles equipped an army, put it under the command of the Duke of Alençon, himself a famous patron of astrologers, and allowed Joan, clad in full armour, to ride with it. On 30 April she entered Orléans and ten days later the English raised the siege. Next month, a French army, with Joan in the van, won a quick victory in the battle of Patay. Having seized the initiative at last, the professional soldiers in Charles's camp wanted to press on with an attack on Normandy, but such was Joan's reputation that she was able to insist that they follow her, as she followed her 'Voices', in advancing into Burgundian territory in order to crown the king at Reims. With little money left in the royal treasury to pay an army, they all to some extent relied on her power to attract volunteers. With banners bearing the name and images of Jesus Christ, with friars marching at the head of the troops singing hymns and anthems, her army has been aptly called 'a revivalist meeting in motion'. On 18 July the meeting ended with the coronation of Charles VII at Reims. And with this ceremony Joan's mission ended too. Her Voices, she said, spoke to her no more. From now on she was in the hands not of God but of men.

For a while longer the war party remained in the ascendant at court, but after an abortive attack on Paris early in September, during the course of which Joan was wounded, Charles VII agreed to a truce. Throughout the winter Joan was kept in a state of frustrated inaction. Then in May 1430, when Duke Philip of Burgundy laid siege to Compiègne, Joan went to help with its defence and there, outside the town walls, she was captured on 3 May. Burgundy sold his

prisoner to the English for £80,000. They were determined to discredit her and, through her, the monarchy of Charles VII. She was put on trial and, in these circumstances, the outcome was a foregone conclusion. That the Duke of Bedford and the English government should have pushed this political trial through to the bitter end may be unpleasant, but it is hardly surprising. In Bedford's own words, 'Everything was prospering until the time of the siege of Orléans; at this time by the hand of God as it seemeth a great evil befell your people which arose in large part, as I think, from the intermingling of false beliefs and mad fears which were instilled in them by a disciple and bloodhound of Satan, called the Maid, who used false enchantment and sorcery.'

But it is salutary to be reminded that of the 131 judges, assessors and other clergy concerned with the trial at Rouen in the spring of 1431, only

Joan at the stake, in the market-place of Rouen. Late 15th-century French manuscript.

eight were Englishmen. Joan was as much a victim of a civil war within France as of a war with the English. Moreover even some of Charles VII's advisers were glad to see her go. In 1430, for instance, the Archbishop of Reims wrote that she had raised herself up in pride, that she would not take advice and did everything of her own will. As for the King himself, he raised no protest against her trial and execution; indeed for twenty years after her capture he made not a single recorded reference to her or to what she had achieved on his behalf. Only in 1450 after his troops had captured Rouen – where the documentary record of her trial was preserved – did he break silence. But in ordering a second trial his purpose was simply to expose the irregularities of the first in order to free himself from the guilt of heresy by association. Eventually the long drawn-out and complex proceedings of the second trial came to an end in July 1456 with the annulment of the sentence of 1431 – but that was all. Although more than 100 witnesses had testified to Joan's purity of life, her integrity, her astonishing physical, mental and moral courage, on these subjects the judges said not one word. They passed no verdict on either her orthodoxy or her sanctity; they merely said that she had been unjustly condemned.

In part their reticence may have been caused by the embarrassing fact that many of the men involved in 1431 were still alive and in influential positions. In part it was because, like all mystics and visionaries, she posed a threat to the hierarchy of the church. If such people could communicate directly with God, through the medium of visions or 'Voices', where did that leave the clergy and the established order of the world? In this sense, all visionaries were uncomfortable people, but what could be more disturbing to the established order than a female visionary leading armies and wearing men's clothes? It is impossible to read the record of her trial and condemnation without being impressed by her quickness of mind and bravery in the most arduous and depressing conditions. That she possessed to an extraordinary degree the qualities of heroism is beyond doubt. Yet what is most extraordinary about her career is that anything like it should have happened at all. Who could imagine the modern French army being led into battle by a seventeen-year-old country girl?

∼ Christopher Columbus ∼

During the hours of daylight on Sunday, 9 September 1492 the sailors in Columbus's small fleet could see the 12,000-foot peak of Tenerife in the Canaries gradually sinking below the horizon behind them, their last sight of the world they knew. Somewhere before them, as they set course westward, lay the fabulously wealthy island of Cipangu (Japan). No one doubted that. The only problem was, how far away was it? And how long would it take to get there? Was it, as Columbus believed, a matter of a few weeks? Or would the voyage, as the experts believed, take at least a year? And was there anything between the Canaries and Cipangu? Optimistic explorers peppered their Atlantic charts with imaginary islands: Antilla (or Atlantis), St Brendan's Isle, Brazil Rock (which was not removed from Admiralty charts until 1873). But if they missed the islands, or there were none, and the experts were right, what then? Only the empty ocean and

Christopher Columbus, by the Venetian painter Sebastiano del Piombo (c. 1485–1547).

the danger of turning back too late, or of being becalmed, so that their supplies ran out and they died of starvation and thirst. They were all of them brave men, none more so than those who lacked Columbus's sense of destiny.

Just when and how Columbus came to be obsessed by the idea of sailing west in order to reach the Far East we will never know; but there are some moments in his life which were clearly important. As the son of the owner of a small textile business in Genoa, his childhood was spent in one of the great ports of the Mediterranean. He went to sea at an early age and in 1476, when he was twenty-five years old, he shipped aboard the *Bechalla*, a Flemish vessel which was joining a Genoese convoy bound for Flanders. Off the coast of Portugal the convoy

was attacked by a French fleet and three ships, including the *Bechalla*, were sunk. Columbus was wounded but, clinging to a piece of wreckage, he managed to struggle the half-dozen miles to shore. And so by accident he made his way to Lisbon where his younger brother Bartholomew was already working in a chart-making establishment. Lisbon at the time was the most active centre in Europe for the organization of voyages of exploration and discovery, the best possible place for Columbus to acquire the knowledge and skills he was to need. He learned to speak and write Portuguese and Spanish, to read Latin; he acquired a considerable book-learning in navigation and geography. In the following years he sailed south as far as the Gold Coast (now Ghana), north as far as Ireland or possibly even Iceland, west as far as the Azores, learning the ways of the Atlantic Ocean. He learned to be a fine ship's captain, considerate of his seamen's welfare. His mastery of the techniques of celestial navigation always remained something less than perfect: a set of observations of the Pole Star made with the quadrant on his third voyage convinced him that one of the earth's hemispheres was pear-shaped with a raised stalk like a woman's nipple. But he was, above all, a superb practical seaman and, when he relied upon his phenomenal skill at dead reckoning, a brilliant navigator.

As for his idea about sailing west to the Indies we have to remember that, as a theory, there was certainly nothing fantastic about it. Ever since the thirteenth century every educated man in Europe had known that the earth was a sphere. Circumnavigation of the globe had been suggested by several travel writers, including Sir John Mandeville, the most popular of them all. In 1474 Paolo Toscanelli, a scholarly Florentine, wrote to a Portuguese friend urging him to persuade the king to organize a voyage west to Japan. That the Far East was well worth reaching no one doubted. The high price of those Oriental goods, spices, drugs, perfumes, silks, fine cloths and precious stones which reached Europe seemed to confirm Marco Polo's description of empires brimming over with luxury goods. The only problem was the practical one. Distance, winds and currents might combine to make the voyage an impossibly long one, above all because ships could not carry enough cargo to feed their crews for several months.

In the early 1480s Columbus wrote to Toscanelli and received in return an encouraging letter and the chart which he took with him on his first voyage. His fleet consisted of the *Santa Maria*, with a crew of about forty crammed into a ship of 100 tons or so, three-masted, square-rigged on fore and main with lateen mizen, and two caravels, the *Nina* and the *Pinta*, coastal traders of 60–70 tons, carrying fifty more seamen between them. They had left their home port of Palos in southern Spain on 3 August and run south before the prevailing northerlies to reach the Canary Islands a week later. On earlier voyages Columbus had observed that at this latitude the trade winds blew from the east. In 1485 King John II of Portugal had authorized two mariners, Dulmo and Estreito, to sail west from the Azores in search of Atlantis, but if they ever sailed they certainly discovered nothing. At the latitude of the Azores the prevailing winds were westerlies. This made it hard to find anything but at least it ensured that, if you were successful, you could get home again. Columbus was taking a greater risk, and he knew it. Four weeks later, when he set sail from the Canaries, he decided to keep two separate accounts of his course.

A partially accurate view of Columbus's experience on landing in the New World: the natives were all 'naked as their mother bore them, including the women' and were 'very gentle', but were unable to provide the explorer with the gold and jewels he sought, much less the intricate treasures of European design which they are seen to offer here.

9 September: He made fifteen leagues [forty-five nautical miles] that day and decided to score up a smaller amount so that the crews should not take fright or lose courage if the voyage were long.

10 September: That day and night he went sixty leagues. But he reckoned only forty-eight leagues so as not to alarm the crew.

(These are extracts from Columbus's logbooks, now lost, but used in the sixteenth century by Bartolomé de las Casas for his *Historia de las Indias*.)

Blessed with fair winds, Columbus made good speed. Almost every day log book entries note indications that they were near land – recently uprooted seaweed, flocks of birds, cloud-banks – but, though these signs helped to reassure the crew, Columbus had no intention of turning aside. He sailed on between these imaginary islands, determined to press on westwards to Japan. By 22 September the crew was agitated about the problem of returning home against the wind and next day Columbus noted:

23 September: As the sea was calm and smooth the crew grumbled saying that since there were no heavy seas in these parts no wind would ever blow to carry them back to Spain. But later the sea rose high without any wind and this astonished them. I was in great need of these high seas because nothing like this had occurred since the time of the Jews when the Egyptians came out against Moses who was leading them out of captivity.

Still he kept on his westward course and by 4 October he believed that he was close to Japan. But they saw nothing and Columbus continued to drive them on due west, despite pleas that he should alter course and look for land. Not for another three days did he agree to change his tack.

7 October: At sunrise the caravel *Nina* which was the fastest sailer and ahead of the others, hoisted a standard at the masthead and fired a gun as a sign that they had sighted land. But in the evening they did not see the land and a great flock of birds came from the north and flew south-west. He knew that the Portuguese had discovered most of the islands in their possession by observing the birds. He decided therefore to abandon his westward course and steer west-south-west.

If Columbus's theory was right they had now reached the longitude of Japan – even by the false calculations which he had been announcing to his men – and the change of course made this public. The atmosphere in the fleet, already tense, became feverish. The crisis was upon them. If nothing was sighted in the next day or two then Columbus was wrong. 8 October, 9 October, still nothing, only the birds flying south-west. On the 9th Columbus accepted an ultimatum from the other two captains: if land were not found within three days he would give up and turn back. On the 10th, despite this promise, the men were in a mutinous mood, and only by reminding them of the wealth of the Indies could Columbus restore discipline. Fortunately on the next day the signs that land was near, particularly branches with leaves on, became so numerous that the mood changed to one of expectation. At 2.00 a.m. on 12 October 1492 Rodrigo de Triana, the look-out on the *Pinta*, sighted land, the sandcliffs on the eastern shore of Watling Island in the Bahamas.

Columbus named the island San Salvador and for the next three days he remained here, causing great excitement among the inhabitants who believed that he had come from the sky. Equally mistaken, of course, was Columbus's own belief that he had reached the Indies and that they were Indians – but the name he gave them has stuck. Almost every aspect of the muddled story of European exploitation of the new continent is foreshadowed in the logbook entries for these three days:

In order to win their friendship, since I knew they were a people to be converted and won to our holy faith by love and friendship rather than force, I gave some of them red caps and glass beads which they hung round their necks, also many other trifles. . . . I watched carefully to discover whether they had gold and saw that some of them carried a small piece hanging from a hole pierced in the nose. . . . They all go naked as their mothers bore them, including the women. . . . They are very gentle and anxious to have the things we bring and they will give all that they do possess for anything that is given to them, exchanging things even for bits of broken crockery or broken glass cups. . . . However should your Highnesses command it all the inhabitants could be transported to Castile or held as slaves on the island, for with fifty men we could subjugate them all.

On leaving San Salvador he sailed south-west, looking for Cipangu, gold and precious stones. For a while he thought that Cuba was Cipangu – and though he later on revised this opinion he died believing it was a part of the Chinese mainland. When the *Santa Maria* ran aground off Hispaniola (Haiti) on Christmas Day 1492 he took this as a sign that he was meant to establish a colony here and, having built a fortified camp on the spot (Villa de la Navidad, Christmas Town), he then set course for Spain. After a stormy return voyage he was given a triumphant reception at court and everything he wanted: a hereditary title and great privileges. He was to be Admiral of the Ocean Sea, and Viceroy and Governor of all that he had discovered.

The coat of arms granted to Columbus by the King of Spain.

In a sense everything after this first epoch-making voyage was bound to be an anti-climax. He made three more voyages and explored a good deal of the mainland coast as well as many more Caribbean islands. But once he became involved in the political management and administration of the new territories things began to go wrong. He decided to blame the relative failure of his second voyage on his own excessive pride and thereafter he always wore the coarse brown habit of a Franciscan. On his third voyage he was accused of illegal actions and sent back to Spain in chains to stand trial. Eventually he was released and given charge of a further expedition, but he was stripped of most of his powers and he never forgot the humiliation. He kept the fetters in his chamber and ordered that they be buried with him.

At one stage Columbus toyed with the idea that he had found the Garden of Eden, but he never once saw what he had come to see – the junks, the temples, the palaces and courts of China and Japan. Even so, while his health lasted, he kept going back to look. He could have settled down in Spain, with money, castles and titles – the very things he had wanted. But if these had been all that he wanted he would never have set out in the first place. Between 1484 and 1492 he had struggled to find the financial support and patronage which was essential for the realization of his scheme. On numerous occasions he faced rejection and ridicule from men who were more learned than he was. But his whole heart was fixed on this idea and despite repeated dis-appointments he never gave up. His sense of mission comes across very clearly in a letter he wrote in 1500 while he was a prisoner. In this he refers to the new heaven and the new earth described in the Book of Revelation and then quotes Isaiah: 'He made me the messenger and He showed me where to go.'

What was it that had made Columbus so certain that he was right? In calculating the degrees of longtitude between Europe and Cathay (China) or Cipangu (Japan), he had followed the calculations of a ninth-century Arab geographer, al-Farghani (whose work was translated into Latin in the twelfth century), who said that a degree was fifty-six miles. Since al-Farghani's unit of calculation was the Arabic mile of 2165 metres, he made it sixty-six nautical miles (whereas in fact it is sixty nautical miles), but Columbus believed that al-Farghani was reckoning in Italian miles of 1480 metres and so he arrived at a degree of only forty-five nautical miles. In other words he underestimated the size of the world by twenty-five per cent.

In addition Columbus made a second colossal error. Following the early fifteenth-century author, Pierre d'Ailly, whose work, the *Imago Mundi*, in the printed edition of 1480/83, was Columbus's favourite bedside reading, he took as his starting point Marinus of Tyre's calculation that Europe and Asia together covered 225 degrees. To this he added a further 58° to allow for Marco Polo's discovery of lands which had been unknown to the Ancient World, in total then 283° from Portugal to Japan. In reality it is about 150°. In his mind Columbus had given such an enormous extension to Asia that, had he been right, Tokyo would now be in the Sargasso Sea and China in Central America. Since he planned to start from the Canary Islands, 9° west of Cape St Vincent, he calculated that a voyage of 2,400 nautical miles would bring him to the shores of Japan. The real distance is 10,600 nautical miles. The experts who rejected his plans had been right. Even in 1493, in Columbus's hour of triumph, one of the scholars at the Spanish court, Peter Martyr d'Anghiera, pointed out that the size of the globe indicated that, whatever Columbus had discovered, it could not be Asia.

But the armchair critics who were right have been forgotten. We remember instead the man of action who was prepared to sail into the unknown in order to put his ideas to the test. It turned out to be one of the most fruitful mistakes ever made – and, as one of Ferdinand and Isabella's advisers observed, their investment in Columbus's expedition cost them less than they spent in entertaining a fellow sovereign for a week.

~ Sir Thomas More ~

Thomas More was born in London in 1477 or 1478. When he was about sixteen he entered New Inn, one of the Inns of Court, and began to study law. As so often in his life, he was probably pulled two ways. He was already attracted to a more literary and philosophical education and felt, as Erasmus put it, that 'the relationship of law to true learning is extremely vague'. On the other hand he was both anxious to please his father, who was himself a successful lawyer, and acutely aware of the social and material advantages which the study of law offered to an ambitious young man. More's own career could hardly have been more successful, culminating in his appointment in 1529 to the highest political office in the land: that of Lord Chancellor. Yet it was not a path which he climbed without hesitation. He always remained true to his intellectual interest, studying theology and Greek writing and giving a lecture course on Augustine's *De Civitate Dei*. Many of his closest friends were among the most learned men in the country: Colet, Grocyn, Lily, Linacre. In 1499 he met Erasmus and forged a life-long relationship of mutual respect and admiration. When Edward Lee, later archbishop of York, attacked something which Erasmus had written, More stepped in to defend his friend's views, but at the same time offered to defend any book which Lee wrote, should it ever be attacked by Erasmus. This combination of tactfulness with the anticipation of pleasure to be derived from an intellectual exercise is very characteristic of the student who had cut his teeth on a defence of Plato's principle of community of property, including wife-sharing, and of the mature writer whose preferred literary form was the dialogue. Most men would find it difficult to combine academic and literary pursuits with the demands of a legal career without becoming weighed down by the sheer hard work of it all, but the impression More left on his contemporaries was one of a gentle, ironic good humour and a lightness of touch. Some found this disconcerting. 'He was too much given to mocking,' wrote Edward Hall, 'which to his gravity was a great blemish.' But all were agreed on the point which Erasmus voiced: 'The most downcast moods and the most irritating situations are not proof against the infectious sweetness of More's disposition. From his earliest youth he took such joy in joking that he often seemed interested in nothing else.' What made this possible was the astonishing quickness of More's intellect. A fellow student commented on his ability to learn Greek: 'Everybody who has ever existed has had to put his sentences together from words, except our Thomas More alone. He, on the contrary, possesses the super-grammatical art of taking in whole sentences at once.' Not surprisingly the scholarly John Colet said of More that he was England's only true genius.

Most of the learned men of the time were churchmen and, given his interests, it was only natural that for several years More considered taking orders or even entering a monastery. Eventually, however, according to Erasmus, 'the attractions of marriage proved so strong that he determined to be a chaste husband rather than a lewd priest.' He married Jane Colt in 1505 and

The Dutch humanist Desiderius Erasmus (c. 1466–1536), the greatest scholar of the Northern Renaissance. Woodcut by Dürer, 1526.

had four children. Within a month of her death in 1511 he married a second wife, Alice Middleton, though his son-in-law and first biographer, John Roper, assures us that he did this 'rather for the ruling and governing of his children, house and household than for any bodily pleasure'. However this may be, he was so attached to his home that later on, when in the King's service, he deliberately curbed his natural light-heartedness so that Henry VIII was less tempted to keep him at court and away from his family.

From 1510 to 1518 More was Under-Sheriff of

London, the City's chief legal adviser, but the fateful turning-point in his life came when he decided to transfer his allegiance from the city's service to that of the King. Erasmus, in a letter written in 1519, says that 'he had several times been pressed into service on embassies and his skill on these missions had so impressed Henry VIII that that monarch could not sit still until he had dragged More to his court. I must say literally "dragged" because no one has ever been as determined to get into court as More was to stay out of it.' It was certainly not as simple as that. An Italian scholar, Ammonio, employed as Henry VIII's Latin Secretary, says that at one time More literally haunted the court of Henry's great minister, Cardinal Wolsey, in the hope of getting recognition and preferment. That More, like Erasmus, was prepared to flatter the powerful is clear from a letter he wrote to Wolsey, recording the King's appreciation of a draft letter which Wolsey had composed on Henry's behalf: 'I never saw him like any thing better and, so help me God, with good reason, for it is one of the best made letters, in words, matter, sentence and couching that ever I read in my life.'

On the other hand, More was certainly under no illusion about the problems involved in entering the King's service. Early in 1516 he refused a royal pension on the grounds that the possibility of a dispute between the king and the City made it incompatible with his office of Under-Sheriff. His doubts on the subject are unforgettably enshrined in the dialogue in Book I of *Utopia*, on which he was working in that very year. The partners in the dialogue are Raphael Hythlodaye, the much-travelled philosopher who had lived in Utopia for five years, and Thomas More himself. More suggests that Hythlodaye could be of great service to mankind were he to put the advice based on his unique experience at the disposal of a king. Raphael thinks it would be a waste of time; amid the jealousies and flatteries of a court, there is no place for honest advice. More disagrees:

You should not, simply because you are unable to uproot mistaken opinions and correct long-established ills, abandon the state altogether. In a storm you do not desert the ship because you are unable to control the winds. Nor should you, on the other hand, impose unwelcome advice upon people whom you know to be of opposite mind. You must try to use subtle and indirect means, insofar as it lies in your power. Where you cannot achieve what is good, you may at least minimize the evil.

These words have often been quoted and are said to have inspired more than one twentieth-century intellectual to enter the precarious world of politics. Less quoted is Hythlodaye's reply:

The only trouble with your approach is that while I would be helping to save others from insanity, I would myself go mad. If I wish to speak the truth, then there are certain things that must be said. However I feel that many clever Christian preachers have followed your advice, for when human morals and Christ's conflict then they compromise by adjusting his standards to human practice. In reaching such a reconciliation they make the law of God a dead letter and as a result they themselves become more deeply immersed in evil. Besides, the king's court is no place for concealing the truth and acquiescing. In many cases a man would be obliged to approve the worst advice and the most terrible decrees or run the risk of being accused of sedition and treason if he only grudgingly approved.

Hythlodaye's diagnosis was to prove all too accurate in later years. In 1532, rather than go mad, More resigned from the King's service, and when he wished to acquiesce in silence he found himself condemned for treason. But in 1517 More took his own advice and went to court.

For years all went well. Henry VIII was still a king who basked happily in the admiration of the world and who had the gift, as More observed, of making each man feel that he enjoyed his special favour. Roper paints an attractive picture of the king liking to take More aside to sit and talk with him, not just of affairs of state, but of astronomy, geometry, divinity and other such subjects. Or taking him on to the roof to observe and consider the movement of the stars and planets.

And for the pleasure of his company the king would sometimes come on the spur of the moment to his house at Chelsea to be merry with him. On one occasion he came unexpectedly to dinner and, after dinner, walked with him by the space of an hour, holding his arm about his neck. As soon as his Grace was gone, I, rejoicing thereat, told Sir Thomas More how happy he was whom the king had so familiarly entertained. 'I thank Our Lord, son,' quoth he, 'I find His Grace my very good lord indeed and believe he doth as singularly favour me as any subject within this realm. Howbeit, son Roper, I may tell thee I have no cause to be proud thereof, for if my head could win him a castle in France it should not fail to go.'

In the event it was not a castle that Henry wanted but a legitimate son. By 1526 he was considering divorcing Catherine of Aragon and by 1527 he had selected Anne Boleyn as her successor. Unfortunately Henry mismanaged the whole business so badly that by 1529 he had no alternative but to blame someone else for the failure. So he sacked Wolsey and in his place decided to make More his chancellor. On both sides it was a strange choice. More had so far refused his support for the divorce; he had refused to speak either for it or against it. Perhaps Henry believed that in time he could overcome his scruples, but for the moment, in order to overcome More's reluctance to take the office, he promised to use other ministers in the 'great matter' of the divorce and not to trouble More's conscience about it. Why did More accept the chancellorship? In the hope of saving Catherine's cause and minimizing the evil? It may be so even though his political role in the next two and a half years was an inconspicuous one. In a private letter he was to refer to 'the liberty which he had always used, in speaking boldly to King Henry in those matters which concerned Queen Catherine'. And certainly at the end he believed, as he told his judges, that the King sought his blood not over the issue of papal supremacy but because he would not agree to the

marriage. But on the whole he seems to have concentrated on rooting out heresy and on the legal side of the chancellor's job – so efficiently indeed that, according to tradition, the day came when, having settled one case and called for the next, he was told that there were none pending. If true, it would have been a unique moment in the history of the law courts. But while More was consolidating his reputation as a great and impartial judge, the King was pressing on with his Great Matter. As Henry lost hope of ever persuading the pope to grant his divorce, so his

Henry VIII, *c.* 1520, by an unknown artist.

desire to possess supreme jurisdiction over the English church became a more urgent need. On 15 May 1532 Canterbury Convocation – or rather the three bishops who were all that remained of that brow-beaten assembly – agreed that in future the clergy could make no laws without the royal assent. The day after this 'Submission of the Clergy', Sir Thomas More resigned.

But resignation did not mean retirement into obscurity. His new freedom from official business had the effect of giving him more time for writing – and writing for More now meant only one thing: the defence of his faith against Lutheranism. Since this was the great controversial issue of the day it kept More right in the forefront of the political life of Europe. Thus, when Anne Boleyn was crowned in Westminster Abbey on 1 June 1533, his refusal to attend the coronation service was bound to cause affront. When, later that year, Elizabeth Barton, the 'Holy Maid of Kent', was arrested and charged with treason, Henry insisted that More, along with Bishop Fisher of Rochester and several others, should be charged with misprision of treason. Not until March 1534 was the baseless accusation withdrawn, but in the same month an Act of Succession was passed, whereby all subjects could be compelled to swear an oath to observe the act – or be guilty of misprision of treason. In April More refused to take the oath and was committed to the Tower where he remained for the last fifteen months of his life. Despite immense pressure on him to change his mind, including pressure from those whom he loved best, he would not. Equally doggedly he would not say why he refused to take the oath. The freedom which he believed in was the freedom to remain silent. The government tightened the screws still further by an act which, after 1 February 1535, made it treason to deny the royal supremacy. The Commons attempted to moderate the act's severity by twice inserting the word 'maliciously' so that the offence was not just denying the supremacy, but denying it maliciously. More and many other victims of Henry

VIII's tyranny hoped that this word might save them. In practice however the King's judges interpreted the statute to mean that whoever denied the supremacy denied it maliciously. Perhaps More remembered Hythlodaye's comment on royal justice in 1516: 'Judges will find loopholes to twist the truth either through love of argument or through desire to win the king's favour. Those who dissent will be persuaded to concur, through shame or fear, and the tribunal will hand down a decision upholding the king. There will be no case, regardless of how blatantly unjust it is, that will be decided against the king.'

Finally, on 1 July 1535, Thomas More was brought to Westminster Hall for trial. He pleaded 'Not Guilty' to the indictment, arguing that treason lay in word or deed, not in silence. At this point the government resorted to perjury. They produced Richard Rich to say that he had heard More deny the King's supremacy. The jury found a verdict of 'Guilty' and, now that it was done, More felt at last that he was free to speak his mind. He made it clear that the reason why he would not support the statute was because it was 'directly repugnant to the laws of God and his holy Church, the supreme government of which belongeth to the see of Rome'. He was then sentenced to death. More fortunate than others condemned under the same law, in his case the sentence of hanging and disembowelling was commuted to one of beheading. On 6 July he was taken to the scaffold. He was told that the king would prefer it if he made no long speeches and, as the king's good servant, he obeyed. He asked the crowd to pray for him and for the King, that it might please God to give the King good counsel, protesting that he died the King's good servant, but God's first. Then laying his head on the block he asked the executioner to wait until he had pulled his unkempt beard out of the way, saying

Sir Thomas More and his favourite child and confidante, Margaret, in the Tower. By John Rogers Herbert, 1844.

that it, at least, had never committed any treason. And so, wrote the disapproving Hall, 'he ended his life with a mock'.

That Thomas More possessed the qualities of greatness hardly anyone doubts. In Jonathan Swift's opinion he was the only great man to have appeared since antiquity. Marxists have admired the man who wrote that 'all the governments that have flourished since the beginning of time have been nothing but a continual conspiracy of the rich to perpetuate themselves under the guise of statecraft.' Roman Catholics have revered the saint – canonized in 1935 – who died for the papacy. Others have seen in More an early liberal who fought for toleration and freedom. A man for all seasons. A man who enjoyed paradox and irony, he was also the prisoner of his unbending conscience and of his reputation. In *Utopia* he condemned those heretics who preached views which led to tumult and sedition; he allowed them liberty of conscience only so long as they kept silent. It was on precisely these grounds that he defended himself at his trial. Yet, as they all knew, he was too famous. His silence resounded around the courts of Europe.

Was this silence finally an acknowledgement that in deciding to enter the King's service he had made the wrong choice? In the last three years of his life he had plenty of cause to recall Hythlodaye's arguments, the arguments which he had rejected in 1517. On the other hand he had enjoyed fifteen years of influence and public esteem. And at the end, though he had remained true to his belief that martyrdom should not be courted, yet he felt he had had martyrdom thrust upon him, and he found that he had the courage to see it through. 'Trouble not yourself,' he said to his daughter Margaret, 'we may meet together in heaven, where we shall make merry for ever, and never have trouble after.'

The Age of Patriotism

by GILA FALKUS

THE STORIES OF the nine heroes and one heroine which follow cover a span of some three hundred years, from the birth of Montrose in 1612 to the death of Florence Nightingale in 1910. At the beginning of this period, broad historical changes were becoming clearer or acquiring new momentum. Throughout much of Europe, territory was consolidated around powerful 'absolute' monarchies. The rise of the nation states, defined by language, geography and obedience to these increasingly 'centralized' governments, gave a developing impetus to a more modern sense of patriotism. The great conflict known as the Thirty Years' War, which disrupted Europe from 1618 to 1648, has been described as the last of the religious wars and the first of the national wars of a more familiar, secular flavour. Meanwhile, the decline of the medieval pattern of social life continued, and feudal links between master and man were ever more subordinated to the interests of the nation states, with loyalties altering accordingly.

Changes such as these are never easy to define; nor are they sharply focused. But the heroes remembered from this age clearly reflect them, just as they reflect the older traditions of nobility, self-sacrifice and courage. Unlike the heroes of previous ages, however, their achievements are to be seen in the context of the aspirations of whole nations: whereas Thomas More spoke for Catholicism, a personal code and a spiritual truth, Nelson spoke for England.

The first, the great Marquis of Montrose, in many ways looks back to the Age of Chivalry. Yet, like Bonnie Prince Charlie, who led another Highland army a hunded years later, his career illustrates the nostalgic face of patriotism, for both men belong to the folklore of a nation that lost its political identity during this time and sought all the more fiercely to cherish the names of the great Scottish leaders of the past.

In sharp contrast to Scotland's loss of independence, these centuries were for England an age of increasing prosperity and power as the nation moved away from the internal dissensions of the seventeenth century into the expansion of the eighteenth. Patriotism acquired a new focus in the epic struggle against France for global domination that lasted for over sixty years, from the outbreak of war in the early 1740s till the defeat of Napoleon at Waterloo in 1815. It was a struggle that shaped the lives of men like Wolfe and Nelson: the first a soldier of genius, the latter probably the greatest sailor in England's history.

Patriotism of another kind gave Lord Byron his place in heroic legend. Rejected by his contemporaries for his scandalous private life, he died abroad in 1820, fighting to free Greece from the oppressive rule of Turkey. His posthumous reputation, in England as well as Greece, demonstrates how the ideals of freedom, and liberation of peoples, had established themselves as part of a wider cause extending beyond national frontiers.

England's struggle against France in the eighteenth century laid the basis for her imperial greatness in the nineteenth, when she influenced the destinies of one quarter of mankind. Such power breeds arrogance, and many of the great empire-builders of the Victorian age seem to us foolishly self-satisfied. It is because David Livingstone combines the great Victorian virtues of enterprise and missionary Christianity without sharing this arrogance that he is included as truly the greatest imperial hero.

The only woman is Florence Nightingale. In her lifetime she was idealized as the symbol of certain womanly virtues, such as healing and compassion. Yet the truth was far more complex and illustrates much that the Victorians sought to repress – the suffocating nature of their family life; the complacency with which the country's army was run; and the fact that a woman could exemplify such 'masculine' qualities as administrative genius.

For America, these years were a time of national birth and astonishing growth as the seaboard settlers pushed their way westwards into the great unknown continent that they had won for themselves. George Washington is widely regarded as the country's first national hero, both as the military commander who won independence from Britain and as the great statesman whose wisdom and dignity gave the nascent country stability and stature during its precarious early years. Another American hero, Davy Crockett, typifies the rougher qualities of the Western settlers who were now able to conquer and settle the new country. But to me the greatest of the three Americans is Abraham Lincoln: the president who, with no more education than Davy Crockett, led his country through the greatest crisis it has yet confronted – the terrible Civil War of the 1860s – and showed himself one of the most compassionate and visionary statesmen the world has ever known.

Gila Falkus

~ *Montrose* ~

Even in his lifetime, Montrose was compared to the great heroes of antiquity and legend, men like Alexander the Great and Roland. Indeed, the worst accusation that his enemies found was that he deliberately led his life 'as in a romance'. Even his birth seemed miraculous, for his mother had been trying for twenty years to produce a male heir for her husband, the 6th Earl of Montrose. Not surprisingly, the young boy was doted on; though his mother died when he was only six, his father and sisters saw that he was provided with everything a young nobleman might need: a lavish wardrobe; an extensive library; good horses; a 'crossbow set with mother of pearl' and a band of devoted attendants. His education took him from a tutor in Glasgow to St Andrews University and finally, at the age of twenty-one, on a Grand Tour of Europe.

It was attention well spent, for the young Montrose was everything that a seventeenth-century aristocrat was expected to be: handsome, cultivated, a generous patron and a fine sportsman. He was not quite seventeen when in July 1629 he won the silver arrow for the best archer at St Andrews University for the second time. In the same year, three years after he had come into his inheritance on the death of his father, he married young Magdalen Carnegie, daughter of his neighbour, David Carnegie. But any hope of a life of quiet domesticity was destroyed by the political troubles that were later to erupt in civil war. In 1637 Charles I tried to impose a new Prayer Book on Scotland, and provoked a storm of protest. Most of his Scottish subjects favoured a Calvinistic form of worship, and they refused to accept the new services which to them smacked of papistry. Ministers who attempted to use the new forms were shouted down by their congregations all over Scotland.

At this early stage Montrose was among those who opposed the King. Loyalty to the crown was an unbroken tradition of his family but so too was loyalty to the freedom of Scotland against interference from England: what was the right course for a Scotsman now that his King was King of England too and was seeking to change the national religion from London? It was not an easy question but Montrose did not hesitate for long. Deciding that resistance was in this case not rebellion but a necessary protest, he threw in his lot with the opposition. In the spring of 1638 he was one of the signatories of the National Covenant, the document drawn up in Grey Friars churchyard, Edinburgh, asserting the inviolability of the Scottish church. And when in 1639 King Charles determined to impose his will on Scotland by force, Montrose took up arms against him.

But as the Covenanting movement fell increasingly into the control of its more bigoted members, so Montrose grew uneasy about his support. In particular he found himself in conflict with the new leader of the movement, Archibald Campbell, the future earl of Argyll whose politics were too extremist for Montrose's taste. This small, lean, red-haired man, with thin bloodless lips and a squint which gave an unattractive leering look to his already plain face, was immensely powerful: he owned a great part of the south-west Highlands and was also head of the large and wealthy Campbell clan. His people's drive to expand at the expense of their neighbours served as both the excuse and the weapon for the acquisitive policy of their chief. The Campbells had already overwhelmed the MacGregors and they were now in the process of overwhelming the Macdonalds. This latter rivalry now began to exert its influence on the broader politics of Scotland. When King Charles, not appreciating the local implications, granted a large tract of land in Kintyre to the head of the Macdonalds, he earned himself the implacable hatred of Argyll.

When civil war broke out in England in 1642, Montrose made up his mind to support the King. Charles was understandably suspicious but in February 1644, after Parliament signed an alliance with the Covenanters, he signed Montrose's commission as Lieutenant-Governor and Captain General of Scotland and Montrose henceforth became one of the staunchest and most steadfast supporters of the House of Stuart.

The plan was for Montrose to invade Scotland via the north-west and to join forces with another army from Ireland, led by the Irish chief of the Macdonalds. His return took Argyll completely by surprise but as the days passed, and the promised reinforcements from Ireland failed to arrive, Montrose was forced to retreat to Carlisle where he received the news of Prince Rupert's devastating defeat at Marston Moor in July. The King's cause was now desperate but his enemies had reckoned without the resolution and skill of Montrose. In the early autumn of 1644, with only two companions, he once more crossed the border into Scotland and began his glorious year of victories. Although completely outnumbered by the Covenanters, he and his small force of Highlanders succeeded time after time in totally outwitting them. His first piece of good fortune was the news that the Irish Macdonalds had at last landed in Kintyre and were striking north-westwards into the Highlands. Swiftly Montrose rode to join them and on 28 August officially raised the royal standard. It was a tiny, ill-equipped army and he knew he must act fast before the enthusiasm waned. His first victory, the result of a speedy and violent attack, was at the little village of Tippermuir, and it enabled him to enter nearby Perth in triumph. Soon the same shock tactics opened the gates of Aberdeen.

But now Argyll in person was hurrying to attack him, at the head of 4,000 well-equipped troops. Montrose knew that a pitched battle would be suicidal and so determined to lead Argyll on a wild goose chase through the Highlands. Throughout the bitter months that followed, in a brilliant series of feints and forced marches, he lured Argyll 250 miles in a circle across Scotland. His advantages were an intimate knowledge of the countryside, daring and mobility. Where Argyll's well-equipped men floundered in bogs and struggled up hillsides, Montrose's forces travelled light, and lived off the countryside. But by mid-November, when the first snow was falling, some of his men could take no more and returned home. With reduced forces Montrose retraced his steps to Blair Atholl in Perthshire, battling through the Grampian passes. There, in council with the Macdonald chiefs, he decided on his next daring move: he would strike at the heart of the Campbell territory. And so, one night, Argyll, sitting at dinner in his castle at Inveraray, incredulously received the news that Montrose was only a few miles away. By the time he realized the truth it was too late to organize any defence and he could only abandon his clansmen to the mercy of the Macdonalds.

Another march in a totally unexpected direction, which led Montrose out of Campbell country and beyond the clutches of another Covenanting force sent to capture him under Baillie, included a breathtaking climb out of the Great Glen that John Buchan in his biography of Montrose has called 'one of the great exploits in the history of British arms'. When they reached Inverlochy, at the south-west end of the valley where Argyll had regathered his troops, Montrose fell on them out of the snow and mist and again took them completely by surprise. Once more Argyll took to his ship and fled but this time his troops fought on without him. 'Like men with a better cause,' said Montrose, and by the end of the battle 1,500 of them were killed.

Montrose next raided and took Dundee, a town that was staunchly for the Covenanters,

Charles I at his trial, by Edward Bower, 1635–67.

again eluding the army sent against him. On 9 May at Auldearn he won a pitched battle against Baillie's second-in-command, Colonel Hurry; then on 2 July at Alford he forced Baillie himself to fight, after drawing him into the Highlands and into a completely unfavourable position.

Montrose's run of victories had now lasted unbroken for eleven months and he felt that the time had come for him to march into the Lowlands. Although Baillie and the Covenanting army hurried after him, anxious at all costs to prevent him taking Glasgow as he had taken Perth, Aberdeen and Dundee, Montrose defeated them at Kilsyth and both Glasgow and Edinburgh opened their gates to his army. But the triumphant entry into Glasgow marked the end of Montrose's successes. General Leslie, a formidable opponent, was marching up the east coast against him and on 13 September, at Philiphaugh, he destroyed Montrose's infantry. Other misfortunes followed. Clan jealousies led

to the desertion of the Gordons and then Alexander Macdonald withdrew his men – still prepared to lay waste to the Campbell lands in Kintyre, but no longer to follow Montrose.

Whether Montrose would ever have recovered the military initiative is impossible to say, for events in Scotland were now overtaken by shock news from England: Charles I had surrendered to the Scots army at Southwell. The King had taken this extraordinary step in the hope of playing off the Scots against the English parliamentary allies with whom they were now at variance. In the hands of his new captors Charles agreed to order Montrose to disband his forces. At first Montrose, believing the King must be acting under coercion, was reluctant to do so, but when Charles twice confirmed the order he had no choice but to obey. Late in July he took leave of the last of his troops and fled to the Continent.

Abroad he found that his fame had preceded him. The one exception to the general acclaim which greeted him was, ironically, the lukewarm reception he received at the shadow court of the exiled Queen Henrietta Maria at St Germain. Undeterred by Stuart coolness, however, he was in Brussels trying to raise troops for an invasion when he heard the news of Charles I's execution in January 1649. According to tradition he fell down in a dead faint and kept to his room for two days, not speaking to anyone, so great was the shock and so deep his grief.

Only three weeks later he was kissing the hand of the new King, Charles II, at The Hague and placing before him his plan to raise the Highlands once more. Charles appeared deeply moved by his loyalty and immediately gave him a commission as Lieutenant-Governor of Scotland. Yet all too soon Charles was to prove even less worthy of Montrose's devotion than his father had been, for at the same time as he was backing Montrose Charles was also entering into negotiations with the Scottish Covenanters, who had now broken completely with their English allies and – on their own terms – were prepared to invite Charles II back to Scotland.

'The Marquess of Montrose carried to execution'. The authorities, hoping to humiliate the Stuart hero, placed him in a hangman's cart and tied his hands so that he would be unable to shield his face from the stones and insults they hoped would be thrown at him; but the mob's anger was directed instead against his captors.

Montrose's final gallant campaign for the Stuart cause was therefore undermined from the start. It began with a bad omen – a storm which depleted his fleet and cost him much of his ammunition. After landing in the Orkneys, he crossed the Pentland Firth to the Scottish mainland and there, on 27 April, he was surprised by one of Leslie's officers. Any chance of recovery vanished as two of the clans supporting him, the Monroes and the Rosses, switched sides in the middle of the fighting. All Montrose could do was escape. For the next few days, weary and hopeless, he eluded his pursuers in the wild passes of Lochaber and the Cairngorms. Then he came to the grim little castle of Ardbreck where he was almost certainly betrayed by the young chief of the McLeods, whose name, in the words of John Buchan, 'lives in Scottish history with that of Sir John Menteith who sold William Wallace'.

Queen Henrietta Maria, by Anthony Van Dyck, 1599–1641. BELOW A contemporary engraving of the execution of Charles I on 30 January 1649.

Over the next few weeks Montrose's heroic qualities were to triumph over the vindictiveness of his captors. His dignity and courage impressed all who witnessed his journey to Edinburgh: 'He sat upon a little shelty horse without a saddle but a quilt of rags and straw, and pieces of rope for stirrups, his feet fastened under the horse's belly, with a halter for a bridle; he wore a ragged old dark reddish plaid. ... yet he never altered his countenance, but with a majesty and state beseeming him, kept a countenance high.'

He arrived in Edinburgh to learn that he had been sentenced, like a common criminal, to be hanged at the Market Cross for three hours on a gibbet thirty feet high; his body was then to be cut down and quartered, the head to be set on the Tolbooth, the limbs on the town gates of Stirling, Glasgow, Perth and Aberdeen. It was a barbaric and insulting sentence, designed by the government to put an end to the magic that Montrose seemed to exert. He was hanged on 21 May. One of his friends had managed to bring him some clean clothes and he prepared himself, it was said, 'like a bridegroom'. As he left his cell he found that all of Edinburgh's militia were there to meet him: 'Are you afraid of me still?' he mocked them; 'My ghost will defeat you yet.'

It was to prove a true prophecy. Through his death Montrose ensured that the struggle to which he had dedicated his life would become a legend in Scottish folklore whose fame would long outlive both the ultimate failure of his own campaign and the efforts of his enemies to destroy his reputation as well as his life.

~ Bonnie Prince Charlie ~

The battle of Culloden in 1746 marked the end of centuries of warfare between England and Scotland, and a lasting acceptance of the bonds created by the union of the two crowns in 1603 and endorsed by the Act of Union of 1707. Never again would Scots confront English on the battlefield and for the first time in living memory peace came to the border lands between the two kingdoms.

For the wild lands of the west of Scotland, the Highlands and Islands, Culloden also marked the end of a distinctive way of life. Perched on the rim of Western Europe, this beautiful but rugged tract of country had bred a society that in the eighteenth century was becoming increasingly anachronistic: a brave, clannish warrior people with their own language and their own laws, who scorned their southern neighbours. Although Lowlanders as well as Highlanders fought against King George at Culloden, the rising had been a sharp reminder to the government that the Highlands were a fertile breeding ground for disaffection. It was therefore decided to destroy systematically their distinctive way of life – to shatter once and for all the clan system which provided such a ready network for raising an army. Laws were introduced, backed by troops to enforce them, forbidding the Highlanders to wear their kilts or tartans, or to speak Gaelic or carry arms; and slowly the position and authority of the clan chieftains were broken down.

But out of this persecution a legend was born. Within 100 years of the carnage of Culloden, the stories of the loyal and daring Highlanders and

Bonnie Prince Charlie.

their Jacobite cause had become the favourite reading of many English as well as Scots, including Queen Victoria. The hero of this tale was, of course, Bonnie Prince Charlie. Fair, slim and with undoubted nobility of bearing – 'born to be King', they said – Charles Edward Stuart was only twenty-four when, in 1745, he returned to the land of his forefathers to reclaim the crown and to lead the Highlanders on their last great adventure.

The Jacobite movement had begun in 1688 when James II was driven into exile by William of Orange. James never abandoned his hopes for a Restoration and his only son, 'The Old Pretender', carried on the struggle after his father's death. Scotland, the ancestral home of the Stuarts and the ancient enemy of England, seemed the obvious place to gain a foothold and twice – in 1708 and 1715 – the Old Pretender attempted an invasion, before retiring to live in regal apathy in Rome. It was there, in 1720, that his son Charles was born. Christened 'Charles Edward Louis Sylvester Maria Casimir', he was brought up a strict Roman Catholic and for the first twenty-four years of his life never left Italy.

The years of Charles's childhood and adolescence were a period of quiescence among the Jacobites, but the movement was far from dead and both Charles and his young brother Henry were brought up to regard their father as the rightful king of Great Britain, and to hope and pray for a Stuart Restoration. And as Charles entered his twenties the European scene was shifting in a way that significantly improved Jacobite prospects: after two decades of peace Europe was once more at war and, as so often before, England and France found themselves on opposite sides. There seemed once again a good chance of securing French backing for a Stuart invasion, and so when, early in 1744, Charles Edward received an invitation to Paris from Louis XV, he set off full of hope.

In faςt, as so often since 1688, the French were interested in the exiled Stuarts only as pawns in a much bigger power game. After months of false promises and broken appointments, Charles finally realized that no French help would be forthcoming. If he wanted to regain his father's kingdoms, he would have to do it alone. And this is precisely what he decided to do.

It was an astonishing decision, brave or foolhardy, whichever way you like to look at it. Charles pawned his jewels and borrowed money to buy a few arms; then, with only a handful of followers, he set out from Nantes in a small brig called the *Doutelle*. He first set foot on Scottish soil on 23 July 1745 on the island of Barra. At first the Scottish chieftains, although they welcomed him, were reluctant to throw in their lot with such a dubious and ill-backed venture and advised him to return to France. But the Prince's own optimism was hard to resist. 'I am come home,' he declared, 'and I will not return to France for I am persuaded that my faithful Highlanders will stand by me.' Few Highland chiefs could resist an appeal to their honour and the turning-point came when Lochiel, chief of the powerful Camerons, announced his decision to join the Prince.

On 19 August, when Charles officially raised his standard at Glenfinnan on the Scottish mainland, his army numbered 1,000 men, and over the next few weeks it continued to grow. On 4 September he occupied Perth and on 17 September he entered Edinburgh. To start with, he encountered little opposition. Although Hanoverian spies had been watching his movements in Paris, his departure had taken the government by surprise. Their forces in Scotland were badly understrength and during the first critical weeks the Jacobites had no difficulty in eluding them.

On 21 September, Charles won his first victory when he routed the elderly and incompetent John Cope at Prestonpans, just outside Edinburgh. It was the climax of his career. In only a few weeks he had, through his own efforts and the appeal of his name and personality, created an army and led it to victory. Installed at the ancient palace of Holyrood, the home of his royal ancestors, Charles was fêted and admired by the ladies of the city.

For all the excitement and enthusiasm, though, the cracks were beginning to appear. Some of the Highlanders began to desert and few Edinburgh citizens came forward to replace them. The army was desperately short of supplies and Charles's more experienced advisers knew that they were in no position to meet with the full force of a Hanoverian comeback. But Charles himself had no doubts as to what to do next. He had come to regain England as well as Scotland and so he must now march south to London before the Hanoverian government had time to ship back their army from Flanders. On 31 October he set off from Edinburgh with about 5,000 troops, crossed the border and without

much difficulty captured Carlisle. By 4 December he was as far south as Derby, and in London the shops were closed and the guards ordered out to Finchley to prepare for the invaders.

But from then on Charles's magic deserted him. His army had attracted almost no recruits on its bold march south. There was certainly no sign of any general Jacobite or Catholic rising in England; nor was there any news of the French help for which Charles still hoped. Instead, every step away from their homes made the Highlanders more reluctant to follow him. And as Charles's army slowly melted away, the Hanoverians were marshalling their forces. Three battalions of guards and seven regiments of infantry were brought back from the Continent and the King's son, the Duke of Cumberland, was appointed to lead them north while the formidable General Wade marched up the east coast at the head of another army. At Derby the Jacobites decided to turn back. It was

Charles enters Edinburgh in triumph, to the cheers of the men and the admiring glances of the women.

a decision forced on Charles by his commander-in-chief, Lord George Murray and his other senior advisers and to the end of his life he maintained bitterly that it was a fatal mistake.

Back in Scotland Charles won one last battle at Falkirk (it lasted little more than twenty minutes) but his situation was desperate. Grimly he retreated northwards, pursued by Cumberland. The final confrontation took place in a snow storm on 16 April, a few miles south of Inverness on Culloden moor. It is one of the most famous disasters in history. Charles's army, half-starved and exhausted, was completely routed and over 1,000 of his men were killed. Those who lived to flee from the battlefield were brutally hunted down on 'Butcher' Cumberland's orders.

Charles survived the battle but was forced to acknowledge defeat. There was no possibility of staying in Scotland to raise another army; indeed, he would be lucky if he managed to escape back to the Continent alive. For over twelve weeks he was a hunted fugitive with a price of £30,000 on his head and 20,000 Hanoverian redcoats searching for him. But although many who aided him were poor, no one betrayed him. He slept rough, went hungry, caught dysentery and was in constant danger of his life. It was a wretched plight and yet the stories of his courage and cheerfulness have become a central part of the legend and testify to the genuine bond between him and the Highlanders. 'Show me a King or Prince in Europe who could have borne the like, or the tenth part of it,' wrote Lochgarry.

As he desperately struggled to evade his pursuers, he fled further into the west, right out to the Hebrides and then, when he was spotted there, back over the Minch to Skye, disguised 'in a flowered gown and white apron' as a serving wench to a young Highland girl, Flora MacDonald, who is today the most famous of all those who helped the destitute Prince. Then at last, early one September morning, Charles boarded a French frigate, *L'Heureux*, and left Scotland for ever.

'Billy the Martial Boy', a caricature of the Duke of Cumberland by his aide-de-camp, George, 4th Viscount and 1st Marquess Townshend, drawn some years after Culloden.

Still only twenty-five years old, he was to live for another forty-two, but the rest of his life was a pathetic anti-climax. His adventures (which he never tired of relating) had created a legend but they had also shown that politically Jacobitism was finished. As the years passed Charles grew quarrelsome, drunk and increasingly ridiculous as he insisted on being treated with the honour due to a king. He died in January 1788. His brother, a Roman Catholic cardinal, conducted his funeral service at Frascati and paid little attention to the few remaining Jacobite exiles who now called him King Henry IX. In 1819, some years after the Cardinal's own death, a monument was raised in Frascati Cathedral to the memory of all three exiled Stuarts – but it was erected not by their Jacobite followers but by the future George IV of England, the Prince Regent.

~ Wolfe ~

For a nation of Britain's great maritime traditions, it is remarkable how many of her warrior-heroes have won their reputations on the battlefield; of these, none is more secure in the memory and affections of his country than James Wolfe, who died at the head of his victorious troops thousands of miles from home at Quebec.

Wolfe's hold on the imagination is not difficult to understand. Only thirty-two when he died, his personal bravery was renowned; he had a high sense of patriotism and duty; his achievements were made despite a permanent struggle against ill-health; and he combined a form of recklessness with infinite dedication to detail. Perhaps, above all, it was his almost poetic streak of fatalism which lent a tragic inevitability to his brief story. He accepted his commission to go to Canada with the comment '... though I know the very passage threatens my life, and that my constitution must be utterly ruined and undone'. Of his ultimate ambition, he wrote with certainty that he would 'find a way to a glorious or at least a fine and manly end when I am of no further use to my friends or country.'

James Wolfe was born in Kent on 2 January 1727 into a military family. At thirteen, he persuaded his father, Edward, to take him on a campaign expedition to the West Indies, though illness prevented him from going. After enlisting two years later, in 1741, he was sent as an ensign to Flanders, where the British and their allies were beginning a protracted if intermittent conflict with France which was to last three generations. Young Wolfe's initiation as a soldier was swift. His regiment was in the thick of the fighting at Dettingen on 27 June 1743. A week later he was

James Wolfe, popularly known after his death as Wolfe of Quebec.

promoted to adjutant and a fortnight after that to lieutenant – at the age of fifteen. Recalled because of the Jacobite rising in Scotland, he was present at the battle of Falkirk and at Culloden, where, according to a famous story, he refused to obey an order from the Duke of Cumberland, his commander-in-chief, to shoot a wounded Highlander, with the reply, 'My commission is at your Royal Highness's disposal, but I can never consent to become an executioner.' Returning to Flanders, he fought and was wounded at the battle of Laffeldt; by the time the first phase of the war was finished in 1748, Wolfe, still only twenty-one, had won a high reputation for

gallantry and resourcefulness and had risen to the rank of brigade-major.

'A View of the Glorious Action of Dettingen'.

Promoted to major, then lieutenant-colonel, Wolfe spent the next years stationed in various towns in Scotland and southern England; but enforcing the destruction of the clan system and suppressing a riot of Gloucestershire weavers were not operations designed to satisfy an eager, restless and ambitious officer, particularly as Wolfe had now developed both a contempt for the prevailing standards of the army and an overwhelming sense of urgency to improve them and himself at the same time. Army organization was ineffective and its prestige low. The gulf between officers and men was enormous; most of

Wolfe's brother officers were idle and uninterested, regarding their military positions merely as sources of income and the men under their command as a bunch of drunken scoundrels. Wolfe used his time to criticize, cajole, reconsider important aspects of tactics and manoeuvres, instruct his regiment and educate himself. He started to read widely, and studied French, Latin and mathematics. He sought permission to go abroad to learn engineering and artillery and when refused wrote, 'This is a dreadful mistake, and, if obstinately pursued, will disgust a number of men of good intentions and preserve that prevailing ignorance of military affairs that has been so fatal to us in all our undertakings.' He dismissed his own high reputation as merely a reflection of the generally low standard of army officers, and when war with France broke out again in 1756, a series of early disasters caused him to write, 'This country is going fast upon its ruin by the paltry projects and more ridiculous execution of those who are entrusted.' In short, Wolfe felt himself and his country to be crippled by inefficiency and lack of visionary leadership at a time of national crisis.

Then, in June 1757, another man of destiny, William Pitt, became Prime Minister, and at once the whole scope of the war effort was transformed. Like Wolfe, Pitt had overcome a fragile body to dominate his contemporaries. He was tireless, imaginative and completely dedicated to victory. He saw the war against France on a global scale, one to be fought on the continent, at sea, in India and in the Americas. Horace Walpole later wrote of Wolfe that he was 'formed to execute the designs of a master like Pitt', and it was certainly a fateful alliance, although its first fruit – a raid on the French coast at Rochefort in which Wolfe served as quartermaster general of the expeditionary force – was a failure which brought him to despair. 'We blundered most egregiously on all sides – sea and land,' he wrote; 'the public could not do better than dismiss six or eight of us from the service. No zeal, no ardour, no care and concern for the good and honour of the country.' A court of enquiry was set up. Wolfe's recriminations naturally made him enemies, answered effectively by George II's comment to the Duke of Newcastle, 'Mad is he? Then I hope he will bite some others of my generals.'

The King's view was shared by Pitt, who had conceived a strategy which could make use of this kind of madness – a confrontation with France in a different theatre of war, Canada. By 1756 Britain and France were vying for dominance in North America. Britain had established a line of flourishing colonies along the eastern seaboard from Newfoundland to Georgia while France, claiming the whole of the Mississippi basin and the lands around the Gulf of St Lawrence in the north, was trying to link her territories by building a chain of forts running down the west of New England, so confining the British colonies to the seaboard and reserving for herself the rich fur trade of the interior. Pitt's plan to conquer Canada and so frustrate this aim involved a two-pronged assault with one force advancing under General Abercromby from the south while General Amherst was to take the fortress of Louisberg, and if possible, proceed up the St Lawrence to attack Quebec from the east. A third force was to capture Fort Duquesne and regain control of the Ohio valley. Wolfe was to be one of Amherst's brigadiers. He received his orders in January 1758, accepted them eagerly, though with foreboding about his own health, and wrote to his parents: 'All I wish for myself is, that I may at all times be ready and firm to meet that fate we cannot shun and to die gracefully and properly when the hour comes, now or hereafter.'

The expedition set sail from Portsmouth in February but, delayed by fogs, gales and contrary winds, did not reach Halifax in Nova Scotia until early May. Wolfe played a leading part in the assault on Louisburg, a seemingly impregnable fortress built upon a craggy promontory overlooking the sea, and it was very largely due to his daring landing and diligence in pressing home the attack that Louisburg fell. The gateway to Canada had been forced. But now once again Wolfe found himself frustrated by the vacillations of his superiors who failed to press home their advantage by immediately moving on to attack Quebec. 'We are gathering strawberries and other wild fruits of the country,' he wrote to his father, 'with a seeming indifference about what is going on in other parts of the world.' He even wrote to Amherst saying that, if nothing else was going to happen, 'I must desire leave to quit the army.' A commission to lay waste the French settlements around the St Lawrence did little to satisfy him and at the end of the year he was glad to sail home on leave for a few months.

Ironically the ship bearing him home crossed with one bearing instructions from Pitt appointing Wolfe as the commanding officer of an expedition to attack Quebec. As soon as he disembarked and realized what had occurred, Wolfe hastened to reassure Pitt that all he required was a brief period to recover his health before sailing back across the Atlantic. He passed his leave with his parents and also in pursuing his courtship of Katherine Lowther and, before he set sail once again from Portsmouth, he had persuaded her to marry him and carried on board with him her portrait in miniature, a lock of her hair and a present from her of a copy of Gray's *Elegy in a Country Churchyard*.

He arrived back in North America at the end of April to find the St Lawrence river still icebound and his army about two-thirds of the size Pitt had originally intended it to be. Moreover, French spies had already learnt the whole British plan of campaign for the year, including the details of Wolfe's amphibious advance up the St Lawrence River. The French commander-in-chief Montcalm had had ample warning to check his defences before, on 26 June,

Wolfe's expedition finally arrived at the island of Orleans, four miles to the east of Quebec. Wolfe found the French encamped on the north bank of the St Lawrence and to the east of the city, with their left flank resting on the Montmorency River. Anxious to act before the river froze, he landed his troops on the opposite bank and tried unsuccessfully to entice Montcalm into battle. But the French commander preferred to rely on the immense natural strength of Quebec as a defensive position: jutting out into the St Lawrence River, it was protected to the north and north-east by a series of rivers, between which, extending along the north bank, was a series of gun emplacements; while to the south and west lay a series of steep cliffs, falling almost sheer into the river and apparently unscaleable.

Wolfe's first moves gave him no encouragement. A landing on the north shore at the end of July resulted in the loss of 400 men and later raids behind the French lines there brought little result. The failures continued throughout

An engraving of the capture of Quebec, based on a drawing by Wolfe's aide-de-camp, Smyth.

August and into September. Some of his senior officers were disillusioned; Wolfe himself was despondent, self-critical – and now, desperately ill. 'I know perfectly well you cannot cure my complaint,' he told the doctor, 'but pray make me up so that I may be without pain for a few days and able to do my duty; that is all I want.' He called a council of his brigadiers, who rejected his ideas and advised a landing some eight miles above Quebec. Wolfe accepted their plan, writing to the British admiral, 'my ill state of health hinders me from executing my own plan; it is of too desperate a nature to order others to execute.'

On 8 September orders for the landing were given, but bad weather caused a postponement. Then, suddenly, Wolfe seems to have recovered his spirits and initiative, for by 10 September he had a new, almost unbelievably audacious plan; and he dismissed the opposition of his officers with the words: 'I have the honour to inform you . . . that it is my duty to attack the French army. If I am mistaken [in my plans] I am sorry for it, and must be answerable to His Majesty and the public for the consequences.' Wolfe's scheme was to take a force up the mountain just a mile and a half above Quebec at a spot so sheer and wooded that Montcalm, the French commander, had declared 'a hundred men posted there would stop their whole army'. Wolfe was going to bring Montcalm to battle by attacking the French at the very heart of their entrenched position and forcing them to fight on the flat land outside the city walls known as the Plains of Abraham.

On the moonless night of 12 September, 5,000 men were ferried upstream. Already Wolfe had had a premonition of his imminent death when, taking Miss Lowther's miniature from his breast, he had given it to one of his commanders, an old schoolfellow, so that it could be restored to her. Then, as the boats moved up the St Lawrence, he spoke some lines from Gray's *Elegy*, saying that he would rather have written those than achieve the glory of victory at Quebec. They landed at a place now called Wolfe's Cove and set ashore to scale the cliffs. Dragging themselves up in the dark by clinging on to trees and bushes, they hauled the guns up on ropes behind them. Almost unbelievably the French sentries were taken completely by surprise and at dawn the next morning Montcalm awoke to find the British army drawn up ready for battle, only a few hundred yards beyond the city walls.

It was in this battle that the famous 'thin red line' formation of the British army was first used. Wolfe ordered his men to stand only two deep and withhold fire until given command. The French, numerically superior, attacked at about ten o'clock and almost at once Wolfe was wounded by a bullet that struck him in the groin, but he scarcely seemed to feel it and continued to walk about, encouraging his men and repeating his order that they should withhold fire. The French opened fire at a distance of about 130 yards. On the British side, the line was continuously replaced as the men behind stepped forward to replace the casualties of the front line. At last, when the French were only 40 yards away, Wolfe gave the order to fire. Nearly every man in the French front line was hit and the attempts of the survivors to close up and reform were pitiable. By the time the smoke cleared, the British gunners had reloaded and they now advanced twenty paces to pour a series of deadly volleys into the remains of the enemy army. The right of the French line was the first to break and flee, and the rest soon followed.

It was after the first British volley that Wolfe received his fatal wound, a musket ball in the chest. He was carried to safety but it was evident that he had only a few moments to live. Blood flowed freely from both his chest and his groin and he appeared unconscious. A messenger momentarily roused him: 'They run! They run!' the newsbearer cried. Wolfe opened his eyes. 'Who runs?' he asked. 'The enemy,' came the answer. The news gave the dying general the strength to issue one final order to cut off the fugitives' retreat. His last words were, 'Now God be praised, I will die in peace.'

Wolfe's death received a bare mention in the official despatch and account of the battle, so great was the ill-feeling towards him among his chief officers. But in Britain the *Annual Register* recorded: 'The effect of so joyful news immediately on such a dejection, and then the mixture of grief and pity which attended the public congratulations and applauses, was very singular and affecting.' His body was brought home and buried in the family vault in Greenwich on 20 November. The day after, Pitt moved an address in Parliament for a national monument to Wolfe. Among the ranks and junior officers of his own troops, the mood was expressed by one of them, Major Know: 'Our joy at this success is inexpressibly damped by the loss we sustained of one of the greatest heroes which this or any other age can boast of.'

∾ *George Washington* ∾

George Washington was America's first national hero. The man who was called on to become the commander-in-chief of the colonies in their fight against their mother country was no military genius like Napoleon or Caesar; but unlike many more brilliant commanders he always kept the issue he was fighting for clear in his own mind and did not seek to feed his personal ambitions. During eight and a half years of war, George Washington always had one aim: to liberate the colonies from British rule; once this object had been achieved, he was positively eager to relinquish his command. As the first president of the new United States of America, he was not a statesman of vision like Pitt or his own successor, Thomas Jefferson. But his caution and moderation shaped the presidency in a way that has proved permanently appropriate for a great democratic nation, and he gave his young country time to breathe, to fashion its own traditions and institutions, and to grow. Above all he provided America, a young, insecure, self-conscious nation, with a folk-hero who was respected in every disparate part of the land.

The young George Washington.

Babies were christened after him as early as 1775 and while he was still president his countrymen paid to see him in waxwork effigy. After his death his surname was commemorated in the naming of one American state, 7 mountains, 8 streams, 10 lakes, 33 counties, 9 colleges, and 121 towns and villages. His birthday is still a national holiday and his calm unruffled face still watches over the life of America on her coins, banknotes and stamps. In the second half of the twentieth century the story of George Washington remains an astonishingly powerful legend.

He was born in the state of Virginia in 1732. His father, who was a man of moderate wealth, died when he was fourteen and the strongest influence during young George's adolescent years was his half-brother, Lawrence. Fourteen years older than George, Lawrence had married into one of the richest families of Virginia, the Fairfaxes, and presided over a generous and sociable establishment at his estate, Mount Vernon, where, at the age of sixteen or there-

abouts, young George Washington came to live. Although a serious if somewhat gauche youth, he was certainly no illiterate backwoodsman, as some of his critics later liked to claim; but his intellectual background could in no way compare with that of his formidable fellow-Virginians, Thomas Jefferson and James Madison, and throughout his life Washington felt ill at ease in set debate or abstract discussion.

He also knew he would have to earn his living, and in 1748 we find him acting as Surveyor, exploring and charting the new lands of north Virginia and, by the end of 1750, staking his own claim to 1,450 acres in the lower Shenandoah. Then in 1752 his prospects were transformed by a succession of family tragedies. Lawrence died, leaving Mount Vernon to his widow in trust for their surviving, rather delicate child; and if this child followed its three siblings to the grave without issue, the estate was to pass to George. As Lawrence had probably foreseen, this is exactly what happened, and so, at just twenty, George was able to take possession of the place that was to be his beloved home for the rest of his life. For the next few years he enjoyed the busy,

Mount Vernon, painted c. 1792, Washington's home until his death in 1799.

comfortable life of a Virginian gentleman planter. Apart from tending and improving his estates at Mount Vernon, and presiding over the affairs of his numerous younger brothers and sisters, he became a Justice of the Peace, a parish vestryman and, in 1758, a burgess at the state capital. In 1759 he made a happy, though childless marriage, to a wealthy young widow, Martha Custis, who added her two children by her first husband to the busy household.

There was one break in this pattern of civilized rural life: from the autumn of 1753 to 1759, George Washington fought in the Virginia militia in the war against the French. It was a rough frontier struggle, often as much against the hostile terrain and the Indians as the French. Washington served ably and quickly rose to the rank of colonel; in August 1755, at the age of only twenty-three, he became commander-in-chief of Virginia's soldiery; and by the time he resigned his commission three years later, he had risen to the rank of brigadier.

Ironically it was partly Britain's success in driving the French out of North America that led to the rebellion of the thirteen colonies. As the crisis that was to bring him to supreme leadership gathered momentum, Washington stood firmly alongside that body of independent men of substance who sincerely believed that Britain's interference in their affairs was both unconstitutional and morally unjustified. He was never an extremist and was described in 1774 as 'a modest man, but sensible and speaks little – in action cool, like a Bishop at his prayers'. But unlike many colonists who shrank from the final, treasonable step of open rebellion, Washington never appears to have had any scruples as to the rectitude of his position: 'The voice of mankind is with me,' he said, and certainly his views reflected those of most of his fellow Virginians.

In the autumn of 1774 Washington was elected one of seven Virginia delegates to a meeting of all thirteen colonies at Philadelphia and again the following year when the congress reconvened. He was not an inspired speaker but in the midst of so many hotheads his sincerity and good sense were reassuring. When, on 15 June 1775, it was resolved that 'a general be appointed to command all the continental forces raised for the defence of American liberty', a unanimous election gave the appointment to 'G. Washington Esquire' – an appointment he accepted on the modest condition that he should be paid no salary, only his expenses.

The war against the British was to last for eight and a half years and for most of that time the American forces were outnumbered and on the defensive. They were also poorly armed and undermined by internal dissensions and suspicions. During this time Washington was most concerned not with any spectacular feat of arms or great victory but with carrying on the struggle and somehow keeping his army together, even during the terrible bleak winter of 1777–8 at Valley Forge when, while Howe and the British redcoats had warm billets in Philadelphia, Washington and his men had to keep watch on a bleak plateau twenty miles away.

But if the odds were against Washington winning any spectacular victory against the British (one observer has commented that it was a war in which the Americans lost every battle except the last), so it was probably impossible for the British generals to crush the rebellion completely. They could capture individual towns but they could not garrison every city and, more important, the war was hardening American opinion. Nor were there any outstanding leaders on the British side: generals like Howe, Burgoyne and Cornwallis were competent but not brilliant. Had Washington been confronted with a Wellington or a Marlborough, history might have been very different.

As a commander, Washington himself certainly made mistakes, but he had some outstanding qualities which rendered him invaluable. Nothing testifies so much to his zeal and conscientiousness during the war as his mountainous correspondence on the subjects of equipment, better supplies, winter quarters,

General Cornwallis's surrender to the American and French armies at Yorktown on 19 October 1781 marked the end of the British cause in America.

uniforms and pay (usually in arrears from Congress) and the need for a regular system of promotions. Moreover, Congress needed a general who could confer stature and soundness on their cause, and Washington managed to impress even hostile Englishmen like Howe. In the House of Lords in 1777 Chatham informed his fellow peers that 'America is not a wild and lawless bandetti ... many of their leaders have a great stake in this great contest: the gentleman who conducts their armies, I am told, has an estate of four or five thousand pounds a year.' Of course it was more useful to impress potential allies, and the French, who signed a formal alliance with the colonies in 1778, and whose help probably determined the outcome of the war, found him a gentleman of quite unusual poise

and integrity and quickly dropped their original proposal that he should be replaced by one of their own experienced generals.

The fighting dragged on for two years after Cornwallis's famous surrender at Yorktown and it was not until December 1783 that Washington, aged fifty-one and spiritually and physically weary, could at last hand in his resignation and thankfully return to Martha and his neglected Mount Vernon estates, content in the knowledge that the independence of the colonies was now formally recognized and that no man's reputation stood higher in the eyes of his countrymen than his own. But it was to be only a brief respite. Freed from the unifying pressures of war and linked only by the Articles of Confederation drawn up in 1777, the colonies rapidly drifted apart. The need for a new constitution was apparent, and Washington's reputation made it inevitable that his opinion should be sought. His

'First in war, first in peace and first in the hearts of his countrymen': Washington, dressed simply in an American worsted suit, takes his oath as President.

sense of duty made it impossible for him not to participate, and so in May 1787 he arrived at the convention in Philadelphia and, having been unanimously elected its president, presided over the heated debates that ensued. When the new constitution was finally forged, providing for a president of the United States to be elected by an electoral college, everyone knew who the first would be. In April 1789 Washington was elected unanimously.

It was due to Washington's preference for simplicity that the office of president was not adorned with the style and trappings of European royalty but that the president was to be addressed just as 'Mr President'. For his inaugural address he wore a worsted suit of American manufacture together with the dress sword and white silk stockings of European court dress. There was nothing particularly inspiring about his speech,

yet most of the watching crowd were deeply stirred. If Washington was a little awkward they forgave him and even trusted him the more, and whatever he might lack in the higher arts of politics, he was an honest, canny and methodical administrator. He was to serve as president for two terms, until 1798. Undoubtedly his prestige lent weight to the new constitution, encouraged its ratification by the individual states, and bound the country together. His administration was not free from strife and Washington found his main problem was to contain the bitter struggle for supremacy between his two rival ministers, Alexander Hamilton and Thomas Jefferson. Somehow he kept both these talented men in his administration but it was only his status and tact that forestalled a violent rupture.

In the field of foreign affairs, his great personal contribution was his proclamation of neutrality delivered in April 1793 to keep America out of the war between Britain and France. France had helped America in her own revolutionary struggle and now the pressure to repay this obligation was strong. But Washington realized that another war would be an impossible burden for his infant country to shoulder and insisted on neutrality. His proclamation together with his great Farewell Address of 1796, in which he sought to establish principles of national behaviour that were based upon national unity rather than party factionalism, have long been regarded as the cornerstones of America's foreign policy: 'Observe good faith and justice towards all nations; cultivate peace and harmony with all. ... In the execution of such a plan nothing is more essential than that permanent and inveterate antipathies against particular nations and passionate attachments for others should be excluded. ...'

Washington died in December 1799, one year after his final retirement. Few have ever claimed that he was a first-rate commander, an original thinker or an inspired orator. His greatness lay in his steadfast belief in the destiny of his new country; in his lack of personal ambition; and in his commonsense. A more brilliant man could not have served his country so well for so long.

∽ *Nelson* ∽

If one name above all others symbolizes Britain's historic greatness at sea, it is that of Horatio Nelson. Born in 1758, in an age when officers were too often idle and incompetent, Nelson, like Wolfe, for whom he had a strong admiration, was unusual for his dedicated professionalism and ambition; also like Wolfe, Nelson had a keen sense of honour and patriotism that, on several occasions when other men would have stayed at anchor, drove him to chase a French fleet vast distances to do battle. And he knew, too, how to immortalize the great moments of his career with the apt phrase or gesture: putting his telescope to his blind eye at Copenhagen; bequeathing his mistress to the nation on the eve of Trafalgar. His faults were many – he could be vain, arrogant and boastful, and his private life, in particular his celebrated liaison with Emma Hamilton, was gaudy and indiscreet – yet they were forgiven him in the wave of grief that swept the nation after his death in the middle of his greatest victory, Trafalgar, and have come down in popular memory as merely the picturesque and human characteristics of a great British hero.

Nelson's apprenticeship started early. He was sent to sea at the age of twelve and, despite his frail constitution and the rigours of naval life, quickly rose to meet the challenge it offered. By the age of eighteen he had already firmly resolved: 'I will be a hero and, confiding in Providence, I will brave every danger.' His first taste of fighting came in 1776 when the American War of Independence broke out and he was sent to the Caribbean where he won rapid promotion, qualifying as a lieutenant well under the regulation age of twenty. Reconnoitring on board

Nelson, by Lemuel Francis Abbott, 1760–1803.

to his family home at Burnham Thorpe in Norfolk. There they spent five years before, in 1793, when once more war broke out between England and France, the Admiralty gave Nelson another ship. 'After clouds comes sunshine,' he wrote enthusiastically but slightly tactlessly to his wife on hearing that he was to be given command of *The Agamemnon*, his first ship of the line, and sent to the Mediterranean. It was a vital area, for the southern French ports provided fine harbours for the French fleet, and Nelson's first task was to go to Naples to persuade the king, Ferdinand, to provide troops to support the British blockade of the French port of Toulon. It was there that he first met the British minister, a distinguished diplomat, Sir William Hamilton – and his much younger wife, Emma, a celebrated beauty. On this first meeting, Nelson reported back to Fanny: 'She is a young woman of amiable manners who does honour to the station to which she is raised.'

Although Nelson's mission was a diplomatic success, King Ferdinand's troops proved of little use in battle and were unable to prevent the French re-establishing control over Toulon. The British fleet now needed a secure Mediterranean base of their own and it was decided to capture Corsica for this purpose. It was there, fighting against the French garrison at the port of Calvi, that Nelson lost the sight of his right eye. This was an injury that was often to be misrepresented in popular portraits, for Nelson confused many people by having a shade made and attached to his hat to shield his good left eye from the sun.

His first full-scale naval engagement came in 1797. Admiral Jervis, Nelson's commanding officer, had withdrawn the British fleet to Lisbon, and it was off the coast of Portugal in February that the great sea battle of Cape St Vincent was fought against the Spanish. In the middle of the fighting, Nelson broke the British line on his own initiative and, in a daring and unorthodox manoeuvre, cut off the escape of the Spanish van. It was unheard of for a naval captain to flout a command in this way and Nelson must have

the schooner *Little Lucy*, he managed to capture several enemy ships and won a considerable local reputation for both seamanship and bravery. In his own memoirs he recalled, not without self-satisfaction: 'I know it is my disposition that difficulties and dangers do but increase my desire of attempting them.'

After the war Nelson secured another commission in the West Indies – and it was during this period that he met and married Frances Nisbet, the widowed niece of the president of St Nevis, on 11 March 1787. It was a happy match for several years even though they had no children and Nelson's career often kept them apart for months at a time. The longest period they spent together was when they first returned to England after their marriage and Nelson took Fanny back

Admiral Sir John Jervis, Nelson's commanding officer who owed his knighthood to Nelson's disobedience of his orders during the battle of Cape St Vincent.

known that he risked disgrace and probably court martial. Fortunately, Jervis was happy to admit the brilliance of an action that had proved so successful, and as a result of the victory Jervis was created Earl St Vincent and Nelson, who by happy coincidence had just risen to the rank of Rear Admiral by seniority, was made a Knight of the Bath.

But the next phase of his career was to be full of setbacks and frustrations. On a disastrous expedition to South America, not only were his men driven off with heavy casualties but Nelson himself was badly shot in his right arm, which was shattered and had to be amputated. For a time Nelson even feared his naval career was at an end, but the reassurances of Lord St Vincent and his own natural ebullience quickly overcame his doubts, and by March 1798 Nelson was ready to rejoin the fleet and St Vincent at Lisbon.

By this date the revolutionary French army

was universally victorious and Napoleon was making a name for himself that would ring around the world. But though Britain now fought alone against him, her greatest weapon, the navy, was flourishing; and among her admirals, Nelson, still a month or so short of his fortieth birthday, was widely considered one of her bravest and most talented officers. The British now knew that Bonaparte was hatching some great design and had heard rumours of his schemes to create a great French empire in the eastern Mediterranean, thereby challenging not merely British power in the Mediterranean but all her interests in the East as well. Nelson's orders were now to pursue the French to any part of the Mediterranean or the Black Sea, to bring them to battle and to destroy them; but they might be anywhere between Sebastapol and Gibraltar. Hunting his prey, Nelson cruised eastwards, picking up the trail at Sicily and then again at Malta. An inspired guess took him to Alexandria; this time he arrived before the French and sailed away again to Syracuse, but somehow he remained convinced that Egypt must be Napoleon's destination and decided to return. There, sure enough, he found the French fleet at anchor in Aboukir Bay, lying in a line nearly two miles long, close into the shallow waters. He immediately sailed in to attack.

The French admiral, de Brueys, had believed that not even an English admiral would risk sailing his ships between the shoals and the French line. But Nelson knew his captains. As evening drew near, five British ships passed in succession on the land side of the French, while Nelson in the vanguard led the rest of his fleet to attack from the starboard side. In the rapidly falling darkness, confusion seized the French fleet. At ten o'clock, de Brueys' flagship, the *Orient*, blew up. The five ships ahead of her had already surrendered; the rest, their cables cut by shot or frantically attempting to avoid the inferno of the burning *Orient*, drifted helplessly. In the early morning three ran ashore and surrendered and a fourth was burnt by her officers. Of the

Emma Hamilton, sketched by Thomas Baxter at the Merton home she shared with her husband, Sir William Hamilton, and Nelson.

great fleet that had conveyed Napoleon to Egypt, only two ships of the line and two frigates escaped, and Britain had established her dominance over the Mediterranean. When news of the great victory reached England, Nelson became a national figure and, to his delight, the King raised him to the peerage.

But over the next couple of years the career of the new Lord Nelson was to pass through its least reputable phase. Once again he found himself at Naples, seeking the alliance of King Ferdinand, and this time he rapidly became infatuated with Emma Hamilton. 'He thinks her quite an angel,'

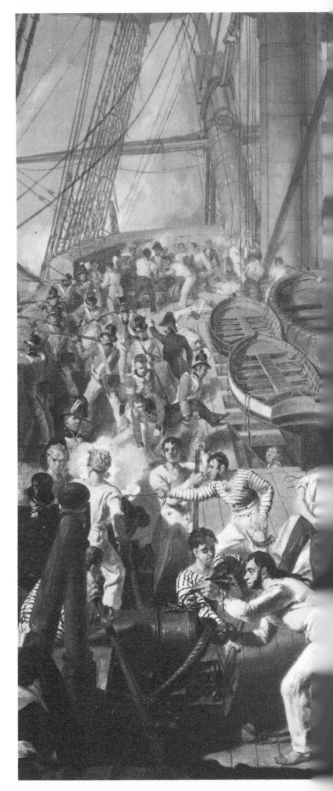

'The Death of Nelson', by Doris Dighton.

wrote one old friend, '... and she leads him about like a keeper with a bear. She must sit by him at dinner to cut his meat and he carries her pocket handkerchief in his pocket.' Soon after his arrival he had allowed himself to become involved with the incompetent Neapolitans in a foolish attack on Rome, one of Napoleon's puppet states; they were rapidly routed and Christmas 1798 saw the victor of the Nile ferrying the King and Queen of Naples along with his mistress and her complaisant husband to the safety of Sicily. The following summer, living happily on shore with Emma, Nelson even directly disobeyed orders to detach some of the ships under his command to defend Minorca. By the time he returned to England in the autumn of 1800 along with the Hamiltons (Emma now carrying his child), he found himself the object of gossip and scandal.

But Nelson was too valuable a sailor to be rejected by a country at war and 1801 saw him posted to the Baltic, as second-in-command to Sir Hyde Parker, a cautious, elderly man whom Nelson immediately eclipsed. When the Danes, determined to resist the British fleet's entry into the Baltic, refused Parker's request that they should cease to co-operate with France, to Nelson's delight Parker decided to leave it to him to teach the Danes a lesson. The battle of Copenhagen, the second of Nelson's great victories, took place in a narrow, shoal-obstructed channel at the entrance of the harbour and was a curiously static fight. The Danish ships were moored in front of the city and were supported by gun batteries on land. Nelson's plan – to sail right in and bring his broadsides against the anchored Danes – was a bold one and made no allowance for retreat. Once fire was joined the struggle was basically a duel between the gunners on both sides and, as Nelson had hoped, the experience of the British gave them the advantage. Then, just as they seemed on the verge of victory, Parker, waiting with a covering force outside the harbour, lost his nerve and hoisted his signal to 'discontinue the action', but, clapping his telescope to his blind eye, Nelson

declared that he could see no signal and carried on fighting. Once again his defiant self-confidence was soon vindicated, for almost at once Danish fire began to slacken.

In the following year, 1802, the Treaty of Amiens brought a few months' peace to Europe and a few months on shore for Nelson. He bought a handsome house at Merton, near Wimbledon, and settled there in an unconventional *ménage à trois* with both the Hamiltons, and with his little daughter Horatia. Relations between Nelson and Sir William appear to have remained perfectly affectionate and when, in the harsh winter of 1802–3, the elderly diplomat died, he left to Nelson in his will a favourite portrait of Emma as 'a very small token of the great regard I have for his lordship, the most virtuous, loyal and truly brave character I ever met with. God bless him and shame fall on those who do not say amen.'

By May 1803 war had been renewed and once again Nelson was sent to the Mediterranean with the mission of destroying the French fleet. Hearing of his imminent arrival, the French admiral Villeneuve withdrew to the safety of Toulon and, knowing that he could destroy the French completely only on the open sea, Nelson stayed some way off, hoping to tempt them out. But by 1805 Nelson had been in the Mediterranean nearly two years without bringing his foe to battle.

It was Napoleon's overweening ambition that at last provided the opportunity. Spain had by now joined France again and Napoleon's scheme was for the French fleet to break out of Toulon, elude Nelson and sail across the Atlantic to rendezvous with the Spanish fleet in the West Indies. They were then, according to his plan, to sail back to Europe together and convey the invasion force mustering on France's northern shores across to England. Thanks to bad weather and fluctuating winds, Villeneuve did manage to slip past Nelson and sail across the Atlantic and back again ahead of him. But then, still fearful of his great British adversary, he took refuge once more in the Spanish port of Cadiz. It was only on the direct orders of Napoleon that in October 1805 the reluctant French admiral abandoned this shelter and Nelson seized his chance.

His battle plan was characteristically bold: to pierce the line of the combined French and Spanish fleets in two or three places by sailing directly at it rather than by cruising down alongside it. This meant that the leading British ships would be exposed to the full power of the enemy's broadsides without being able to bring their own guns to bear. The result was a triumphant success and, after about four hours' intensive fighting, eighteen French and Spanish ships had struck their colours and surrendered while no British ship had been lost. But casualties had been heavy and Nelson was among them. At about 1.15, as he was pacing the quarter-deck with Hardy, his flag-captain, Nelson was struck by a bullet. 'They have done for me at last, Hardy,' he said as he fell. 'My backbone is shot through.' He was carried below, his face hidden with a handkerchief so that the men would not realize that their great leader was no longer with them, and he lived for another three hours, long enough to know that victory had been won.

The battle of Trafalgar was one of the most decisive battles of the Napoleonic wars. Although Napoleon was not to be brought to his knees on land for another ten years, England was henceforth safe from invasion, and the English navy which Nelson had done so much to create and inspire was to dominate the seas for the next 100 years. 'If ever there was a man who deserved to be praised, wept, honoured, it is Lord Nelson,' wrote *The Times* on 7 November 1805. 'His three great naval achievements have eclipsed the brilliancy of the most dazzling victories in the annals of English daring.'

∼ *Davy Crockett* ∼

'I had gone about six miles up the river, and it was then about four miles across to the main Obion; so I determined to strike across to that, as I had found nothing yet to kill. I got on to the river, and turned down it; but the sleet was still getting worse and worse. The bushes were all bent down, and locked together with ice, so that it was almost impossible to get along.... In a little time I saw a bear climbing up a large black oak-tree, and I crawled on till I got within about eighty yards of him. He was setting with his breast to me; and so I put priming in my gun, and fired at him. At this he raised one of his paws and snorted loudly. I loaded again as quick as I could, and fired as near the same place in his breast as possible. At the crack of my gun here he came tumbling down; and the moment he touched the ground, I heard one of my best dogs cry out. I took my tomahawk in one hand, and my big butcher-knife in the other, and run up within four or five paces of him, at which he let my dog go, and fixed his eyes on me. I got back in all sorts of a hurry, for I know'd if he got hold of me, he would hug me altogether too close for comfort. I went to my gun and hastily loaded her again, and shot him the third time, which killed him good.'

'After all this, the reader will perceive that I am now here in Congress, this 28th day of January, in the year of our Lord one thousand eight hundred and thirty-four; and that, what is more agreeable to my feelings as a freeman, I am at liberty to vote as my conscience and judgment dictates to be right, without the yoke of any party on me, or the driver at my heels, with his whip in hand, commanding me to ge-wo-haw, just at his pleasure. Look at my arms, you will find no party hand-cuff on them! Look at my neck, you will not find there any collar, with the engraving

MY DOG.

Andrew Jackson.

But you will find me standing up to my rack, as the people's faithful representative, and the public's most obedient, very humble servant,

DAVID CROCKETT.'

These quotations come from Crockett's *Autobiography* and illustrate something of the phenomenon he was to himself and to his contemporaries. At the time his book was published, Crockett even imagined he might be required to take the 'White House' – he would have made the most improbable of presidents. Indeed, it was to be his tragedy that the very appeal of his simplicity brought him into a political arena for which he was completely ill-equipped; yet those who used him for political ends helped to make him a national figure and so to create the legend which survives today.

David's grandfather, an emigrant from Ireland, was among the earliest of those who crossed the barrier of the Appalachian mountains in search of a new life in the vast tracts of unexplored lands which came to be called the Wild West. In 1777, a year after the Declaration of Independence, his home was overrun and he

David Crockett, the pioneer turned legislator whose lack of political sophistication was the cause of both his success and his downfall.

was killed in an attack by Creek and Cherokee Indians. His son John – David's father – was away patrolling the frontier outposts or he too might have fallen in the massacre. And John continued the westward trek, restless and optimistic, living in poverty, speculating in land, suffering from floods and other disasters but always prepared to move on with hopes of better things to come. David himself was born on 17 August 1786 and grew up in the rough, uneducated style inseparable from the lives of such families. At the age of twelve we find him being hired out by his father to help a fellow-pioneer drive a herd of cattle to Virginia; and after a few months we learn of his escaping from his new master and returning home after several dangerous adventures. A year later David, in trouble at school and fearing a beating from his father for truancy, ran away, only returning home some two and a half years later. During that time his activities – as a cowhand, farm boy, often merely as a survivor – all helped to forge that immensely hardy, self-reliant character which was to become part of the legend.

David's homecoming lasted long enough for him to acquire a modicum of education; and to fall in love unsuccessfully at least twice before his marriage to Mary Finely in August 1806. Mary's family was as poor as his own, her marriage portion consisting of 'two likely cows and calves'. They rented some farmland and tried, with great difficulty, to earn a living from the soil. But after a few years David had had enough; already his wife had presented him with two sons, John and William, and 'before my family got too large, that I might have less to carry,' he decided it was time to move. And so, some time during 1811, they settled themselves in a new homestead in Middle Tennessee, part of that inexorable westward trail which was re-shaping a continent.

David applied himself energetically to life on the new frontier. 'It was here that I began to distinguish myself as a hunter and to lay the foundations for all my future greatness.' But the settlements were not won without blood, and it was not long before David, as a volunteer, was called upon to defend the land he and his contemporaries were taking from its proprietors. During the Creek Indian War of 1813–15, David combined the roles of pioneer farmer and frontier soldier. He participated in the terrible Battle of Tallussahatchee, and left a vivid account: 'We shot them down like dogs,' he wrote, including a squaw who 'had at least twenty balls blown through her.' He was then involved in hunting down and killing refugee Indians, finally returning home in the early part of 1815. It was at about this time that his wife gave birth to her third child, Margaret; it was to be her last, for within a few months she had died, leaving David an impoverished backwoods widower with three young children to care for.

Pioneer life did not allow for prolonged grief; within a year he was married again, to a widow called Elizabeth Parton who was socially above him. Perhaps as a result of his new wife's influence, David's affairs began to take a different turn. By the end of 1817 he had moved yet again, to what is now Lawrence County, and become a Justice of the Peace and colonel of the local militia. Four years later he was elected to the state legislature for Tennessee – his public life had begun.

David's formal qualifications for office of any sort were negligible, but then the people he was representing looked for someone who shared their fears and concerns, not a remote figure whose knowledge of life came from books and theories, and David had a good campaigning style, with homespun humour and a feel for his audience. As a member of the state legislature he took up the cause of the new settlers in Tennessee. He had great fellow-feeling for the pioneers and the poorest of the settlers and throughout his life advocated that they should be allowed to settle on their lands with security and not be taxed on their improvements, a cause in which he did not succeed, any more than he was to succeed as a political careerist.

But David's political life was only one of his concerns. In 1822 he moved yet again to the far west of Tennessee and he set up a homestead near the Obion river. It was in the wildest of country, teeming with game and a land in which the Davy Crockett of popular imagination flourished in his true environment. He became increasingly renowned for his skill as a hunter, recording that he once killed 105 bears in seven months. He hunted bear and deer and boasted that he paid for his political campaigning from the three-dollar bounties offered for wolf scalps; he was continually looking for opportunities to improve his always precarious financial position – once embarking on an enterprise to make barrel staves which ended in fiasco when the boats taking his cargo to New Orleans sank at Memphis.

By now Crockett's reputation, which stretched from East to West Tennessee, was sufficient for him to think seriously about national politics. Although he failed in 1825, two years later he was

The battle of Tallussahatchee, 3 November 1813, a horrific episode in the war with the Creek Indians.

elected as one of the Tennessee representatives to Congress, finding himself in the very unfamiliar surroundings of Washington. In Congress he returned to his theme of the Tennessee lands but here he was at odds with his fellow-representatives, and above all with their Democratic leader, Andrew Jackson. This breach was to lead to an almost pathological hatred of Jackson and almost all David's activities in Congress – whether the question was roads, the West Point Military Academy or his Tennessee land proposals – were to be dominated by his antagonism. For Jackson represented the party machine whose interests embraced the whole state, not just the impoverished western areas which provided David's constituents.

It is in this context that we must see not only David's defeat in the Congress elections of 1831 but also his adoption by the eastern Whigs which later played such a significant role in his

downfall. For the Whigs, seizing on the opportunity to create a national hero out of an anti-Jackson westerner, took him under their wing. When he was re-elected to Congress in 1833, the Whig Press supported him enthusiastically and his *Autobiography* was partly ghosted by a Whig propagandist. On a tour of the east to promote his book, he was fêted and banquetted everywhere – apparently never realizing that his proud boast of independence of party politics had led him to become a tool of eastern interests. The result was predictable: he lost the support of his own people in the west for whom Jackson, elected president in 1828 and re-elected in 1832, was a hero. David failed in his next and last bid for Congress in 1835, losing to Adam Huntsman, a Jacksonite with a sharp wit and a wooden leg received as a

Davy Crockett at the battle of the Alamo. Woodcut from the Davy Crockett *Almanacks*, 1835–38.

result of an injury in the Creek Indian war. David remarked, 'Since you have chosen to elect a man with a timber toe to succeed me, you may all go to hell and I will go to Texas.'

Thus David set out on 1 November 1835 with a small party of friends to explore yet another frontier. His movements are difficult to trace and only a shadowy figure emerges at different places and times in Red River country until he arrived at San Augustine. Perhaps hoping still to further political ambitions, he volunteered to serve under the commander-in-chief Sam Houston in the endemic war that was being waged against the Mexicans under their general, Santa Anna. David wrote his last letter home:

My dear Sone [*sic*] and daughter
This is the first I have had an opportunity to write to you with convenience. I am now blessed with excellent health.... I must say as to what I have seen of Texas it is the garden spot of the world. The best land and the best prospects for health I ever saw and I do believe it is a fortune to any man to come here. ... I have taken the oath of government and have enrolled my name as a volunteer and will set out for the Rio Grand in a few days with the volunteers from the United States.

David's arrival at the Alamo and the circumstances of the famous battle are shrouded in mystery. It seems possible that he was among those who defied an order from Houston to blow up the fortress and retreat. Whatever the truth, the Alamo fortress was surrounded by Mexican forces led by Santa Anna himself; David and another famous frontiersman, James Bowie, were among the defenders who refused to surrender. On 24 February 1836 the bombardment began and on 6 March the garrison was stormed. Every one of the 150 able-bodied defenders was killed while some 2,000 Mexicans died in the attack.

There is no evidence that Crockett played any spectacular role in the battle of the Alamo; he seems to have been one of the first to fall, possibly unarmed. But the death of the famous frontiersman defending his country at its border lived on to combine with the legend of Crockett the Bounty Hunter and Crockett the Pioneer. To disentangle truth from myth is not easy – but what is certain is that Crockett's name has come to symbolize the very essence of that lonely, homely frontiersman whose virtues embody not only the spirit of the pioneer but that of American democracy itself.

~ *Byron* ~

Nelson's private life may have been irregular but his liaison with Emma Hamilton was innocent compared with the rumours of sodomy, incest, orgies and cruelty that surrounded Lord Byron: his was a heroism spiced with debauchery. He was born George Gordon Byron in 1788 in London, the child of a wild, spendthrift father known as 'Mad Jack' Byron and a rather plain but rich young Scotswoman called Catherine Gordon, whom Mad Jack evidently married for her money. Mad Jack died in France when Byron was only four but not before he had spent his wife's fortune and run the family into debt. Byron's early years were spent in genteel poverty in Aberdeen in the care of his hysterical and unbalanced mother and a dour Calvinistic nurse. It was a strange household and the boy had another disadvantage to fight, for he had been born with a club foot. The precise extent of this malformation is not known but Byron was extremely sensitive about it all his life and strove both to conceal it and to overcome it.

The death of his cousin William in Corsica in 1793 made Byron heir presumptive to the family barony, and in 1798 on the death of his grandfather he became Lord Byron, inheriting Newstead Abbey in Nottinghamshire, a Gothic ruin that could have been built specially to inspire the poetic imagination of an adolescent boy. His formal education was completed at Harrow and at Trinity College, Cambridge, where he met other young aristocrats eager to overspend their inheritances and cut a dash in the world. By the time Byron left Cambridge at the age of twenty-one, he was heavily in debt, led the life of a rake, and had already discovered that he was sexually attracted to men as well as women. One of his most passionate attachments formed while he was at Cambridge was with a

Byron, aged 25, by R. Westall, 1765–1836.

young King's chorister, John Edleston; 'It was', claimed Byron, 'a violent, though pure, love and passion.'

As soon as he came of age he was entitled to sit in the House of Lords and for a while played with the notion of a life in politics, as a member of the Whig party. But, perhaps unfortunately, Parliament was not destined to be the arena for his undoubted oratorical talents. The ambition to become a poet was already bearing fruit and Byron's first two volumes of verse, *Fugitive Pieces* and *Poems on Various Occasions*, appeared in 1806 and 1807, both privately printed and distributed. The eroticism of the first volume caused some consternation which provoked Byron, always sensitive to criticism, to have the book recalled and to burn many of the copies. The

An engraving of Newstead Abbey, the romantic ruin which Byron inherited with his title at the age of ten.

second volume, he assured a friend, was 'vastly correct and miraculously chaste'. But his next publication, *English Bards and Scotch Reviewers*, again caused offence, for it was an attack on the literati of the day, including such venerable figures as Wordsworth and Walter Scott.

A restless search for novelty in both people and places was already one of Byron's most prominent characteristics and he decided to go on a journey to the East, accompanied by a Cambridge friend, John Hobhouse, and a handsome young page, Robert Rushton. He was away for almost exactly two years and during this time he visited Portugal, Gibraltar, Albania, Greece and Turkey; swam the Hellespont; had various sexual adventures with partners ranging from a Mrs Constance Spencer Smith on the island of Malta to a fifteen-year-old Greek boy, Nicolo

Giraud; and first became aware of the oppression that Greece was suffering at the hands of her Turkish rulers. He also wrote the first two cantos of one of his finest poems, *Childe Harold's Pilgrimage*.

It was this poem that transformed his life. It was published after his return to England, by John Murray on 10 March 1812, and to quote Byron's own celebrated description of its reception, 'I awoke one morning and found myself famous.' The poem was an instant success, selling 5,000 copies in the first month. Suddenly Byron became the darling of society and found himself pursued by women. He was certainly not the man to turn down such opportunities but perhaps he was unlucky in his next celebrated love affair. 'Mad, bad and dangerous to know' was Lady Caroline Lamb's famous description of Byron, but he could justifiably have said the same of her. Caroline Lamb was twenty-seven when they met, with slim, boyish looks and an eccentric, neurotic temperament. She was married to William Lamb, the future Lord Melbourne and prime minister, who seems to have had a curiously detached attitude to her passion for Lord Byron. Their attraction was mutual and they were soon in the middle of an intense, passionate and very public love affair. Then Byron's feelings began to cool and quickly he found the intensity of Lady Caroline's passion irksome. Distraught, she tried various hysterical ruses to win him back and refused to accept that their relationship had ended, even when Byron told her that he now loved another woman – Lady Oxford, a mature society beauty who conducted her infidelities with a calmness and discretion that probably even Byron found a welcome contrast.

But his next emotional entanglement was to be even more scandalous. Byron had a half-sister, Augusta, Mad Jack's child by an earlier marriage; he had seen her intermittently when they were children, but not since his return from Greece or since her marriage to Colonel Leigh. She was beautiful, unhappily married, and they established an instantaneous and dangerous rapport which it seems certain developed into an incestuous sexual relationship. By August 1813 Byron was confessing to a friend that he was in 'a far more serious and entirely new scrape than any of the past twelve months – and that is saying a good deal.' The same year he wrote *The Bride of Abydos*, the story of a love between a brother and a sister, although in the end it turns out, probably to avoid shocking an inflammable public, to be no more than the permissible passion felt for each other by cousins. By the autumn Augusta was pregnant and the two retired to Newstead to spend a snow-bound winter together. In April 1814 Augusta gave birth to a girl, Medora.

This passion was certainly one of the most powerful (perhaps because the most dangerous) of Byron's life. But even when the relationship was at its height, he was pursuing at least two other women: Lady Frances Webster and the woman who was shortly to become his wife, Annabella Milbanke. In many ways Annabella

An engraving of Lady Caroline Lamb, one of Byron's mistresses whose behaviour was a perfect illustration of William Congreve's dictum, 'Heav'n has no rage, like love to hatred turn'd, Nor Hell a fury, like a woman scorn'd'.

was precisely the type of woman Byron most disliked – priggish, prejudiced, virtuous and plain – and why Byron decided to marry her remains a mystery, though he was almost certainly swayed by a feeling that it was time he married somebody, a view Augusta shared. Whatever his motive, the ceremony took place on 2 January 1815. Hobhouse recorded, 'I felt as if I had buried a friend.'

Not surprisingly, the marriage was a disaster and lasted only one year before Annabella removed herself and their baby daughter Ada and travelled back to her parents' home, never to see Byron again. In her demands for a separation she accused him of brutality and insanity, saying that while she was in labour he threw bottles at the ceiling of the room below that in which she was lying. The scandal created by Annabella's accusations and by the rumours spread by a vindictive Caroline Lamb ruined Byron's reputation completely. Heavily in debt and with nothing to keep him at home, Byron decided that the only course open to him was to go abroad and on 24 April 1816 he left England for ever.

In a vast travelling coach, modelled on Napoleon's, Byron wended his way to Switzerland where he rented the Villa Diodati on the shore of Lake Leman and set to work on the third canto of *Childe Harold*. Among his neighbours at Geneva was his fellow-poet Shelley, with his mistress Mary Godwin and her step-sister, Claire Clairmont. Claire had already pursued Byron just before his departure from England and was now expecting his child. 'I was not in love,' Byron reported in a letter to Augusta, 'nor have I any love left for any, but I could not exactly play the Stoic with a woman who had come eight hundred miles to un-philosophize me.' But in August Shelley and his household left for England while Byron moved on to Italy. Although his spirits had revived since his departure from London, he was becoming conscious of his physical decay: 'My hair is growing grey and *not* thicker; & my teeth are sometimes loosish though still white and sound. Would not one think I was sixty intead of not quite nine and twenty?' But in Venice he fell in love again – with a draper's wife – and was cheered to hear of the successful publication of both the third canto of *Childe Harold* and of his shorter poem, *The Prisoner of Chillon*, and of the sale of Newstead which cleared his debts. He was apparently not very interested in the news that Claire Clairmont had given birth to his third daughter, Allegra.

He continued to write poetry and over the next two years produced the mock-heroic poem, *Beppo*, and then probably his greatest work, the vast spoof-epic, *Don Juan*. He also formed the final serious attachment of his life with a young, married Italian countess, Teresa Guiccioli. Their relationship was to last for almost six years, but by 1823 Byron had tired of her and was restless to get away.

His opportunity came with a visit from Edward Blanquiere, of the London Greek Committee, a group of Greek exiles dedicated to the cause of freeing their country from Turkish rule. Byron's sympathy with their cause was well known and Blanquiere had come to appeal for his help. In July 1823 Byron set sail for Greece on board the *Hercules*. He landed to an enthusiastic welcome in the officially neutral Ionian islands, where he helped to raise funds and personally made a loan of £4,000 to equip the Greek navy. In November he received a message from the Greek senate at Salamis asking him to go to Missolonghi, which was considered an essential base for any attack on Patras and Lepanto, the last remaining Turkish strongholds on the Greek mainland.

But the enthusiasm of his welcome when he arrived there on 5 January 1824 could not conceal the fact that Missolonghi was a dingy and extremely unhealthy place. While the Greeks were still preparing their expeditionary force, Byron fell ill. On 15 February he apparently had some kind of epileptic fit, and although he seemed to recover he remained weak. On 9 April, after returning from a ride wet through, he came down with a severe fever. Death was clearly in his thoughts and seemed not unwelcome. 'I am not afraid of dying,' he told his servant on the evening of the 17th; 'I am more fit to die than people think.' By the next day he was delirious and on the 19th, at six o'clock in the morning, he died without regaining consciousness.

It was hardly a heroic ending, yet the circumstances of his death were completely overshadowed by the single fact that he had given his life to the twin causes of nationalism and liberalism that were to shape the future of Europe for the next half century. In Greece itself Byron was instantly honoured as a national martyr; in England, although the Dean of Westminster refused to bury his body (brought back to England by his loyal friend Hobhouse) in

Westminster Abbey, many Whig and radical peers attending the lying-in-state in Great George Street and a large crowd gathered to watch the funeral cortège on its slow route north to the Byron family vault near Newstead. But his influence was not to be confined to Greece and England. Throughout Europe over the next few years Byron became a source of inspiration to artists and poets as diverse as Lamartine and Dostoevsky, Goethe and Pushkin, while his name was to be invoked by those struggling to liberate themselves from oppressive regimes throughout the Continent. The myth of the Byronic hero was raised above time and place to become a romantic symbol of the world's eternal struggle for freedom.

～ *Abraham Lincoln* ～

Abraham Lincoln was born on 12 February 1809 in a log cabin in the backwoods frontier community of Kentucky. His early life was one of struggle, hardship and rootlessness as his father, Thomas, moved ever westwards with that frontier optimism which sought prosperity beyond the next mountain range. His formal education was negligible – just one year at a local school; and as he grew into a gangling youth ('a tall spider of a boy,' recalled one neighbour) his talents were those of the logsplitter and farmhand rather than a future president. But he did acquire a local reputation as a storyteller, a raconteur of homespun yarns tinged with fantasy and imagination which not only made him something of a leader among the boisterous companions of his youth but remained to give colour to the simple philosophizings of his later years.

When he was nineteen Lincoln left the narrow confines of his family life for the first time, taking a flat-boat trip to New Orleans where he saw slavery in operation. At the age of twenty-one, he moved away from home to the small town of New Salem where he worked as a partner in a general store and also at numerous odd jobs, including surveying and bricklaying. He ran up debts but steadfastly and with great difficulty managed to repay them over a period of fifteen years. It was about this time too that his life-long dissatisfaction with his own education and knowledge began to express itself in ever-wider reading and it was not long before, entirely self-taught, he turned himself into a lawyer, finally receiving his licence to practise in 1836. He also began to develop an interest in politics, and from the age of twenty-six to thirty-four served in the Illinois stage legislature. He made an improbable politician, retaining his coarseness, earthy humour and high-spirited conviviality both in his public utterances and in seclusion with his colleagues. But he was also affected by something else – a deep streak of melancholy which once led him to confide to a friend that he dare not carry a penknife for fear that in one of his moods he might decide to end his life with it.

When the state capital was moved to Springfield in 1837, Lincoln moved with it; and there he continued his excursions into local politics, developed his reputation as a lawyer and, after a series of strange and somewhat unhappy love affairs, plunged into marriage. His wife, Mary Todd, who was by all accounts his social superior, was something of a tartar and created considerable domestic unhappiness; once, when

The earliest known photographs of Congressman Lincoln and his wife, Mary, probably taken in Springfield in 1846.

asked why she spelt her name with two 'd's, Lincoln replied that one 'd' was enough for God but not for the Todds.

In 1846 Lincoln was elected to Congress but during two undistinguished years in Washington he gained little more than a certain unpopularity for his pacifist stance over America's war with Mexico. Returning to Springfield, he concentrated on building up a highly successful legal practice, attracting those with whom he came into contact by his compelling presence and simple, thoughtful capacity to go right to the heart of any particular problem. In this way he became something of a local character, if not exactly a celebrity, at precisely that moment when great issues in the rest of America were about to transform him into a national figure. For the great cleavages between the Yankee north and the southern states were being altered by a shift in the balance of power caused by the flood of immigration and the opening up of the vast territories of the west. Hitherto, the Democratic

party which, although it had supporters in the north, mainly represented the cultured, wealthy and sophisticated peoples of the south, had held sway over preponderately northern Yankee 'Whigs'. The north was more populous, more industrialized and its economy quite independent of the slave system which was at the root of the cotton plantations of the south. The opening of the western territories – the lands of the Louisiana purchase west of the Mississippi – held a grave threat for the south; if they were to ally themselves politically with the north, then the south could easily find itself outvoted in Washington. It was a question which was to revolve around slavery, with the north increasingly in favour of abolition, the south determined on its continuation, and the west holding the key to which side would end up victorious. It was out of this political conflict that the south began to talk of an issue more fundamental than slavery, that of secession from the Union itself.

Although Lincoln is remembered today as 'The Great Emancipator', he was never a fanatical abolitionist. His position was that although he had no wish to abolish slavery in the south, where he still trusted it would die a natural death, he was certainly not going to tolerate its extension into the new territories now being opened up. His re-entry into politics was thus precipitated in 1854 by the introduction of the Kansas-Nebraska Bill which, if passed, would allow the western territories to decide for themselves on the question of slavery. This contravened the famous Missouri compromise of 1820 whereby slavery was prohibited in the northern part of the Louisiana purchase and permitted in the southern part. Despite Lincoln's brilliant performances in a series of public debates with his opponent, a Democrat called Stephen Douglas, the bill was passed. But Douglas, who had supported the bill in the hope of winning southern support for his presidential ambitions, found that he had alienated not only the abolitionist north but also most of the south, which wanted a much stronger pro-slavery line than simply the right for individual territories to decide for themselves, and the west, which suspected him of merely propagating southern supremacy. As Lincoln put it, 'You can fool all the people some of the time; some of the people all of the time; but you cannot fool all the people all of the time.'

Lincoln's opposition to Douglas had made him more than just a local figure. It had also helped to crystallize his own unusually broad views on slavery which he related to the freedom of whites as well as blacks: 'As a nation we begin by declaring that "all men are created equal", we now read on "all men are created equal except negroes". When the Know-Nothings get control it will read "all men are created equal except negroes and foreigners and Catholics".' He now decided to join the newly created Republican party, the extremists of which were far more abolitionist than Lincoln, and he was chosen as a senatorial candidate for Illinois. His remorseless logic and practical, almost simplistic phraseology secured his position as a man of the future; talking of the divisions and uncertainties created

Springfield c. 1845.

by the conflict between north and south, he made one of his most famous remarks: 'A house divided against itself cannot stand. I believe this government cannot endure permanently half slave and half free. I do not expect the Union to be dissolved – I do not expect the house to fall – but I do expect that it will cease to be divided.'

In 1856 the south won a notable if transient victory when the Democratic candidate, Buchanan, was duly elected president. But before long there was a fatal split in the Democratic party, as the northern Democrats, whatever their views on slavery, began to oppose the political ambitions of the south. At the next presidential election, three years later, both north and south put forward Democratic candidates, and it only needed a Republican who could command the west and secure the allegiance of anti-slave factions in the north to ensure a Democratic defeat. The nation was on the verge of disintegration. Southerners knew perfectly well what was happening and threatened to secede from the Union if a Republican occupied the White House. In Virginia John Brown's abortive attempt to free slaves by force ended in his execution by the state government. It was amid these tribulations that Lincoln was adopted by the Republican party as presidential candidate and, although not a single southern or border state voted for him, he was duly elected on 6 November 1860. 'Well, boys,' he told newsmen the day after his election, 'your troubles are over, mine have just begun.'

In the limbo between his election and inauguration the following March, he had to watch helplessly as the country drifted inexorably towards civil war. The first of the states to fulfil their pledge to secede in the event of a Republican victory was South Carolina; soon seven others followed, and a separate government, the Confederate States of America, was formed under Jefferson Davis, and its army mustered under the great generals, Lee and Jackson. For all the natural advantages in wealth and population enjoyed by the north, the south was now better prepared, better led and better

armed. But Lincoln's troubles were not confined to the inadequacies of his own armies: within the government there was hostility from some Republicans who wanted a far more intransigent line to be taken against the institution of slavery. Lincoln made it clear that he was prepared to accept slavery in the states where it already existed and that he saw his main task as the preservation of the Union: 'If there be those who would not save the union unless they could at the same time save slavery, I do not agree with them. If there be those who would not save the union less they could destroy slavery, I do not agree with them. My paramount object in this struggle is to save the union and is not either to save or destroy slavery.'

Meanwhile, as the war continued, Lincoln assumed powers that were almost dictatorial, such as the suspension of habeas corpus, confident that the verdict of the people would justify his measures, provided that in the end he was victorious and the union was preserved.

Lincoln and his generals, October 1862.

Gradually the advantages of the north began to prevail, and in Grant and Sherman he found leaders capable of turning the tide of war in favour of the federal government. After the momentous victory at Gettysburg in November 1863, he made one of the great statements of war aims which established in characteristically plain language the democratic ideal allied to magnanimity which marked his leadership:

Four score and seven years ago our fathers brought forth to this Continent a new nation, conceived in liberty and dedicated to the proposition that all men are created equal.... It was for us, the living, rather to be dedicated here to the great task remaining before us – that from these honoured dead we take increased devotion to that cause to which they gave the last full measure of devotion; that we here resolve that these dead shall not have died in vain; that this nation, under God, was for a new birth of freedom; and that government of the people, by the people, for the people, shall not perish from the earth.

At this time, Lincoln realized the logical conclusion of his earlier remarks about the collapse of a house divided against itself, and so in 1863 he officially announced his change of policy on slavery and proclaimed the famous Emancipation Act, guaranteeing freedom to the slaves in all states of the union at the conclusion of the war. It was a momentous decision; it meant that under his leadership the war was to be fought not just for a united America and not just for the survival of democratic institutions but for the ideal that all men are created equal.

By 1864 it was clear that the war would soon be won and Lincoln's mind turned both to his own prospects for re-election later that year and to the prospects of peace and reconciliation when the war was over. Although he had made many enemies in high-ranking government circles, his own homely observation that 'it was best not to swap horses when crossing a stream' proved to be the advice accepted by the electorate and he was returned with an overwhelming majority. In his second inaugural address, a moving appeal to

Slaves in Virginia newly freed by Lincoln's troops.

his fellow-countrymen, Lincoln looked to the future:

With malice towards none, with charity for all; with firmness in the right as God gives us to see the right, let us strive to bind up the nation's wounds; to care for him who shall have borne the battle and for his widow and his orphan – to do all which may achieve and cherish a just and lasting peace among ourselves and with all nations.

Following the election Lincoln took a brief holiday in the spring of 1865. He returned to Washington in time to receive the news that on 9 April General Lee had surrendered at Appomattox and to prepare for the task of reconstructing the union. But that challenge was not to be his. One morning soon after, Lincoln dreamt that he had been assassinated. A day or so later, on the evening of 14 April, he and his wife went to the opera, where a fanatic, John Wilkes Booth, fired a shot at him at point-blank range. Before the morning Lincoln was dead. America had lost a president who both articulated for his nation and exemplified in himself the virtues of ordinary people, a man of the people, working for them with the authority of their support.

∼ *Livingstone* ∼

The life of David Livingstone is an astonishing monument to the Victorian ideals of self-sacrifice and enterprise. During the thirty years he spent in Africa, he explored thousands of miles of the interior virtually single-handed and did more than any other European to open up the continent. By the time of his death he had added a million square miles to the known surface of the earth. His single-minded dedication and his unwavering acceptance of the superiority of his own civilization and religion made him a very Victorian figure, and yet he had none of the arrogance of many nineteenth-century imperialists. Instead he made a thorough and sensitive study of the Africans he met as well as of their country, and always behaved towards them with honour and civility.

Livingstone was born in 1813 in Blantyre, a Scottish mill town south of Glasgow. His ancestors had been poor crofting folk from the small island of Ulva, near Mull, and his grandfather had fallen at Culloden. Like so many other Highlanders, poverty and the industrial revolution had drawn them south and David's father was a tea-vendor, a pious but unsuccessful man who could afford only one room in a grim tenement block for his family of seven children. Money was short and at the age of ten David went out to work as a 'piecer' in the local cotton mills and, according to tradition, spent his first week's wages on a Latin Grammar. True or not, the story certainly testifies to the extraordinary curiosity and thirst for knowledge that was to turn the ten-year-old factory hand into a qualified doctor and one of the greatest explorers of the age.

When Livingstone was twenty, he underwent some kind of intense religious experience, and from this time on he was convinced that he had

A miniature of Livingstone, aged 27, painted for the London Missionary Society before he sailed for South Africa.

been singled out to serve God in some special way. An appeal by a missionary home on leave from China first planted in his mind the idea of spreading Christianity overseas and his first practical step was his decision to study as a doctor to fit himself for missionary work. For two years, while still working as a cotton piecer during the summer, during the winter he attended lectures in Glasgow on not just medicine but divinity and Greek. In 1838 he applied for membership of the London Missionary Society which sent him on a year's probation to study under the Reverend

Richard Cecil at Chipping Ongar before giving him the time to complete his medical studies in London. He finally qualified as a doctor in 1840 and, only a few days after receiving his licence to practise, he had said goodbye to his family, taken holy orders and set sail for Cape Town to his first post as a missionary.

The station to which he was sent was run by Robert Moffat, a South African missionary whom Livingstone had met in London, and was at Kuruman in Bechuanaland, north of the Orange River and on the frontiers of civilization. Although the coast of Africa had been settled and charted by 1840, almost the whole of the interior south of the equator was unknown to Europeans, and it was commonly believed that the Kalahari desert, which no white man had ever crossed, merged with the Sahara. From the first, Livingstone wanted to be the first missionary to carry the word of God into these vast new lands, and within two months of his arrival in Africa, he had set off into the wilderness. With an ox-wagon, one colleague and two native converts he trekked 700 miles to the north-east – 'further in that direction than any missionaries have yet been' – to select a site for a new mission. On a

second trip a few months later he spent six months alone with the Bakwena tribe 'in order to obtain an accurate knowledge of the language'. He also made friends with the paramount chief of the Bakwena, Sechele, by curing his son of dysentery; seven years later, Sechele became one of Livingstone's most influential converts to Christianity. A more immediate result was that during these months Livingstone gained an insight into the 'habits, ways of thinking, laws and language' of the Africans that was to be invaluable to him in the years ahead.

The site he selected for the new mission station was at Mabotsa, about 200 miles to the north of Kuruman, and in 1843 Livingstone and a colleague, Roger Edwards, started to build a hut there and to construct a watercourse. But before it was finished Livingstone was attacked by a lion that badly mauled his left arm. It had to be set by Edwards without any anaesthetic and for the rest of his life Livingstone was unable to raise it higher than his shoulder. In a weak state he returned to Kuruman to recuperate and there he fell in love with Robert Moffat's daughter, Mary. In a letter home he confessed: 'It will comfort all your hearts to know that I am become as great a fool as any of you. ... In love! Words, yea thoughts fail. ...' The couple were married in January 1845 and Livingstone took his bride back with him to Mabotsa to build their first

'Bird's-eye view of Kuruman', the mission run by Robert Moffat who, according to one report, had made only one convert in the seven years preceding Livingstone's arrival.

Livingstone's friends, Chief Sechele and his wife.

home: a mud-walled shack roofed with reeds.

It was a marriage that was to bring Mary much hardship, for Livingstone, though he loved her dearly, had little thought of providing for her and the children she bore him. Frequently pregnant, she accompanied him on many of his journeys and helped him establish a new mission at Kolobeng, surrounded by the Bakwena and Chief Sechele. Then in 1852 they decided that Mary and the young family should return to Britain where she stayed for the next few years, first in Scotland, then in England, often on the verge of destitution and seldom hearing from her distant husband.

Between 1849 and 1856, when he made his own first trip home, Livingstone made a number of journeys into the interior. After several abortive attempts he managed to cross the Kalahari and discovered that to the north lay, not the Sahara, but some of the most beautiful and fertile lands in the whole of Africa. He also discovered Lake Ngamai and some 200 miles beyond the lake he met the legendary chief Sebituane, head of the Makololo people, with whom he established a close friendship. Then in 1853, accompanied only by Makololo tribesmen, he travelled halfway across the continent from the interior to the west coast, across the great rain forests to Luanda in Portuguese West Africa.

This was one of the most important journeys of his career and a landmark in opening up the interior. Livingstone's journals describing it rank among the classic records of expeditions. Although his health was already undermined by the hardships of the climate, with unflagging care and interest he observed and recorded everything he saw: flora, fauna, geological phenomena, the customs of the tribesmen. The hardships he suffered were daunting: African fever, shortage of food, clothes rotting in the damp of the rain forests, hostility of the local tribes. At one point the Makololo tribesmen wanted to turn back but when Livingstone told them that in that case he would go on alone, they loyally decided to stay with him – and in March 1854 were rewarded by their first-ever sight of the sea. Livingstone repaid their devotion when he rejected an offer made by two British ships in Luanda harbour to take him home. Although by now he longed for news of his family, he feared that without him the Makololo would not survive the journey home and insisted on accompanying them back to the interior. The return journey proved as arduous as the outward one. Livingstone caught a bad bout of rheumatic fever and, while he was still recovering, he and his party were attacked by bands of armed villagers and only just escaped with their lives. But he was still observing and reflecting on everything he saw and one of his great achievements was to solve the riddle of the watershed in central Africa and to realize that this was not a range of as yet undiscovered mountains, as most people thought, but that the great African rivers, like the Congo and the Zambezi, rose in a plain only about 4,000 feet above sea level.

His next expedition was a journey in the opposite direction, to the east coast. Again he was accompanied by a party of Makololo tribesmen and together they followed the course of the Zambezi, giving Livingstone his first sight of the magnificent Victoria Falls. Early in 1856 he reached the coast where again he was warmly received by the Portuguese and then, at last, he set sail for home.

On his return to London in December, to his surprise he found himself acclaimed as the greatest explorer of the age. He was made a Fellow of the Royal Society, given honorary degrees and everywhere fêted and listened to; even Queen Victoria wished to meet him and laughed heartily when he told her that the Bechuana, informed that Livingstone's own chief was very rich, inquired how many cows she had. When he published an account of his travels, it immediately became a bestseller, selling out the first edition of 12,000 copies in only a few weeks. However, the London Missionary Society was unimpressed by all this attention and had come to the conclusion that its famous member had become first and foremost an explorer rather than a missionary. So sadly Livingstone severed his links with it and when, in 1858, he returned to Africa, it was as the leader of an official government expedition whose brief was to explore the Zambezi and to 'extend the knowledge of the geography and minerals and agricultural resources of East and Central Africa'.

Unfortunately this expedition was far less successful than his earlier ones. Livingstone was accustomed to travelling with natives, not to organizing a full-scale European expedition, and he soon fell out with many of his companions, one of the most uncooperative and unpopular of whom was his own brother, Charles. It quickly became evident too that the difficulties of getting up the shallow waters at the mouth of the Zambezi had been underestimated. The boat they had brought out with them in pieces from England and re-assembled on arrival, the *Ma-Robert*, kept breaking down and was quickly nicknamed the *Asthmatic*. A message was despatched to London requesting a better vessel and meanwhile Livingstone determined to explore the Shire River, one of the tributaries of the Zambezi, and to search for the great lake

reputed to lie at its source. Struggling up almost impassable cataracts and rapids, he eventually discovered Lake Nyasa and the Shire Highlands, a region of great fertility and beauty. But he also discovered to his dismay how great the slave trade now was in the interior. Since he had first come across it on his great journey to the west coast, it had extended its tentacles right across the land that Livingstone was exploring. His hostility towards this cruel trade was to crystallize into a crusading passion to exterminate it completely from the face of the continent. He first intervened actively to stop it in July 1861, releasing eighty-four captives whom he came across in the forest.

In January 1862 Livingstone was joined by his wife who had come out from England with him

The Great Western Fall, Victoria Falls, by T. Baines, painted in 1863.

but had gone to Cape Town for the birth of her last child. In April, after a tragically brief reunion, she caught malaria and died. She was buried under a baobab tree in Shipanga, leaving her husband desolate and perhaps remorseful for the suffering her marriage had brought her: 'For the first time in my life,' he wrote, 'I feel willing to die. . . . I feel as if I have lost all heart now . . . I shall do my duty still but it is with a darkened horizon that I shall set about it.'

By 1862 the British government had grown disillusioned by the expedition's lack of success. It had been planned to last only two years and now in 1863 it was officially recalled, and Livingstone went back to England. He was only fifty but prematurely aged and in poor health. But when his old friend and fellow explorer, Sir Roderick Murchison, suggested that he should return to Africa to search for the source of the Nile, he was unable to resist the opportunity. In 1865 Livingstone was back in Africa.

In fact he was to spend the last years of his life exploring the headwaters not of the Nile but of the Congo. This time accompanied only by Africans, he went up the river Rouvma from the east coast and then across to Lake Nyasa which he had previously reached by going up the Shire from the south. Then he pushed on north and west, discovering lakes Mweru and Bangweulu. His health was now constantly on the verge of collapse and, among the many difficulties and setbacks he met, none hit him harder than the theft of his medicine chest. 'I feel as if I had now received a sentence of death,' he recorded.

But somehow he was to survive for another six years. During that time nobody in England heard any news of him and most people had given him up for dead. Then, in 1871, an American newspaper, the *New York Herald*, decided to send their correspondent, Henry Stanley, to search for him. All the odds of geography and timing were against him, yet finally, after months of looking, Stanley tracked Livingstone down at Ujiji, on the shore of Lake Tanganyika, and uttered his celebrated greeting, 'Dr Livingstone, I presume?' Stanley provided the doctor with much-needed stores and medical supplies and the two men, so different in age and background, took an immediate liking to each other. For a few months they explored the northern end of Lake Tanganyika and when Stanley decided he must return to report to his newspaper, he tried to persuade Livingstone to come with him. But the old man refused and reluctantly, in March 1872, Stanley set off for Zanzibar alone. He was the last white man to see Livingstone alive.

After Stanley's departure, still obsessed with his search for the head of the Nile and convinced, quite wrongly, that it must lie to the south, Livingstone set off for the last time. Racked by malaria and dysentery and bleeding incessantly from an internal haemorrhage, he was in constant pain. 'It is not all pleasure, this exploration,' he recorded on 19 April 1873 in one of the great understatements of history. Two days later he fainted and fell off his donkey, and on 1 May, in a small village hut and attended by his devoted African servants, he died. Afraid that they might be accused of murdering him if they returned without his body, they embalmed it and carried it down to the coast where it was shipped back to London. In 1874 David Livingstone was buried in state in Westminster Abbey.

Ironically the tragedy of his death gave others a renewed impetus to fulfil his ideals. Within two months the Sultan of Zanzibar yielded to pressure and signed a treaty prohibiting the export of slaves from his dominions. Once the great slave market in his capital was closed, the end of the Arab slave trade was in sight. Livingstone's argument too that by opening up the African wilderness he was laying a trail for Christianity rapidly bore fruit and within a century of his death missions and churches were established all over the vast areas where he had been the first Christian to tread.

~ *Florence Nightingale* ~

Florence Nightingale's early life seems to have been blessed with every material advantage that English life could offer. Her parents had two country houses, a comfortable, unearned income and a wide circle of well-connected relations and friends, and as Florence and her sister Parthenope grew up, they joined a pleasant, and not unstimulating, round of visits to relations, dinner parties, opera-going and foreign travel. Both girls were pretty but Florence was clearly exceptionally attractive, with brilliant chestnut-coloured hair and wistful grey eyes. She soon became a figure in London society and numbered among her friends Lord Palmerston, Elizabeth Barrett Browning, George Eliot, Lord Shaftesbury and Cardinal Manning. Bachelor admirers were not lacking and it seemed only a question of time before a suitable engagement was announced.

Yet just as she was tasting the pleasures of social success, Florence's ambitions were secretly

Florence Nightingale and her sister, Parthenope, *c.* 1836 by William White.

turning in another direction. Fortunately, we know a great deal about her private thoughts and emotions from the copious series of 'Private Notes' which she wrote throughout her life and which still survive among her papers. In one of these, written when she was only sixteen, she had recorded: 'On 7 February 1837, God spoke to me and called me to his service.' It was the turning point of her life. For the next sixteen years, although outwardly she followed a conventional routine, inwardly Florence was in turmoil. Psychologically, her struggle to break free from the cocoon of Victorian family life was in its way as hard as anything suffered by Livingstone or Lincoln and on several occasions the strain caused a complete nervous collapse. But to start with, although she never seems to have doubted the authenticity of her 'call', she had no idea what form her service to God should take, or what practical steps she should take to further it. It was not until sometime in 1844 that the firm knowledge came to her that nursing was to be her vocation. 'From then on', she wrote in her Notes, 'there was never any vagueness in my plans or ideas as to what God's work was for me.'

But it was another eleven years before Florence found a way of translating this into action. When, in December 1845, she announced to her family that she wanted to spend three months in Salisbury Infirmary to learn about nursing, the news was greeted by her mother with a hysterical outburst that fast changed to anger. The prospect of a daughter becoming a professional nurse would have appalled any middle-class Victorian family. In the mid-nineteenth century, hospitals were squalid, dirty and positively dangerous, caring (if that is the right word) only for the poor. The nurses were untrained, often drunk and dishonest and certainly not drawn from well-to-do families like the Nightingales. Permission was refused and Florence thought that her life was pointless.

Marriage might have been an alternative but in 1849, after much heart-searching, Florence turned down her last serious proposal, from Richard Monckton-Milnes, a talented man whom she admitted she adored. The strain of this sacrifice for a destiny which remained hopelessly unfulfilled proved too much for Florence's health. In an attempt to distract her, two friends, Mr and Mrs Bracebridge, invited her to accompany them on a visit to Egypt. Out of desperation and pity, Mrs Bracebridge suggested that on the way home Florence should spend two weeks at Kaiserwerth, an institution in Germany 'for the practical care of deaconesses ... embracing the support and care of a hospital, infant and industrial schools and a female penitentiary'. Florence responded to her new environment immediately and by the time she left she felt 'so brave as if nothing could ever vex me again'. In 1851, despite family disapproval, she returned to Kaiserwerth for a second visit, this time for three months. 'This is life,' she wrote happily. 'Now I know what it is to live and to love life ... I wish for no other earth, no other world than this.' A final letter to her mother and sister pleading for their blessing went unanswered. She never appealed to them again.

In 1853 Florence's first real opportunity arose when she was appointed Superintendent of the Institute for the Care of Sick Gentlewomen in Distressed Circumstances. She started work in August in their Harley Street premises and was quick to grasp the fundamental principle that effective organization was of greater benefit to her patients than sitting holding their hands. She devised schemes for piping hot water to every floor, and a lift to bring up patients' meals; she reorganized the accounts, meticulously checked the stores, and realized that vast sums could be saved by negotiating contracts for bulk purchases.

Yet within only a few months she seemed restless. The home was running smoothly and she was looking for greater challenges. The cholera outbreak of 1854 found her helping in the Middlesex hospital; she visited other London hospitals too and started to collect evidence to support her view that widespread reforms were vital – and to look for a hospital post for herself

British soldiers in the Crimean Peninsula, photographed by Roger Fenton.

where she hoped she would be able to train a new type of nurse. But fate, which had kept her waiting for so long, was now about to confront her with a gargantuan task.

In March 1854 England and France had declared war on Russia and in the autumn the allied armies landed in the Crimean Peninsula in southern Russia. The main army hospital was at Scutari, back across the Black Sea on the Asian shore of the Bosphorus. The plight of the sick and wounded who were sent back there was one of horrifying misery. There were not enough boats to cope with the load, and so the wounded and diseased were all crammed in together in squalid conditions. Once they reached Scutari, there was not enough of anything from water to doctors and the vast barracks quickly became a ghetto of suffering and disease which no one seemed able to combat.

In fact other British armies in the past had

probably suffered equal hardships but previously the British public had known little about them. Now for the first time there was with the expedition a war correspondent determined to reveal the suffering he was witnessing and to expose the shortcomings of those responsible – William Howard Russell of *The Times*. The nation was outraged at the lack of nursing for British troops and demanded action. By a stroke

'An Angel of Mercy', by Butterworth, published in June 1855 together with the following extract from a letter to *The Times* from Scutari: 'When all the Medical Officers have retired for the night, and silence and darkness have settled down upon those miles of prostrate sick, she may be observed alone, with a little lamp in her hand, making her solitary rounds.'

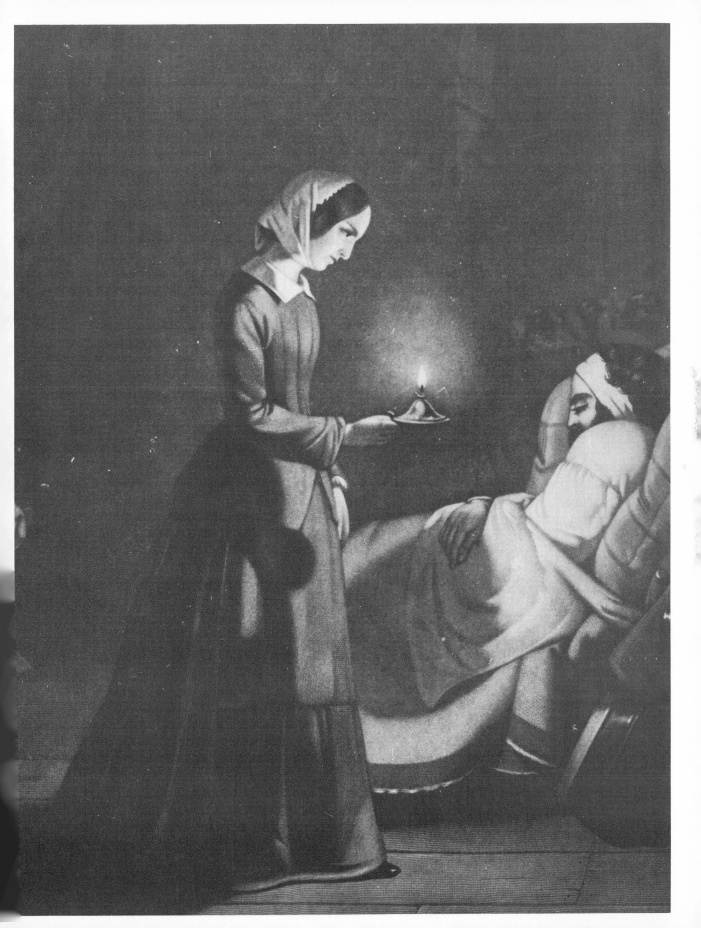

of fortune, the Secretary at War, Sidney Herbert, was a close friend of Florence Nightingale. On 15 October he wrote to her asking her to go out to Scutari in charge of a party of nurses. In fact Florence's mind was already made up and his letter to her crossed with one to him announcing her determination to go. But Herbert's letter gave her official backing and unlimited power to draw on government funds.

Before Florence set sail, four days later, she had to recruit her party of nurses. The original plan had been to choose forty applicants but in the end only thirty-eight suitable ones could be found. The nurses were to be paid between 12s. and 14s. a week with board, lodging and uniform. Each of them signed an agreement submitting herself absolutely to Miss Nightingale's authority. Misconduct with the troops was to be punished by instant dismissal, and was in any case rendered improbable by the selection of 'old bodies' rather than young women.

On 5 November 1854, after a stormy voyage that prostrated Florence with seasickness, this strange band of women arrived at the Barrack Hospital at Scutari and began to assess the task ahead of them.

The real tragedy of the Crimean War was that so much of the suffering was caused not by enemy wounding but by the administrative bungling of the British army. Three separate departments were in charge of the army medical services: the Commissariat, the Purveyor's Department and the Medical Department. There was no logical division of functions between them and during the years of peace since Waterloo a series of economies had deprived them of almost all staff, equipment and funds. Relations with the medical staff were poor. No one could do anything (a doctor could not even obtain a bandage) without filling in a form and getting it signed by the correct authority, and many surgeons spent more time dealing with form-filling than with patients, even at the height of the crisis. The officials running the system were not malevolent but they were overworked and unimaginative.

But there was also a second and more subtle reason for the tragedy of the Crimea, and that was the attitude of the officers towards their men. The idea that they had a right to be treated with consideration off the battlefield was considered as not just odd but positively dangerous. It was probably Florence Nightingale's greatest achievement in the Crimea that never again would the British soldier be treated in such a callous way.

The first task she faced was to gain acceptance

for herself and her nurses from the army authorities and the doctors. Smarting at the newspaper criticisms, the doctors bitterly resented her arrival. Florence had government backing and therefore she could not be openly rejected, but she could be ignored. It says much for her tactical skill that she managed to survive this initial hostility. She decided that the only way to win the confidence of the doctors was to do nothing till they asked for help. No nurse was to enter a ward unless she was invited to do so by a doctor; instead, they spent their time sorting

linen, counting stores and practising bandaging. Only in the kitchens did Florence gain a foothold. With inspired foresight she had bought large quantities of invalid food and other supplies at Marseilles on the voyage out. She was careful to supply nothing without receiving the correct official requisition form but within a week her quarters had become a special diet kitchen, providing the only decent food available. Yet still the nurses were kept out of the wards.

By 9 November, two weeks after the battle of Balaclava and four days after the battle of Inkerman, the stream of casualties arriving at the hospital became a flood. There were more victims of disease and exposure than of battle wounds (no one, it seems, had foreseen the bitter cold of the Crimean winter). Within days the hospital became a charnel house. Fever, dysentery and gangrene spread like wildfire – and the death rate rose inexorably. This was Florence Nightingale's opportunity. Under this pressure, the hospital staff were prepared to turn to the nurses, and Florence emerged as the one person who had ample funds and was ready to spend them. At Constantinople she bought shirts, socks, nightshirts, plates, cutlery, bedpans. By December it was Florence Nightingale, not the army purveyor or commissary general, who was supplying the hospital. And at last, as they worked twenty-four hours a day, the doctors began to accept the help of the nurses.

The amount of work that Florence managed to get through was phenomenal. Every day literally thousands of words poured from her pen in both official reports and private letters to Sidney Herbert. Somehow too she found time to visit the wards, and it was there, in these terrible winter months of 1854–5, that the legend of Florence Nightingale was born. The men adored her. 'If she was at our head,' they said, 'we'd be at Sebastopol next week.' When a batch of new patients arrived at the hospital she would often be

Florence (at the window) and nurses from her school, 1887.

on her feet for twenty-two hours out of twenty-four, spending as long as eight hours dressing wounds. As she went about the wards, she radiated an extraordinary charisma. 'What a comfort it was to see her pass even,' wrote one soldier. 'She would speak to one, and nod and smile to many more ... we could kiss her shadow as it fell and lay our heads on the pillow again, content.' She calmed men before operations; she wrote letters home on their behalf to their wives; she held their hands as they died.

Her heroism and self-sacrifice at this time are unquestionable. Yet there were still those who opposed her and persisted in obstructing her. Her biggest enemy was the Chief of the Medical Staff of the British Expeditionary Army, Dr John Hall. Hall was not just a stern disciplinarian opposed to pampering the men in any way; he was almost certainly a sadist. He was also haunted by a rash statement he had made in October 1854 that the hospital at Scutari had 'now been put on a very creditable footing and that nothing is lacking'. Florence Nightingale's very arrival, let alone the tasks she performed, were a standing indictment of his judgment and his competence.

By the spring of 1855 the situation at Scutari had slowly improved and, characteristically, Florence felt it was time for her to find some fresh challenges. She decided to visit the two hospitals at Balaclava on the Crimean itself, one of which was in the personal charge of John Hall. When she got there she found, as she had suspected, that the hospitals were dirty and inefficient and once again she set to work with plans for diet kitchens and prepared herself to do battle with Hall. But this time, before anything could be achieved, her health gave way; for two weeks her life was feared for and it took her several months to recover. She was shipped back to Scutari and

there in September her aunt Mai arrived to join her. But no one could prevent Florence from overtaxing her strength and she soon insisted on returning to the hospital. In March 1856 she was even back at Balaclava.

By now, however, the war was almost over. A peace conference was held in Paris and on 29 April a treaty was proclaimed. Florence Nightingale's mission to the Crimean War was over. She was now thirty-six years old and was the only participant on the British side to emerge from the war with an enhanced reputation. After Queen Victoria, Florence Nightingale was probably the most famous woman in England. Poems and books about her poured off the presses. Staffordshire figures of her sold in their thousands and, once again, social invitations poured through her letter-box.

Florence was to live for another forty-five years, until she was ninety. For most of this time she was an invalid, confined to her couch, maintaining that her health had never recovered from the strains of war. Yet she did not cease to work. On the contrary, she produced an enormous report on the whole subject of army medical and hospital administration; she founded a nursing school at St Thomas's; and gave the government her advice on public health in India. None of this really added to her reputation, however, as most of it was done behind the scenes, and when, in 1907, Florence was awarded the Order of Merit, many people were startled to realize she was still alive. It was her work in the Crimea that had made her a national heroine, yet at the heart of the legend lay a fundamental contradiction: the image of Florence cherished by the public on the one hand, 'that gentle vision of female virtue', and the formidable administrative genius of reality on the other.

The Modern Age

by ALAN PALMER

*E*VERY AGE SALUTES valour and every generation idolizes those who bring glory to its most cherished pursuits. In retrospect, however, it is sometimes difficult to see why some deeds stand out more sharply than others. Although the qualities of concentrated courage which breed heroism are as immutable as the human spirit, fashions in hero-worship change with even the shortest passage of time. The turn of the nineteenth century saw a new type of name on the roll call of honour. Since then, generals rarely seem to have made the grade, though the courage of individuals continues to shine proudly through the fog of two world wars. After 1900 there are fewer enterprises designed to boost national dignity: the great Antarctic Expedition came to a tragically heroic end, but Captain Scott's primary objective was not to 'show the flag' at the South Pole, but to conduct a scientific survey. In scope and purpose Scott's last expedition to Antarctica has more in common with the Apollo 11 mission of 1969 than with Major Marchand's brave trek bearing the French tricolor from the Congo to the Nile only a few years previously. Certainly by 1912–13 the curtain had come down on the pageantry of overseas Empire. The heroes of the new age were, for the most part, ordinary people who had expected to live out their lives peacefully at home, never donning uniform or seeking adventure. Many went to nameless graves; they are remembered in collective anonymity as 'the men of . . .' the Marne, or Ypres, or Verdun, or Gallipoli, or the Somme, or of a dozen other giant battles, on land and at sea.

More women's names are inscribed on the rolls of honour of the twentieth century than those of earlier ages. This is not surprising, for women played a greater part in public life during these years. The courage of the militant suffragettes at the start of the century created very different heroines from those whom the Victorians admired. Florence Nightingale had won fame by nursing soldiers fresh from the battlefields of the Crimea, but she was never in any sense a combatant. Nor, indeed, was Nurse Edith Cavell. Yet in Brussels in 1914–15 Nurse Cavell found her sense of patriotic duty too intense to maintain the neutrality of her profession; and commitment was enough to bring her a martyr's death and the posthumous glory of a national hero. During the second of the world wars, against Hitler, a succession of remarkable women showed the undaunted and sustained courage of resistance to enemy occupation: some, like Andrée de Jongh, helped allied airmen along the escape route from Belgium southwards and across the Pyrenees into non-belligerent Spain; others, like Odette Sansom and Violette Szabo, faced death or the inhumanities of capture by working as allied agents within occupied France. Nor was the heroism of women limited to the European theatre of operations. Across the world, in China, a simple woman, astonishingly naive politically and impressively resolute in her religious faith, found herself outwitting the Japanese invaders with a price on her head. Gladys Aylward, so deceptively lacking in sophistication, remains an enigma. Perhaps the great women of the nineteenth century would have understood her more easily than many of us can do. But what would they have made of Rosa Luxemburg, a militant agnostic so loyal to her convictions that she courted death in the aftermath of revolution rather than compromise her individuality? 'Red Rosa', heroine of the dissident Left for more than half a century, believed in the dignity of the human being. Among the Berliners of 1919, that was an unfashionable article of faith.

The coming of powered flight in December 1903 was the key technological achievement of the century. Only sixty-six years separate Orville Wright's forty yard heavier-than-air long jump at Kitty Hawk from mankind's 'giant leap' to the Sea of Tranquillity. These two airborne events are linked by an impressive roll of heroic names: pioneers like Blériot before 1914 or Alcock and Brown after the Armistice; Sir Alan Cobham, and others who opened up the world with long-distance flights; women pilots, such as Amelia Earhart and Jean Batten; experimental scientists risking disaster; and more recently a long list of Soviet and American astronauts. If Lindbergh, Amy Johnson and Neil Armstrong are names springing readily to mind, it is because their achievements were dazzling triumphs of willpower, although Armstrong of course shares the glory of his moonflight with his colleagues, Aldrin and Collins. Powered flight also brought a new dimension into warfare. Among air aces in the two world wars, 'the few' of 1940 reign supreme, not only the British fighter pilots but the Canadians, Australians, South Africans, Frenchmen, Poles and Czechs who fought beside them in the Battle of Britain. It might seem invidious to select any one hero from such a band were it not for the unique distinction of Douglas Bader in mastering physical disabilities as well as outwitting the enemy, both in the skies and as a prisoner of war.

It is indeed a sad commentary on 'the modern age' that five of the ten heroes and heroines in this section should have found their liberty curtailed by prison walls, four of them as victims of war. The fifth captive hero, Martin Luther King, stands in a class of his own. Like Rosa Luxemburg he scorned the society around him, placing his zeal for human dignity higher than all material comforts; and, again like Rosa, he fell victim to an assassin's bullet. He preached, however, not the divisive bitterness of class war, but the racial brotherhood of man under the fatherhood of God. The passive resistance which he urged on the American Negro exposed the soullessness of a system based on discrimination. The more successful King's campaign – and the more he became a revered hero of liberals, whether black or white – the more certain it seemed he was drawn to follow the terrible path to a personal Golgotha. To those who were privileged to hear him in the full flight of inspired rhetoric during his later years, Martin Luther King stood out as a hero, not of any 'modern age', but of the centuries. The characteristic virtue of the greatest heroism is persistency to the bitter end.

Alan Palmer

～ *Captain Scott* ～

In the first week of August 1901 an unusual wooden vessel, with stubby masts and a single short funnel, sailed slowly through the lines of yachts assembled off Cowes for the annual regatta. On the bridge of *Discovery* was Commander Robert Falcon Scott, RN. Ahead lay a 14,000-mile cruise to New Zealand, followed by twenty-six months in the white solitude of the furthest South.

'I may as well confess that I had no predilection for polar exploration,' Scott was to write a few years later. Until the previous year he had been serving as torpedo officer aboard the flagship of the Channel Squadron, a good appointment with every prospect of rapid promotion, for it was an advantage to have a specialist's understanding of the navy's newest and deadliest weapon. But Scott was fired with an ambition quite distinct from the normal dream of flying an admiral's flag before one's fiftieth birthday. A naval officer's life proved for him a severe financial strain: no private income or parental allowances helped him through his first years in the wardroom; and he knew that at times his mother and sisters were virtually penniless, for his father had lost all his savings some three years before his death in 1897. Scott became a recluse from necessity: he could not buy his brother officers a round of drinks; and he certainly could not contemplate marriage. He looked for an outlet for his abilities which would enable him to make his name and free him from the embarrassment of threadbare life in a smart flagship. Long ago his seamanship had been admired by Sir Clements Markham, the President of the Royal Geographical Society, and a fanatical advocate of Antarctic exploration. A chance meeting with Sir Clements in Buckingham Palace Road in June 1899 gave Scott the opportunity for which he was seeking. Markham told him that he was hoping to fit out an Antarctic expedition. 'Two days later I wrote applying to command it,' Scott confessed later. He was just thirty-one at the time.

Funds for the proposed expedition came only slowly. African exploration brought the profits and prestige of Empire, but government ministers could see little material benefit coming from the Great Ice Barrier. Royal and princely patrons gave a lead which the government followed with some reluctance. Scott, however, was easily fired by Markham's enthusiasm. If Sir Clements wished the Southern polar regions methodically explored by a British expedition, then Scott was prepared to master the techniques of Polar study as he had mastered the novelty of torpedo warfare. During the twelve months before the expedition sailed, Scott set himself to acquire new skills, learning how to travel by sledge and how to meet the challenge of marathon journeys by ski. Yet when *Discovery* reached the frozen South and found an ice-anchorage in McMurdo Sound, Scott was still aware of being the pupil of Nature's elements. For an officer born and brought up near Plymouth Sound, it was a strange world. Even familar tasks of seamanship were changed beyond recognition: the cruise of ironclads across the Bay and into the Mediterranean had none of the problems faced by *Discovery* as she sailed slowly between the icebergs into a sea where the difference between the magnetic pole and the geographical pole made the compass a topsy-turvy instrument of navigation. Each man aboard *Discovery* – and there were forty of them in all – needed to show the heroic fortitude of a pioneer. Command of the expedition called for greater qualities still: the inspirational lead of a romantic visionary who could exalt his men beyond the common run of human feelings while himself remaining soberly constrained by the logic of the possible. Commander 'Con' Scott was endowed with just such a rare duality of temperament.

The *Discovery* expedition of 1901–4 achieved more than any previous scientific survey of the South. Scott and his men discovered a large tract of land (the peninsula named after King Edward VII); they proved that the Great Ice Barrier was a floating and frozen shelf, not a continent; they confirmed that the geographical pole lay on a glacial plateau approached through a mountain range higher above sea level than the French Jura; and they assembled detailed information of great value to geologists and ornithologists. These facts, prosaic though they looked on paper, were established in the face of constant hazards. In all, the expedition made twenty-eight journeys by sledge and, although only one life was lost while Scott and his men were in the polar

Captain Scott aboard *Discovery*, then frozen in McMurdo Sound during his 1901–04 Antarctic expedition.

regions, they had to battle endlessly against snow-blindness, hunger, scurvy, and the danger of falling headlong into ice crevasses. It was never intended that the expedition should make a sustained thrust to reach the South Pole, but Scott himself with two companions (Shackleton and Wilson) penetrated 300 miles farther into Antarctica than man had yet reached – and still the Pole lay nearly 500 miles beyond them.

The dynamic force of Scott's character, which ensured success for the expedition, also made him personal enemies at home. Hence, although the public was thrilled by Scott's feat, he was cold-shouldered by the government and, surprisingly, his name was not submitted to the sovereign for a knighthood. He went back to sea in August 1906, with the rank of captain, and was given command of a battleship. In exercises off Portugal six months later his ship, HMS *Albemarle*, was in collision with another vessel. Although Scott was cleared of all blame, worry over the episode intensified his determination to return, as soon as possible, to the polar regions. Meanwhile he remained with the Atlantic Fleet until March 1909, when he accepted a high appointment at the Admiralty, which kept him in London for the following nine months.

Polar exploration again attracted public notice in the newspapers that year. In March it was announced that an expedition headed by Scott's former companion, Shackleton, had come within 100 miles of the South Pole; and a month later the American, Robert Edwin Peary, claimed that he had reached the North Pole. On 13 September 1909 Captain Scott – by now a married man and about to become a father – launched a public appeal for £40,000 for an expedition, the main object of which was 'to reach the South Pole and secure for the British Empire the honour of that achievement'. The response was slow, but in January 1910 the government announced it would contribute £20,000 for what was now called the National Antarctic Expedition. Scott was able to purchase the former whaling vessel, *Terra Nova*, which had come to the assistance of the earlier expedition as a relief ship: *Discovery* had been sold to the Hudson's Bay Company and was not available.

The *Terra Nova* sailed from Port Chalmers in South Island, New Zealand, on 29 November 1910. Within three days a severe storm almost wrecked the ship and 65 gallons of petrol intended for the new motor-sledges went overboard. At the time it seemed an ominous development: great hopes had been placed on motor transport. Yet one sledge was lost when it fell through the ice on landing in McMurdo Sound, and the other two sledges broke down completely after covering less than 80 miles of

the frozen Antarctic. Ultimately the success or failure of the expedition depended, as had its predecessors, on dogs and ponies (Siberian animals, in both cases) and above all on human endurance and willpower.

Despite the emphasis which Scott had made publicly on the honour of 'reaching the South Pole', the expedition was fundamentally a scientific project. Its members were constantly engaged in practical research, collecting samples of fossils, studying birds and penguins, examining rocks, probing the secrets of the silent South, as in the *Discovery* expedition nine years before. Yet the challenge of the South Pole loomed larger and larger in their commander's thoughts. From McMurdo Sound to the Pole and back was over 1,500 miles, a journey as long as a return trip from Calais to Genoa or from San Francisco to Salt Lake City. It could be made only in the summer months, November to mid-April; and there was now a need to make the journey speedily. Unexpectedly a Norwegian expedition, under Roald Amundsen, had anchored in the ice of the Bay of Whales, 60 miles nearer the Pole than McMurdo Sound; and Scott learned that the Norwegians had plenty of dog-teams better trained to pull sledges than his own Siberian dogs, and in better physical shape. He resolved to set out from Cape Evans in McMurdo Sound on 1 November 1911 with nine men, each leading a pony, and with six other men following the main party with dogs and man-hauled sledges. Every mile across the windswept and icy plain had to be made on foot and, though it was summer, the snow continued to fall as they moved southwards towards the 100-mile-long Beardmore Glacier and their ascent of the polar plateau. Five days were lost in a blizzard and it was necessary to shoot the ponies, storing their carcasses for meat on the return journey. At last, 170 miles short of the Pole, Scott selected four companions who would continue alone with him, sending the rest of the party back to base. On 3 January 1912 Captain Scott, Edward Wilson (a Cambridge zoologist), Captain Oates of the Inniskilling

The *Terra Nova*, a former whaling ship purchased by Scott for his second polar expedition, anchored near Cape Evans.

Dragoons, Lieutenant Bowers of the Royal Indian Marine and Petty Officer Edgar Evans set out on the decisive march, with enough food for a month.

They hoped to reach the Pole in eleven days. But it was bitterly cold for midsummer and they were tiring rapidly. Another blizzard left the snow soft and for a week there was no sun. At last, on 16 January, they had a good and fine day; but that afternoon they saw, ahead across the snow plain, a Norwegian flag and the marks of a camp. Amundsen had forestalled them by a month. It was a bitter blow for their hopes; and, as a force five gale swept down on them, Scott wrote in his diary, 'Great God! This is an awful place.' The Union Jack was planted in the snow beside Amundsen's flag and, after three nights near

the Pole, Scott and his four companions started the homeward journey which they were never to complete.

The tragic chronicle of Scott's last weeks of life may be read in his own diary and in the journals kept by Wilson (until 27 February) and by Bowers for a brief seven days. The temperature dropped and they were soon suffering from severe frostbite. Evans, a heavy man, had a bad fall in a crevasse on 3 February. His health rapidly deteriorated and the rest of the party were held back by concern for their sick comrade. In the small hours of 18 February he died, almost at the foot of the long glacier. Thereafter conditions should have improved, but the cold became more intense and it was impossible to pull sledges more than six miles on any day. Captain Oates, his frostbitten feet turning

Captain Scott writing his diary in the hut at Cape Evans, 1912.

gangrenous, could go no farther: walking out into the snow, he sought death in the hope of saving his companions. 'Though we tried to dissuade him, we knew it was the act of a brave man and an English gentleman,' wrote Scott in his journal.

It was almost the end. Although within eleven miles of supplies at 'One Ton Depot', the survivors were halted by a fresh blizzard. They had covered 600 miles since leaving the Pole, but they were still 150 miles short of McMurdo Sound and too weak to march farther. Meticulously, as they awaited death, they completed official letters and set out beside their tent the third of a hundredweight of geological specimens they had dragged back with them over the snows. For at least ten days the blizzard howled around the tent before death claimed them, Scott outliving his two companions by some hours. Seven and a half months later a search party from *Terra Nova* found their bodies, and set up a snow cairn where they had died.

Captain Scott's fate was not known in London until the third week of February 1913. The honours denied him in life were readily forth-

coming for a man who had struggled so heroically to the Pole. Technically he had failed, but morally he had triumphed. He became the last hero of the long years of European peace, an exemplar for a generation soon to find, nearer at home, challenges to mind and spirit as torment-ing as those Scott had suffered in the solitude of Antarctica.

Scott's disappointed party at the South Pole, (left to right) Oates, Bowers, Scott, Wilson and Evans.

~ *Edith Cavell* ~

Among the thousands of English women thrilled and saddened by Scott's abortive expedition was the forty-seven-year-old matron of the first teaching hospital set up in Brussels, Edith Cavell. Like Scott, she had grown to maturity under the

blossom of Victorian imperialism, when the British public shared vicariously the deeds of bronzed heroes east or south of Suez and serenely ignored those heavily-armed nations competing for mere mastery within Europe. Not that Edith

For the time being, however, she was content to mould the characters of young children, first in Essex and Norfolk, and from 1890 onwards as governess in the family of a Brussels lawyer. Nearly half a century previously another clergyman's daughter, Charlotte Brontë, had taught in the Belgian capital, and by a coincidence Edith later found herself working with the son of the unscrupulous headmistress portrayed by Charlotte Brontë in *Villette*, but otherwise their experiences had little in common. In sixty years as a capital city Brussels had spread outwards, acquiring the dignity of boulevards, in one of which Edith found her home. She liked Brussels, its people and its public places, and she enjoyed riding out with the children in her charge through woodland to the rolling pastureland around the battlefield of Waterloo. Once she painted the famous farmhouse of Hougoumont in water colours; so, no doubt, had other daughters of Victorian gentlefolk gifted with brush and palette. Edith Cavell was an archetypal respectable middle-class spinster, temporarily resident abroad.

In the summer of 1895 she returned to Norfolk, for her father's health was failing. The following December, around her thirtieth birthday, she decided to train as a nurse. There followed twelve years of practise in English hospitals: a long spell at the London Hospital; the award of a commemorative silver medal for 'loving services' to the people of Maidstone in the typhoid epidemic of 1897; and routine work in the wards of infirmaries at St Pancras, Shoreditch and Manchester. Yet she had developed an affection for Belgium and, in September 1907, she was glad to have the chance of returning to Brussels with responsibility for turning a private nursing home (*clinique*) in the suburb of Ixelles into a teaching hospital. For the next seven years this task absorbed her energies, winning her widespread professional recognition. She was invited to address the International Congress of Nurses in London, and told them of her plans for expansion in the centre of the Belgian capital and

Edith Cavell.

herself ever despised 'abroad'. She was born the second daughter of the vicar of Swardeston, a village four miles outside Norwich, and she passed her early years in East Anglia; but on inheriting a small legacy, when she was twenty-two, she immediately spent it travelling through the Rhineland, Austria and southern Germany. So attracted was she by the people of Bavaria that she gave a sum of money to purchase medical equipment for a new 'Free Hospital' there. It is curious that this earliest sign of her vocation manifested itself in the Kaiser's Germany.

Edith Cavell and her student nurses in Brussels.

in the suburbs. Each summer she returned for a holiday to Norfolk and she was there, beside the sea at West Runton, when Germany's mobilization on 1 August 1914 brought war to western Europe. Two days later she was back on duty in Brussels. German troops crossed the frontier next morning and at midnight that same Tuesday (4 August) Edith Cavell's homeland came to the aid of 'brave little Belgium' in resisting the invader.

As yet there was no indication in Edith's single-minded devotion to nursing that she possessed special qualities of heroism. Her sense of Christian service had prompted her to hurry back to Belgium; it now induced her to stay with her nurses when German troops marched into Brussels on 20 August. If there are hints in her letters of inner fears, they were mastered by rigid self-control. So it had been with the nurses who accompanied Florence Nightingale to Scutari;

and so it was, too, with the other English nurses in Brussels, none of whom wished to escape from the doomed city as the Germans drew nearer and nearer. They had proud traditions of their own to maintain and were prepared to tend German wounded as well as any allied soldiers taken prisoner. There was work for them also among the refugees. The Germans inspected the hospital but imposed no greater restraint on its nurses than on the general public of the occupied city.

On 1 November 1914 two British veterans of the fighting around Mons, seriously wounded and disguised in civilian clothes, arrived at the hospital in Ixelles and sought the matron's assistance. As a matter of course she took them in, dressed their wounds, allowed them to recuperate, and eventually sent them by secret couriers to the frontier of neutral Holland. By the end of the year the two men were back in England. From now on, for more than eight months, 'Nurse Cavell' – as everyone was soon to call her – helped a succession of British, French and Belgian soldiers escape into Holland so that they could, in due course, resume their fight against the enemy. At times there were as many as eighteen allied soldiers hidden in the buildings of the hospital, and several hundred were able to follow the secret escape route worked out by the Belgian resistance and by Edith Cavell herself. From Brussels they were escorted to Harcourt and then on to Turnhout and through marshes across the frontier to sanctuary in a Dutch town, Breda or Tilburg or Eindhoven. Some fugitives were able to supply British intelligence with valuable information, notably about the Zeppelins based on the airfield at Evere, a mere nine miles north of the Ixelles hospital. Although Edith Cavell was not herself in any sense a spy, the men whom she helped, and the members of the Resistance, were determined to ensure that London knew as much as they could learn of German intentions. For the first half of the year 1915, the hospital she had built up in Brussels

was the most important staging-post on the underground escape route.

'We are bound to be caught one of these days,' she remarked with resignation to one of her English ward sisters, Elizabeth Wilkins. The escape movement was loosely knit, stretched over a wide area and easily penetrable by German agents. Moreover security in and around the hospital itself was strangely lax, and Nurse Cavell fell under suspicion long before the German authorities arrested her. In July 1915 it became clear that the secret police were closing in; on the last day of the month some of her closest associates in the Belgian Resistance were taken into custody. Stoically she prepared for the worst. On 5 August the hospital buildings were raided and Edith Cavell and Elizabeth Wilkins driven away to the Brussels Kommandantur. Sister Wilkins was soon released; but not Nurse Cavell. She was treated courteously but received the impression that others in the underground movement had already implicated her. Quite freely she admitted having assisted fugitives on their way to the frontier. After two days at the Kommandantur she was sent to St Gilles and housed in the grim and overcrowded thirty-year-old prison.

Nurse Cavell spent ten weeks in St Gilles

German troops enter Brussels, August 1914. An English witness commented on the quality of their equipment.

awaiting trial. She remained eminently composed in character, reading again and again her copy of Thomas à Kempis's *The Imitation of Christ* and marking many passages which seemed to her of particular significance in these weeks of strain. To her gaolers she seemed fearless and cheerful, and she came to regard her enforced inactivity as an opportunity for spiritual retreat. There was a crucifix on the wall of her cell and she spent many hours in prayer and meditation. Occasionally she sent eminently practical and precise notes of advice to the Sisters still running her hospital. No despair entered her correspondence, or her conversation with those who were permitted to visit her.

Thirty-four other members of the underground escape movement were charged along with Nurse Cavell. She was the only person of English nationality: three were French, the remainder Belgian; and thirteen in all were women. The trial, a court martial before five German officers, was held in the Belgian parliament buildings on 7–8 October 1915. Edith Cavell was interrogated for a mere five minutes: she admitted having sent to the frontier 'about 200' English, French and Belgians of military age; but she claimed that she was merely assisting wounded men who had asked for help to reach the border – 'Once across the frontier, they were free,' she said. On the second day of the court martial, the prosecutor demanded the death penalty for nine of the accused, including Nurse Cavell. It is probable that, until this moment, she had expected a term of hard labour in a German prison, not knowing that in the German Military Code 'conducting soldiers to the enemy' was a capital offence. The accused had to wait three more days before learning their fate. Then, at a quarter past four in the afternoon of Monday, 11 October, Edith Cavell learnt that she was to be shot, with four others among the accused. Even at this terrible news, she maintained the statuesque calm she had shown throughout her ordeal.

That night, neutral diplomats still in Brussels made strenuous efforts to save her. The Spanish ambassador, the Marquis de Villalobar, even asked the Military Governor of Brussels to telephone directly to the Kaiser, who was at his headquarters at Charleville, some ninety miles away. But the Governor maintained that there was no reason to refer a court-martial verdict of this kind to the All Highest War Lord, adding that he himself had no power to remit a sentence made under military law. Neither the Kaiser nor anyone at his headquarters knew of the court-martial of Nurse Cavell until five days after her execution.

She refused to plead for mercy, saying that she was convinced the German authorities wished to kill her because of their hatred of England. Her last hours at St Gilles were spent in writing farewell letters and in religious observance. An English chaplain, the Reverend Stirling Gahan, administered the sacrament of Holy Communion in her prison cell. To him she gave a final message for the outside world: 'Standing as I do in view of God and Eternity, I realise that patriotism is not enough. I must have no hatred or bitterness towards anyone.' Next morning – 12 October 1915 – she was driven to the principal rifle range, the Tir National, and executed by firing squad. Philippe Baucq, a Belgian architect who had been one of the chief organizers of the escape route, died beside her. The three other death sentences were never carried out.

The London newspapers broke the news of Nurse Cavell's fate on Monday, 18 October, almost a week after her execution. Her death was seen as an act of glorious martyrdom: 'Judicial murder,' howled the British press; 'another outrage committed by the crowned criminal in Berlin'. Thursday of that week was Trafalgar Day, when the nation traditionally remembered an earlier brave offspring from a Norfolk vicarage, and in the pulpit of the church beside Nelson's column, the Bishop of London declared: 'The cold-blooded murder of Miss Cavell, a poor English girl deliberately shot by the Germans for housing refugees, will run the

May 1919: crowds line the streets as the coffin carrying Edith Cavell's remains leaves Westminster Abbey.

faithfully caught the mood of the country. More than a century previously the cynical Talleyrand had condemned Napoleon's execution of the Duc d'Enghien as 'worse than a crime – a mistake'; so heartless a verdict on Germany's shooting of Nurse Cavell was, of course, unthinkable in 1915, but it would have been apt, none the less. Her most recent biographer, Rowland Ryder, calculated from War Office records that 'the propaganda drive following Edith Cavell's death brought in about 40,000 extra recruits to the army alone'. In 1919, after a burial service in Westminster Abbey, her remains were reverently re-interred outside the south transept of Norwich Cathedral. Four years later a statue to her – the first to any 'Great War' hero in London – was unveiled in St Martin's Place. Gradually people began to ponder her final message: no hatred, no bitterness; and, as an afterthought, the Labour Government of 1924 added to the plinth of her memorial the four words of her great injunction, 'Patriotism is not enough'.

sinking of the *Lusitania* close in the civilized world as the greatest crime in history.' Edith Cavell, executed eight weeks short of her fiftieth birthday, was hardly a 'girl', nor was her offence the housing of refugees, but the bishop's words

~ *Rosa Luxemburg* ~

Today the town of Zamość lies in south-eastern Poland, not far from the Soviet frontier, in an agricultural region remote from all the excitement of Warsaw. In the last century the town was within Tsarist Russia, a trading centre whose inhabitants spoke Polish and were proud of their Polish heritage. More than a third of the population was Jewish, among them a family of timber merchants, originally called Luxemburg but now accepting Luxemburg as a more familiar spelling. In March 1871 Line Luxemburg, wife of the head of the family, gave birth to her fifth child and named her Rosa. Husband and wife

were not popular with the leaders of the Jewish community: the Luxemburgs felt no reverence for the Synagogue; and, though they read their Pentateuch, they treated all religious writings as a form of literature, which they enjoyed along with the German and Polish classical authors. This enlightened view made life difficult for Rosa's three elder brothers and her sister, Anna; and in the winter of 1873–74 the Luxemburgs were glad to move from Zamość to Warsaw, where they could find other intellectuals who thought little of established religion.

Here, in Warsaw, Rosa spent a materially

Rosa Luxemburg, photographed in 1912, aged forty-one.

joined the rump of the Revolutionary Proletarian Party to which the executed men had belonged; and in her last year at school she was an active agitator among students at Warsaw University. With her tidy hair, trim dresses and vivacious manner she did not look a revolutionary, as she made her way home to the family apartment in a fashionable district of the city. Police spies thought her too young to take seriously, but the family sensed that arrest was close. Shortly after her eighteenth birthday Rosa was safely smuggled across the frontier, hidden beneath the straw of a peasant's cart. Since Russia alone demanded a passport in 1889, it was easy for her to travel farther in Europe. She settled in Switzerland, enrolled at the University of Zurich, and for eight years studied philosophy and law, gaining a doctorate for a thesis on the industrial development of Poland. Life was pleasant in Zurich, where her apartment windows faced the distant lake and a vista of mountains; and in a community of émigré Poles and Russians she also maintained her intense interest in politics.

In 1890 Rosa fell in love with Leo Jogiches, a Jew of twenty-three with years of conspiratorial experience in his native Vilna. Her attachment to Jogiches intensified her Marxism, for he was one of the earliest active Marxists in their homeland. Both, however, sought a unified and socialist Poland in place of the downtrodden nation partitioned between the Russian, German and Austro-Hungarian empires. The key to the future lay, they believed, in Germany, the most highly industrialized of these three powers, and Rosa decided to settle in Berlin and co-ordinate Polish and German socialist activity. Permanent residence in Germany was, however, permitted only to German nationals. To secure this right Rosa married an indolent German émigré, who agreed to leave her on the steps of Basle registry office after the ceremony, on 19 April 1898. A month later Rosa found apartments in Berlin. Although she frequently travelled abroad, the city was to be her home for the rest of her life.

Imperial Germany was the most militaristic

comfortable childhood. Physically she was weakened by a bone disease in the hip, which left her undersized and with a permanent limp. She was precocious; even before going to High School she could write verses which were astringent in tone, not sentimental as with so many gifted children from plush homes. Yet at High School she suffered from three disadvantages: she was too clever for the self-esteem of her teachers; she was not a Russian; and she was of Jewish race. The gold medal for academic attainment, which was hers by right, was withheld, on political grounds. Soon she was intellectually and emotionally a rebel against the system, even though her family remained politically conformist. The execution of four Polish socialists in Warsaw in 1886 – the first hangings for over twenty years in Russian Poland – deeply stirred the adolescent girl. Secretly she society of modern Europe: it needed courage for a young woman to denounce the trappings of imperialism at public meetings in city parks. And she was at heart a very feminine revolutionary, who missed Jogiches and regretted that her formal marriage could not be annulled before 1903. He sent her, as a twenty-eighth birthday present, an edition of the works of the German economist, Rodbertus, and she in reply sent a touching letter in which she dreamt of 'our own little room, our own furniture, a library of our own, quiet and regular work ... perhaps even a little, a very little baby. ... Will this never be permitted?' she asked pathetically. A year later Jogiches joined her in Berlin; neither of their temperaments were suited to domestic felicity, and their relationship was frequently stormy.

In Berlin Rosa became less interested in Polish questions and increasingly convinced that capitalism was spiralling down to disintegration. Rosa's pamphlets made her a European figure: at meetings of the Second International her independence of mind and lack of respect for established reputations were matched by a Jewish sense of humour and a warm sensibility not readily discernible in the earnest theorists of other delegations. Lenin was impressed by her powers of analysis when she met him in Finland in 1906; so, too, was the virtually unknown Stalin on the only occasion on which he heard her speak – improbably, at a nonconformist tabernacle in London's Whitechapel district, where the Russian Social Democrats were holding their fifth congress (May 1907). Gradually, however, she was developing political and economic theses of her own: on the value of a general strike as a revolutionary weapon; on the decline of purchasing power in capitalist societies; on the wrongheadedness of Marx over the national question; and on the folly of imposing a dictatorship of the

Rosa Luxemburg speaks to a rally in Stuttgart in 1907.

proletariat. Quixotically she attacked the great French parliamentarian, Jaurès, while deviating doctrinally from Lenin, at the other end of the socialist spectrum. She was imprisoned for six weeks in Berlin in 1906 for having insulted the Kaiser by suggesting, in a speech, that he knew nothing of the real life of a German worker. The German authorities found 'Red Rosa' co-operative and placid in prison; and minimized her danger.

From 1911 onwards Rosa Luxemburg began to campaign against the threatened call to serve Germany in a European war. 'If they think we are going to lift the weapons of murder against our French brethren, or others, then we shall shout, "We will not do it",' she declared in a speech at Frankfurt-am-Main on 16 September 1913. For this call to disobedience she was prosecuted in February 1914, making a speech at the end of her trial which magnificently ridiculed militarism, as expecting 'commands from above and blind obedience below'. The speech publicized her beliefs throughout Germany, and much of Europe, too. She was sentenced to a year's imprisonment but appeal procedure left her free until February 1915. Hence when war began in August 1914 and the majority of German socialists pledged their support to the Kaiser's government, Rosa was still free to denounce what she stigmatized as the treason of the social democrats. In this she was vigorously supported by some half a dozen prominent radical socialists, headed by the Reichstag deputy Karl Liebknecht and the distinguished elderly historian Franz Mehring. All three signed an open letter announcing their opposition to the war on 4 September 1914, and Liebknecht voted against further war credits in the Reichstag. By the spring of 1915 these dissidents, calling themselves the 'International Group', had become a headache to the security police, although Rosa herself was in prison when her revolutionary periodical *Die Internationale* appeared on the streets in April 1915. All copies were soon seized but the Group then began to publish a series of

letters, smuggled out of prison, and named after Spartacus, leader of the slave revolt against Rome in 73 BC. These Spartacus Letters, at first roneo-copied and from September 1916 secretly printed by Jogiches, provided German left-wing radicals with a revolutionary programme: a mass rising of workers and soldiers to overthrow the imperialist government, end the war, and set up a decentralized socialist system. Apart from five months of freedom in 1916, Rosa spent the rest of the war in prison, on the outskirts of Berlin, at Poznan or in Breslau. Yet somehow she continued to send epistles to the faithful, often using a primitive invisible ink on the pages of innocent-looking volumes of poetry. Her ingenuity and courage were remarkable: she may not have won the mass following which her theory of revolution demanded; but the verve and style of her pamphleteering made her an idol of the intellectual Left, both then and later. It is extraordinary that the German authorities allowed so intransigent an enemy to survive and flourish in their jails.

Rosa learnt of the Bolshevik revolution in 1917 while in the town prison at Breslau, and while physically weak from the poverty of a criminal's wartime diet. At first she welcomed Lenin's success, but by January 1918 she had become highly critical: she deplored the decision of the Soviets to sign a peace treaty with Imperial Germany; and she wrote that Lenin was 'completely mistaken' to rule by terror and deny freedom of the press and of public assembly. This was not her ideal of communism. Yet when in November 1918 the moderate German socialists participated in the revolution which forced the Kaiser into exile and established a German Republic, she was no less critical of their preoccupation with 'bourgeois parliament-arianism' and the summoning of a constituent assembly rather than Workers' and Soldiers' Councils.

She was released from Breslau Prison on 9 November 1918, and was back in Berlin by nightfall. On 11 November (Armistice Day in the

West) the members of the 'International Group' formally adopted the name 'Spartacus' and pledged themselves to put pressure on the other socialist groups and work for a specifically German form of communism. Conflicts soon developed between the Spartacists and the republican authorities, while from Moscow Lenin sent a top-level Bolshevik to cast an experienced eye on the activities of comrades Liebknecht and Luxemburg. Rosa was convinced that it would be a mistake to attempt a left-wing seizure of power in Berlin, similar to Lenin's 'October Days' in Petrograd. She had always argued in favour of a mass rising of workers throughout Germany; and she did not believe that the time for this upheaval had yet come. On 29–30 December the Spartacists held a Congress which accepted Rosa's reasoning, but – largely as a gesture – proclaimed the establishment of a German Communist Party. Yet the situation was really beyond control of any loosely-knit organization. On 4 January 1919 the government dismissed the chief of Berlin's police force, who was sympathetic to the Spartacists. Radical socialists and communists called for a mass demonstration: 700,000 workers turned out

A Spartacist march in Berlin, 7 January 1919.

in the Berlin streets on 5 January, a Sunday; and it was rumoured that the garrison was about to mutiny. The Spartacists were swept along on a tide of revolutionary fervour. There was a week of strikes and demonstrations. Since the Government was uncertain of the regular army it summoned volunteer 'Free Corps', nationalist brigades of veterans led by officers who felt their old regiments betrayed by agitators of the Left. Three thousand Free Corps men made an ostentatious entry into Berlin on Saturday, 11 January; and one fanatically right-wing unit, the 'Cavalry Guard Sharpshooters Division', set up its headquarters in the fashionable Eden Hotel, facing the zoological gardens.

Rosa Luxemburg and Karl Liebknecht, unable to calm the mob or to direct its energies constructively, were forced into hiding, first in working-class Neukolin and from Tuesday, 14 January, in respectable bourgeois Wilmersdorf. Their block of flats was little more than a mile from the Eden Hotel. On Wednesday evening they were visited by a veteran Spartacist, Wilhelm Pieck, travelling with forged papers under an assumed name. His arrival was followed by the entry of a detachment of sharpshooters, who arrested Rosa, Liebknecht and Pieck, leading them to the Eden. There Rosa was roughly handled and told she would be taken to the Moabit Prison. As she emerged through a side door a sharpshooter clubbed her with his rifle butt. Half-dead she was bustled into a car and shot by one of the officers. Her body was thrown in the Landwehr Canal, remaining undiscovered until washed against a lock gate twenty weeks later. Liebknecht suffered a similar fate, though his executioners left his body at a mortuary. Pieck talked himself out of the Eden: he re-appeared in Berlin in 1945; and for the last eleven years of his life he was East Germany's Head of State.

Few people remember President Pieck. Rosa Luxemburg, however, has achieved a martyr's immortality of name. She was venerated by party men whom she had inwardly despised and claimed by disillusioned idealists as a lost, unheeded prophet. Artists and poets of protest have found her an inspiration in the East and the West. Yet, as with most saints, it is hard to recognise the figure beneath the halo. For Rosa Luxemburg, indomitable heroine though she became, was always a mightily propellent individualist and never a doctrinaire sycophant. 'Now tell me,' asks Shaw's St Joan, 'shall I rise from the dead and come back to you a living woman?' Aghast, Bishop Cauchon replies, 'The heretic is always better dead.' There are Cauchons around Rosa's shrine in the Friedrichfelde Cemetery of East Berlin.

Rosa Luxemburg's funeral procession, June 1919.

~ *Charles Lindbergh* ~

When in April 1917 President Woodrow Wilson asked the United States Congress for support in declaring war on Germany, only 50 of the 423 members of the House of Representatives declined to back him. Prominent among them was an outspoken Republican pacifist in his late fifties who for the previous ten years had represented a district in Minnesota: Charles Augustus Lindbergh, Senior, was too independently minded to allow his principles to be swayed by the emotive oratory of a Democratic president. The vote cost him his political career; it also made life hard for his schoolboy son, Charles Augustus Lindbergh, Junior. With patriotic sentiment erupting in flag-waving parades and banner-carrying marches, a fifteen-year-old whose father was 'anti-war' could not be sure of

that easy popularity which adolescence craved and his own good looks readily merited. To have a German-sounding name did not help, either – even if you were of impeccably Scandinavian descent. Lindbergh, Junior, the shy and diffident son of elderly parents, retreated into a defensive isolation of spirit: he enjoyed ornithology, he was good at mathematics, and his long, thin fingers might have made him a pianist had they not worked so deftly and confidently with machines. He was not unhappy, so long as he could watch the flight of birds and tinker with engines.

His father died in 1924 and Lindbergh returned, with his mother, to Detroit, where he had been born. By now, small private air lines were coming into being and he decided to leave Detroit for a flying school at Lincoln, Nebraska.

Charles Lindbergh.

The final stimulus for Lindbergh's dream of emulating or surpassing Alcock and Brown came from the French. Since the summer of 1777, when the Marquis de Lafayette's volunteers had arrived to fight for the Americans in their war of independence, Lafayette's name had continued to symbolize Franco-American friendship: a 'Lafayette Squadron' of American volunteers was raised to fight with the French Flying Corps on the Western Front in 1916, while the United States was still a non-belligerent. To a French hotel proprietor it therefore seemed appropriate that the 150th anniversary of the Marquis's arrival in America should be commemorated by a prize of 25,000 dollars which would go to the first flier, or crew of fliers, to cross directly from New York to Paris. It is one of the gentler ironies of history that the son of the consistently non-belligerent Congressman Lindbergh should early have emerged as principal contender for the Lafayette prize.

Two other pilots were excited by the challenge, but neither possessed Lindbergh's devotion to meticulous planning. In an era when flying was a craze, he showed a professional attention to detail which marked him off from the stunt fliers of the air circuses. Lindbergh himself said that the personal prestige of being 'first to Paris' mattered less to him than the potential effect of such a flight on the American public. He was convinced that a sensational feat would make Americans, individually and in corporate bodies, aviation-minded: the new aeroplane industry could be built up; and municipal and federal funds would help turn primitive flying-grounds into airports for all the commerce of the skies. This missionary objective appealed to the business instinct of the Ryan Airlines Company, who backed his proposal to construct an aeroplane capable of crossing the Atlantic. But Lindbergh personally supervised every detail of work on the high-wing monoplane, *Spirit of St Louis*: nothing was left to chance, or to anybody else. His navigational scheme, his estimate of petrol consumption, his interpretation of me-

The skill came easily to him; and so, too, did the maintenance of engines and basic cross-country navigation. In 1925 he joined a struggling air line based on St Louis, Missouri. That year Congress authorized the transfer of airmail from government-operated aeroplanes to private air lines who initially would receive federal subsidies to build up their services once the contracts for airmail had been concluded. It was as an airmail pilot, operating mainly over the Midwest with occasional trips to Mexico or Canada, that Lindbergh discovered how best to meet the challenge of flight. Once, as he emerged triumphant from the buffetings of a thunder-storm, he began to wonder if he might not pit his skills against the winds and air-currents of the great ocean. Alcock and Brown, two officers in the Royal Air Force, had made the first Atlantic crossing, from Newfoundland to Ireland, in a Vickers Vimy bomber in 16½ hours on 14 June 1919: but since then no one had bridged the Atlantic in an aeroplane.

teorological reports, his chain-and-container toilet arrangements – all were his own. He was pilot, engineer, navigator and inventor, as much a solo performer as the pioneers who had thrust westwards his country's great frontier. Should he disappear, as he flew alone over the Atlantic, the failure would be his own, too.

Onlookers who had come out to Roosevelt Field, Long Island, on that wet May morning in 1927 were inclined to place heavy odds against Lindbergh. The *Spirit of St Louis* looked smaller than any other plane on the muddy runway: it was twenty-eight feet long, had an instrument panel less complicated than that of a family car, lacked wireless and, for that matter, even a sextant. Navigation depended on the stars, on compass readings and on the pilot's intuitive sense of direction. Whether it depended, too, on the pilot's eyesight was doubtful, for extra petrol tanks were fitted ahead of his cockpit, partly to balance the aircraft and partly because there was nowhere else for them to go; but the effect of the extra tanks was to prevent him seeing clearly ahead. Small wonder if, as Lindbergh took off, it seemed a miracle that he avoided the telephone wires around the airfield. But the *Spirit of St Louis* was safely airborne: field-glasses followed the plane as it turned north-eastwards and disappeared, a greyish-white speck, hardly distinguishable from the mist and murk above the Sound. Perhaps someone might spot 'Lucky Lindy' from Cape Cod or Nova Scotia, or hear the plane as it crossed the Avalon peninsula on Newfoundland; but, after that, there would be no news for many hours as the *Spirit of St Louis* swept in a rhumb-line arc through a night and a day of Atlantic cloud and rain. It is said that, as night fell, thousands of baseball spectators at a New York stadium stood in prayer for the young

Lindbergh receives congratulations in Paris after his record flight.

airman alone above 3,000 miles of ocean.

Black waves were pounding empty beaches as Lindbergh's plane flew into a second dusk above Britanny. It was the evening of Saturday, 21 May 1927, and the Paris airfield at Le Bourget was not equipped for night flights. The army and the *gendarmerie* turned out as thousands of cars headed for the landing ground at the news that the monoplane was over French soil. A double line of car headlights made a flarepath for the hero; and the *Spirit of St Louis* touched down at 10.24 p.m. after $33\frac{1}{2}$ hours in the air. Lindbergh, stiff and numb with cold, was lifted in triumph from the cockpit, and the lone eagle of the Atlantic found himself encaged by 100,000 excited Parisians, most of them French but many American expatriates. Back in the States, newspapers came out in special editions and cheering crowds filled the streets: there had been nothing like it since Armistice Night in 1918.

Lindbergh was fêted in Paris, in Brussels and in London. He was a guest of President Doumergue in the Elysée Palace, of King Albert of the Belgians, and of King George V, who described him in his diary as 'a very nice boy and quite modest'. President Coolidge sent an American warship to bring him back up the Potomac for a reception in Washington. Lindbergh had been commissioned in the Air Corps Reserve in 1925, and Coolidge presented him with a high decoration to honour his flight. It was characteristic of the publicity thrust on Lindbergh that the award of the medal was made three times: once privately in the White House, then on the lawn in front of reporters and cameramen, and yet again on the lawn in case the first filmed version proved imperfect. New York, angry that the President had whisked off its hero to Washington, gave Lindbergh the noisiest and most enthusiastic ticker-tape parade of all time with nearly two million people crowding Broadway to cheer him to and from the City Hall. The *New York Times* that day saluted the hero with sixteen extra pages of 'human interest' gossip and photographs.

Although Lindbergh, a serious young man and naturally reserved, hated the publicity, there was no doubt that his solo flight had caught the imagination of his compatriots. They became, as he had wished, air-minded. But he could never again retreat into privacy. In May 1929 Lindbergh married Anne Morrow, the daughter of an American banker and diplomat. She became his co-pilot in other pioneer flights, doubling up as radio-operator and navigator as well. Together they flew to China, by way of Alaska, in 1931 and from equatorial Africa to Brazil. In March 1932 the publicity which hounded their life brought them tragedy: their baby son was kidnapped; a ransom was paid; but the child was not returned, and was eventually found dead in undergrowth four miles from their home. An emigrant carpenter from New York was arrested more than two years later. His trial dragged on until February 1935, and even then fourteen months of legal appeals intervened before his execution. Throughout these four years the Lindberghs remained front page news, never allowed to forget their sorrow. To escape from the press, they leased a cottage in the Weald of Kent in the spring of 1936; that summer they went to Berlin for the Olympic Games.

Lindbergh was impressed by Nazi Germany. He visited the country again in 1938 and was awed by the displays of German military air power. Hitler wished to give him a high Nazi distinction, making him a 'Knight of the Golden Eagle'. Lindbergh consulted the American ambassador who recommended him to accept the decoration in the interests of Germano-American understanding. But, once back in America, Lindbergh became a vigorous isolationist, opposing Roosevelt's foreign policy as his father had opposed Woodrow Wilson's. The press turned against him. Although technically a colonel in the Air Reserve, he was employed in a purely civilian capacity throughout the war. His advice to the U.S. government on aeronautical matters was of high value: he flew and tested aircraft; and, with his old inventive skill, helped perfect a pump for mechanical hearts. Little fuss was made over these achievements although his judgment was much respected.

In his last years, content to be out of the public eye, Lindbergh became an enthusiastic conservationist, helping the World Wildlife Fund. As millions of Americans responded vicariously to the thrills of space travel, he seemed to survive like a pioneer from an earlier age. When he died, in August 1974, obituaries recalled the courage of his solo flight as though delving into a forgotten past. But worthwhile legends invariably possess a lively resilience, and four years later his name was back in the newspapers. Three American balloonists, making the first non-powered aerial crossing of the Atlantic, drifted in over the Normandy coast and sought to reach Le Bourget in emulation, they said, of Lindbergh's achievement. They fell short of their target by some sixty miles; history is, perhaps, too possessive of its heroes to repeat itself precisely.

~ *Amy Johnson* ~

The success of Lindbergh's flight from New York to Paris stimulated an interest in aviation on both sides of the Atlantic. In Britain races, air pageants, joy-rides – five shillings for a single circuit, ten shillings for a circuit and looping the loop – became familiar features of the weekend's entertainment. In 1928 Hollywood cashed in on the craze: *Wings*, the first film awarded an 'Oscar', featured spectacular (though silent) stunt flying in a tale of Western Front heroism. Among the audience in a London cinema on the last Thursday of April that year was a Yorkshire girl of twenty-four, a graduate of Sheffield University with an honours degree in Latin, French and Economics now working as secretary in a solicitors' office. Eighteen months previously Amy Johnson had duly paid the standard five shillings for a joy-ride near her native Hull, but it was *Wings* that first turned her imagination excitedly skywards. The following Saturday she took a bus to Hendon and on to the Stag Lane aerodrome at Edgware, determined to join the London Aeroplane Club and learn to fly. Two years and one month later newspapers throughout the Empire were hailing her as 'Queen of

'Queen of the Air' Amy Johnson, pictured in the *Illustrated London News* in 1930, only two years after her first flying lesson.

the Air', 'a heroine to match Colonel Lindbergh in courage and in skill'. By then she had achieved lasting fame as the first woman to pilot and navigate an aircraft halfway round the world.

Women were responding to the exciting challenge of flight for more than twenty years before Amy Johnson ever went solo; but, almost without exception, they had possessed both wealth and social status. The first woman in the world to pilot a plane (in 1909) was Louise de Laroche, a French aristocrat. Later Lady Bailey, wife of a rich mine-owner in the Transvaal, the Duchess of Bedford and Lady Heath pioneered, independently of each other, air routes from London to the Cape; while Amelia Earhart, the first woman to fly the Atlantic (as a crew member in 1928, solo in 1932) was married to a wealthy American publisher. By contrast Amy Johnson was the daughter and grand-daughter of Hull businessmen whose trade had prospered, but not to excess, from herring fishing. Her father would lend her money to live in London and later promised her help, 'limit £800', to purchase a plane; but ultimately her career depended on her enterprise, her self-salesmanship and her tenacity of purpose. Much of the adulation heaped on Amy Johnson in the summer of 1930 sprang from a popular belief that she was 'one of us', 'an ordinary girl around the corner'. In reality she was a very extraordinary girl – persistent, possessed by the ruthless energy of a fanatic, outwardly ebullient and at times arrogant, inwardly pent up and uncertain of herself or of her background.

Amy Johnson took her first lesson at Stag Lane aerodrome on 15 September 1928. Ten and a half months later she qualified for an Air Ministry licence to pilot 'flying machines'. This was, in itself, an achievement: she found it hard to master so strange a technique, and she had to overcome much anti-feminist prejudice in men still encouraged by the popular press to look on women of her age as 'flappers'. Throughout these months Amy was fighting her emotions, trying to forget a love affair which had brought fleeting moments of ecstasy over seven years. It is probable that the psychological shock of this faded romance steeled her will to triumph in a man's world, to be accepted as 'Johnnie' rather than as 'Amy' by her new friends at Stag Lane, and to win recognition, not only as a pilot, but as engineer and navigator too. A fortnight before Christmas in 1929 she became the first woman to receive a ground engineer's licence from the Air Ministry; a fortnight after Christmas she was studying meteorology, direction-finding, morse code and all the regulations which governed international flights. That month a London journalist featured her as the girl who 'intended to fly alone to Australia'. This feat had already been accomplished by an Australian test pilot, Bert Hinkler, but no woman had considered such an undertaking; it seemed ludicrous for this youngster from Yorkshire, with under eighty hours solo in her logbook and no single flight longer than a hundred miles, to challenge Hinkler's record of fifteen and a half days from London to Darwin. But Amy Johnson's indefatigable spirit was beginning to win her influential backing: Sir Sefton Brancker, director of civil aviation at the Air Ministry, was impressed by her determination to succeed, and he secured support from Lord Wakefield of Hythe, the Castrol Oil magnate, who agreed to meet the outstanding costs of her venture. At Easter she purchased, for £300, a two-year-old Gipsy Moth biplane which she named *Jason*, a trademark of the family firm in Hull. She was left with a fortnight in which to familiarize herself with the machine for, if she was to avoid the monsoon in the tropics, she needed to start no later than the first weekend in May.

Jason took off from Croydon at a quarter to eight on Monday morning, 5 May 1930. The first lap, about 780 miles, took her by late afternoon to Vienna, where she spent the night. Next day another 800 miles brought her to San Stefano, an airfield beside the Sea of Marmora and within sight of Istanbul. On Wednesday she flew through the Taurus range in Asia Minor: unable

Amy Johnson sets out for Australia from Croydon.

to climb over the mountains, she followed the route of the famous Baghdad Railway along winding gorges and between sheer faces of rock, sometimes wreathed in mist, until she could turn southwards to Aleppo. On Thursday she was caught in a sandstorm and forced to land in the desert until it had blown itself out, and at Baghdad one of *Jason*'s undercarriage struts broke after a fast landing. The strain on the Gipsy Moth was considerable: there was another minor mishap at Bandar Abbas and, as she approached Karachi, the engine began to sound ominously rough. Yet, against all odds, 'Johnnie' reached the Indian sub-continent on Saturday 11

May in a record six days from London, forty-eight hours quicker than Hinkler. But then trouble started: a forced landing at Jhansi on a regimental parade ground damaged a wing and, as she flew along the coast of Burma, she encountered such heavy rain that she was virtually flying blind with no navigational aids apart from a compass. She had to land on a playing field north of Rangoon, ran into a ditch and smashed propeller, undercarriage supports and a section of wing. Within sixty hours, the plane was repaired sufficiently for her to continue the flight to Bangkok; then, on down the long finger of Malaya to Singapore, which she reached fourteen days after leaving Croydon.

By now the changing fortunes of the 'lone girl

flyer' were arousing wide interest in Britain and Australia. She was surprised by the excited warmth of the greeting accorded her in Singapore, not least because she knew she could not now beat Hinkler's record. Ahead of her there still lay 2,400 miles, over the Dutch islands of Indonesia and the shark-infested Java Sea. The approach of monsoon weather led to freakish conditions of wind and rain: at times she was tossed around, momentarily lost, in the cone of a storm. She had to make yet another forced landing on Timor, where she was surrounded by such fierce natives that she drew her revolver out of its holster, fearing they were headhunters in search of an unexpected trophy. But the Portuguese authorities on Timor soon established contact with her and, though the landing strips on the island were mere swathes in the jungle, *Jason* took to the air again for the last 500 miles across the waves. In the afternoon of Saturday 24 May, Amy Johnson finally touched down on Australian soil at Darwin. Crowds greeted her rapturously. Overnight she found herself idolized, thrust from obscurity into prominence. It was a transformation with which she never quite came to grips.

There followed six weeks in Australia, fêted as a public figure. Telegrams poured in from all over the world; messages of congratulation arrived from royalty, from statesmen, from famous entertainers, and from ordinary people whose horizons had been momentarily lifted by the shared excitement of her adventure. From Darwin she flew on to Brisbane but there she crashed badly on landing. Although she was unhurt, *Jason*'s starboard wing was crumpled and Amy Johnson gave up her earlier thought of flying her plane back to England. Six days later came news that she had been awarded the C.B.E. 'for services to aviation' in the King's Birthday Honours List. She returned from Fremantle to Port Said as honoured guest of the P & O steamship line and then she continued by the Imperial Airways flights from Egypt to London by way of Athens, Vienna and Cologne. It was

late on Bank Holiday Monday, 4 August, before she arrived at Croydon; thousands of well-wishers lined the streets of south London to give her a conquering hero's triumph. Already Lord Rothermere's *Daily Mail* was extending to Amy Johnson a generous, if sometimes heavy-handed, protection: she was presented with a cheque for £10,000 and a gold cup which would remain as a symbol of her 'British courage and endurance'. A long tour of England, Wales and southern Scotland was planned for her, with the *Daily Mail* encouraging old and young alike to become air-minded for the sake of Britain. 'Amy, wonderful Amy, How can you blame me for loving you?' ran the popular song hit of the moment. As one of the *Mail*'s rivals informed its readers, it was a pity that she preferred to be called Johnnie.

Amid all this hullabaloo, the heroine of the day began to wilt. She had defeated the snares of mountains and rainstorms, pressed on across seas and deserts but now the endless speeches and interviews prying more and more into her inner life robbed her of vitality, and she collapsed, physically and mentally exhausted. Gradually she recovered her eagerness to fly. Soon she was planning attacks on new long-distance records and with Jack Humphreys, the chief ground engineer of the London Aeroplane Club, she flew from Lympne in Kent to Tokyo across Siberia in the summer of 1931 in under ten days. In March 1932 she fell in love with Jim Mollison, a good-looking rival flyer two years her junior in age. They were married four months later in a blaze of publicity, which to their dismay continued throughout their married life. Joint flights of Jim and Amy were newsworthy events, but rarely happy: an air crash at Croydon on take-off for a round-the-world flight; a worse crash at Bridgeport, Connecticut; and at Allahabad, India, irreparable damage to the engine of the plane in which they were winning the Mildenhall to Melbourne Air Race of 1934. Only on two occasions, when she flew solo to Capetown and back, was it possible for her to re-capture some of

Amy and her husband, Jim Mollison, eight months after their marriage.

the magic of her great flight to Darwin. Her marriage proved a mistake: it ended in divorce, and a decision that she should revert to the use of her maiden name.

It was thus as Amy Johnson that she figured for the last time in the headlines. Wartime needs turned her into a ferry pilot, flying new planes from factories to airfields as First Officer in the Air Transport Auxiliary. On Sunday, 5 January 1941, she was delivering an Airspeed Oxford twin-engined trainer from Blackpool to Kidlington, Oxfordshire. That afternoon – in snow showers and a biting east wind – her plane was seen to crash in the Thames Estuary; she appears to have come down by parachute half a mile from an armed trawler, which tried in vain to rescue her in the heavy swell. No one, then or later, could understand why she was more than 100 miles off course; and no one knows if she crashed from icing, from lack of fuel or was shot down by an aircraft raiding the Kent coast. There was newspaper speculation even under the restraints of censorship, but these mysteries remain unresolved in the silence of death.

Since her body was never recovered, she has no gravestone. Perhaps that is appropriate. For Amy Johnson won fame as an active force, someone for whom a carved name looks incongruously static. Her memorials are in being, none the less: trophies and mementoes exhibited at Sewerby Hall, Bridlington, in her native Yorkshire; and *Jason* housed proudly at the Science Museum in Kensington. The girl thrilled by *Wings* that April evening more than half a century ago would be content with her niche in history.

～ Gladys Aylward ～

It was clear to the crowds at Liverpool Street that the diminutive, soberly-dressed woman with two bulging suitcases knew her way around the station. For almost all of the thirty years of her life, 'home' was just twenty minutes up the line at Edmonton: she had come this way to work, first in a shop and then as a parlour-maid; and here, too, she had changed on to the underground for the monthly gospel rallies at Kingsway Hall. All the smoky bustle of the London terminus was familiar to her. But now on this particular Saturday – 15 October 1932 – she was setting out on a longer journey: the boat train for Harwich and the Hook of Holland, and then twelve days and nights across the railways of two continents. In her purse she carried tickets for Moscow and for the Trans-Siberian route to Chita and eventually south to Tientsin. Some years previously a newspaper paragraph on the impact of the twentieth century on China's traditional way of life had aroused in Gladys Aylward's spirit a determination to carry her bible to the Far East. She felt compelled to preach the Christian gospel to some among these millions of peasants who were content to believe in ancestral worship and the rites and teachings of Confucius.

Christian missionaries, Catholic or Protestant, had laboured on the Chinese mainland since 1552, many meeting martyrs' deaths. In October 1930, while Gladys was saving her earnings to buy a ticket for Tientsin, English newspapers were shocked at the murder by Chinese bandits of two missionaries, Edith Nettleton from Yorkshire and Eleanor Harrison from Worcestershire, both of whom had been abducted and held captive for three months before execution. Their fate strengthened Gladys Aylward's certainty that the Almighty was calling her to help fill the depleted ranks of His crusaders in the East. As she set out from Liverpool Street she feared she would never again see her family in Edmonton; she was allowing her simple life to assume heroic proportions, should that be the will of God.

Gladys Aylward had never been farther from London than Swansea; she knew nothing of foreign places or foreign politics. On the day her train went through Berlin and she commented on the cleanliness and orderliness of the city, over 100,000 young Germans were marching past Hitler in an election rally less than a dozen miles away, and within a few months Germany passed under Nazi dictatorship. Moscow, in the grip of an 'anti-God' propaganda campaign, made a less favourable impression on Gladys: she never wavered from her conviction that communism, Soviet or Chinese, was an evil creed. World affairs first made an impact on her plans at Chita: the Japanese, who had occupied Manchuria a year previously, closed the shortest rail route to Tientsin, and Gladys Aylward was forced to continue along the Trans-Siberian Railway to Vladivostok. There she was alarmed by the menacing attitude of the authorities and was glad to find passage on a ship to Japan, where she liked the country and the people – a judgment she was soon to revise. At last, three weeks after leaving London, she reached the Missionary Society Home in Tientsin. Ahead of her there still lay a five-day bus journey into Shansi province to the city of Tsechow. Finally she travelled for two days in a mule litter to the walled mountain town of Yangcheng where Mrs Jennie Lawson, a Scottish widow who had preached the gospel in central China for more than fifty years, needed a young, keen helper.

In 1932 China was a 'Nationalist Republic' under the presidency of General Chiang Kai-shek, with his capital in Nanking. Two years previously (23 October 1930), Chiang had been baptized by a Methodist minister of Chinese birth at Shanghai: Madame Chiang was born a Methodist, and at the time of his conversion her husband was anxious to show his government's abhorrence of the murder of Edith Nettleton and Eleanor Harrison by 'red brigands'. But a Christian president brought no special privileges to missionaries in China. Chiang's authority was disputed by warlords in the south and, more significantly, by a Chinese Soviet Republic established by Mao Tse-tung along the provincial borders of Hunan and Kiangsi. The weakness of China's central government left considerable responsibility to the local magistrates ('mandarins'), who perpetuated many of the habits associated with the old Manchu Empire, nominally overthrown in 1911. Gladys Aylward was shocked to discover that in Yangcheng criminals were still beheaded publicly with the sword or kept fettered in dungeons, and that the feet of baby girls were bound, since husbands-to-be rated small feet highly when seeking a wife. She was surprised to find such suspicion of Christian missionaries among the Chinese peasants that Mrs Lawson was forced to convert her mission courtyard into a hostel for muleteers – 'The Inn of the Sixth Happiness'. Only thus could the missionaries gain an opportunity to preach the gospel of Christ.

Within a few months of Gladys Aylward's arrival in China, Mrs Lawson died and she was left alone with responsibility for the primitive mission in Yangcheng. By now she had mastered the local dialect and allowed her own name to be rendered into Chinese – Aylward became 'Ai Weh Teh' (The Virtuous One). The Yangcheng mandarin, stirred into action by decrees from Nanking, asked her to serve as Inspector of Feet, travelling through the surrounding countryside with powers to insist that the custom of foot-binding should at last be discarded. This strange appointment made her known and respected in the mountains of Shansi. At the same time she

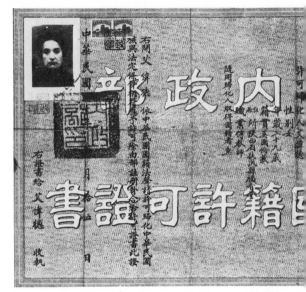

Gladys Aylward's certificate of naturalization as a Chinese citizen, 1936.

discovered the nature of the terrain and began to understand the people among whom she moved. So closely did she come to identify herself with the local peasantry that, after four years in China, she successfully applied to Nanking for naturalization as a Chinese citizen. Few missionaries ever took such a courageous step: it removed her totally from British protection, should China be invaded or devasted by civil war. In 1936–37, with the Japanese massed in Manchuria and with Mao's communists settled in northern Shensi after their epic Long March from Hunan, it seemed probable that Ai Weh Teh would be confronted by both these terrifying challenges to her newly adopted way of life.

On 7 July 1937 Japanese troops on manoeuvres north of Peking clashed with units of Chiang Kai-shek's army. There was no declaration of war but full-scale fighting followed: Peking and Tientsin were in Japanese hands by the end of the month, the whole of north-eastern China by the end of the year. War came to Yangcheng in the spring of 1938, two bombers leaving the defenceless town pitted and scarred. Gladys Aylward's mission compound suffered with all the other buildings; she cared for the wounded and for orphans as well as seeking to organize rescue of the injured from under the rubble. The air raid was followed by weeks of ground fighting as the Japanese pursued the Chinese Nationalist army through the mountain towns and villages. Gladys Aylward, in Chinese dress, moved fearlessly around the countryside, seeking to bolster and maintain the spirits of her small Christian community. For some weeks she was in Japanese-held Tsechow, helping refugees survive on totally inadequate rations. Once the fighting caught her in an isolated village, where she took refuge for two months until the tide of battle ebbed and she was able to see for herself the carnage and destruction left in its wake. The record of Japanese atrocities appalled her. Against the advice of other missionaries, she identified herself closely with the Chinese Nationalist cause. Colonel Lin, intelligence officer of the Shansi army group, became a close personal friend, and she had no hesitation in letting him know all that her sharp eyes perceived of Japanese troop movements as she wandered around the country. By the beginning of 1940 she was known to the Japanese as a dangerous spy. They posted placards in the villages offering a reward of a hundred dollars for the capture, alive, of 'the small woman, known as Ai Weh Teh'. Had she been seized by the Japanese, she would have suffered torture and, eventually, the mercy of death.

It was under the menace of this terrible fate that the ex-parlourmaid from Edmonton began the adventure with which her name became most closely associated. In April 1940 she led a hundred Chinese children, many of them orphans, away from the battle zone in northern Shansi and across the mountains to the comparative safety of Sian. This long trek, sleeping sometimes in Buddhist temples but more often in the bleak shelter of rocks, was undertaken with only two days of food and in the knowledge that, at any hour, they were likely to be overtaken by Japanese forces advancing to the Yellow River.

With aid from sympathetic villagers and from small bands of Chinese soldiers in retreat, the pathetic column of young refugees reached the great river, only to find that all ferries had been removed to the farther shore as a means of keeping the Japanese from crossing this last defensive moat of inland China. For three agonizing days and nights the refugees waited beside the river, praying for a miracle. At last it seemed as if God answered their prayers: a Chinese officer appeared and arranged for a small ferry to cross and re-cross the river until all the children were safely on the farther shore. Even then there remained a nightmare journey, for Sian was overcrowded with refugees, and the children had to be taken still farther inland, to Fufeng. There, with her young charges safe, Gladys Aylward's physical and nervous strength gave way. She collapsed with typhus fever and pneumonia, and only the care of the American Red Cross and missionaries in Sian saved her life.

She remained in China, already a legendary figure to the Christian community, throughout the years of war with Japan and the uncertainties of the post-war conflict between Chiang Kai-shek's Kuomintang and Mao Tse-tung's communists. Until 1944 she was in Sian, then in north-western China at Tsingsui, and finally in Chengtu, over 400 miles to the south, where dialect and climate were new to her. At last, in the spring of 1949, friends found funds for her to return to London. She arrived at the once familiar terminus, unrecognized by her family and so prone to culture-shock that she found herself more naturally speaking Chinese than her native tongue.

Mrs Aylward had often spoken to ministers and friends at church of her daughter's exploits, and a nonconformist religious newspaper duly carried a brief notice that Miss Gladys Aylward had returned to her home in Edmonton after many years as a missionary in China. The paragraph was seen by a BBC producer, Alan Burgess, who was preparing to dramatize true stories of courage in a radio series, *The*

Gladys Aylward with some of the children she led across the mountains to Sian.

Undefeated. Mr Burgess came out to Edmonton, interviewed Gladys Aylward several times, and found her saga unique. China was a newsworthy topic that summer: from 20 April until 31 July 1949, the frigate HMS *Amethyst* was hemmed in by Chinese communist guns on the Yangtze Kiang, after being fired on while bringing supplies to the British community in Nanking; and the subsequent escape of the *Amethyst* by running the gauntlet of five riverbank forts was greeted with jubilation and pride throughout the country. When Gladys Aylward was featured in *The Undefeated* the public mood was therefore especially receptive to tales of courage in China; a heroine who was by birth London working-class and by conviction staunchly anti-communist could be certain of a wide and sympathetic audience. Almost overnight Gladys Aylward, for so long a lone pilgrim crusader,

found herself in great demand as a speaker. Her simplicity, her biblical imagery and her unquenchable certainty of faith made her story unforgettable. It appeared as a best-selling booklet, *Gladys Aylward, One of the Undefeated*, on the eve of the Korean War; and it was turned by Alan Burgess into a book, *The Small Woman*, which sold well on publication in 1957. Finally in 1958 a glamorized version, *The Inn of the Sixth Happiness*, featuring Ingrid Bergman and Robert Donat, became popular in the cinema – popular, that is, with most seekers after family entertainment, although hated on hearsay by Gladys Aylward herself. She refused ever to see the film.

In April 1957 she sailed back to the Far East, not to communist China, but to Hong Kong where she spent her energies and her money helping destitute families from the mainland. A few months later she settled on Taiwan (Formosa), the island refuge of Chiang Kai-shek's defeated Nationalists. There she continued her work as a missionary and built up an orphanage. On several occasions she travelled to Britain, to America, Canada, Australia and New Zealand, as well as to Japan and Korea, supporting evangelical crusades and raising funds for her orphanage and for a mission she ran at Kowloon. Once, while in England, she was invited to luncheon with the Queen at Buckingham Palace; and she always received good publicity from the BBC, who had first made her famous. Yet she never relaxed her sense of mission. If she could not set foot again on the Chinese mainland, at least she would travel among the offshore islands, bringing the gospel both to the simple peasantry of her adopted country and to the American servicemen and their wives based in Taiwan. Suddenly, in the first week of January 1970, she developed pleurisy and died in her sleep. They buried her on the hillside near Taipei; her memorial looked out towards the coast of Fukien and the land to which God had summoned His 'London sparrow' nearly forty years before.

An extract from a letter to her parents in Edmonton reveals the strength of Gladys Aylward's sense of personal mission.

~ *Douglas Bader* ~

One morning in August 1930, while London was fêting Amy Johnson on her return from Australia, a newly commissioned pilot officer reported for flying duties with 23 Squadron of the RAF at Kenley, in Surrey. At twenty, Douglas Bader already enjoyed a reputation among his contemporaries as a sportsman and a daredevil. He had distinguished himself as a cricketer at St Edward's School, Oxford; and at the RAF College, Cranwell, he was reckoned the best player of his year in the cricket, rugby and hockey teams as well as a good middleweight boxer. It seemed likely he would win an international cap as a fly-half at rugby. He had been in trouble at Cranwell for escapades on motorbikes: he was, officially, 'plucky, capable and headstrong'. At Kenley, where they flew highly manoeuvrable biplane fighters, his chief ambition was to become one of the two pilots chosen for the aerobatics team in the annual Hendon air display. That ambition was fulfilled the following summer, when he threw his Gloster Gamecock

Bader (fourth from right) and some of the (mainly Canadian) pilots of his 242 Squadron, 6 October 1940.

through ten minutes of exciting trick flying before hundreds of thousands of spectators. Soon afterwards 23 Squadron was equipped with the more modern, but heavier, Bristol Bulldog. On 14 December 1931 Bader was asked to give an unofficial demonstration of aerobatics at an aero club near Reading. The Bulldog crashed and disintegrated. It seemed incredible that Bader survived: but so grave were his injuries that when he reached hospital both legs were amputated.

This terrible blow was met by the young man with indomitable determination. As soon as he was convalescent, he acquired such mastery of his artificial legs that he was able to drive a car

and take part in dances. Before long he could play golf and squash as well. By the summer of 1932 he was able once again to fly an aeroplane. Since, however, there was no provision in air force regulations to cover his case, he was invalided from the service in March 1933, much against his will. For six years he worked for the Asiatic Petroleum Company (Shell, as it became later), but he continued to seek re-entry into the RAF and, on the outbreak of war, found means of by-passing the medical authorities. In November 1939 he returned to flying duties. Within three months he had been posted to a squadron flying Spitfires, far more sophisticated machines than the Gamecock or the Bulldog he had known nine years before.

To have triumphed over these injuries was in itself an astonishing achievement. Even more remarkably, within the next year, he was to become as famous as any fighter pilot in the world, known and respected alike by senior officers on Britain's Air Staff and by the enemy. At first, in the spring of 1940, he chafed at lack of action as the 'phoney war' gave way to German onslaughts on Norway and the old, familiar battlefields of the Western Front. Bader was based at Duxford, in Cambridgeshire, the most southerly airfield in No. 12 Group's zone of England's air defences, a region which covered the whole of the Midlands and much of Yorkshire but not London and the south-east (which formed No. 11 Group). Although Bader was in action above the Dunkirk beaches at the end of May, most cross-Channel fighter sorties during the crucial weeks of battle were flown from 11 Group airfields in Kent, Sussex and Essex. Even when, on 16 June, he was given command of a squadron of eighteen Hurricane fighters, he remained within 12 Group, and was stationed at Coltishall, near Norwich. Since 12 Group's task was to protect the industrial Midlands, Squadron Leader Bader thus missed the first month of fighting in the Battle of Britain. It was only when the burden on 11 Group became excessive that support for its weary squadrons was sought from 12 Group. On 30 August Bader and his Hurricanes were ordered back to Duxford; and on that same gloriously sunny Friday they were in action over the copses and ploughed furrows of the Essex countryside. When they returned to Duxford the squadron claimed twelve enemy planes destroyed, two by Bader himself. No bombs had fallen on North Weald aerodrome, the principal German target; and all eighteen Hurricanes landed safely, virtually unscathed.

This success reflected credit on Bader in two important respects. He had found his command, 242 Squadron, in poor shape: its pilots, mainly Canadian, had fought in France and lost all their equipment in a chaotic retreat from one improvised landing ground to another; and only a commander of resource, energy and determination could have toughened this demoralized

group of men into a crack unit in a mere ten or eleven weeks of inspired leadership. Moreover Bader had introduced valuable new tactics into air warfare. He kept his planes on a tight leash, concentrated on attacking the centre of the enemy bomber formations so as to break them up, and sought to intercept them before they reached their targets, preferably by diving at them out of the sun. These tactics updated the style of combat first perfected by the ace pilots of the First World War, but they profoundly changed the character of the later stages of the Battle of Britain. For Bader's initiative was taken up by the commander of 12 Group, Air Vice-Marshal Leigh-Mallory, who ordered his squadrons to operate together as a wing, so as to get as great a number of aircraft as possible concentrated at one strategically vital defensive point. By 15 September, the climax of the Battle of Britain, Bader had five squadrons operating from Duxford under his command, enabling him to meet the enemy bomber formations which swept in over Kent and the Thames Estuary that Sunday morning with a massed pack of sixty fighters. The pilots of Bader's wing believed they had shot down 52 enemy planes, with eight other probables, that Sunday. In all, the British claimed 185 enemy aircraft destroyed on 15 September. After the war, it became clear that this figure exaggerated German losses, which seem to have been little more than 50 – a distortion caused primarily by duplication of claims during the heat of battle. Yet the actual number is less important than the longterm effect. German losses were sufficiently heavy for Hitler to accept the impossibility of gaining air supremacy over the Channel that autumn; and two days later he indefinitely postponed the projected invasion of England.

Significantly, Squadron Leader Bader was awarded the Distinguished Service Order (a decoration given for leadership) some weeks before he gained the Distinguished Flying Cross (for individual initiative in action), although both ribbons were on his tunic before the end of the year 1940. He remained with 242 Squadron until March 1941 when he was promoted Wing-Commander and transferred to Tangmere, near Chichester in Sussex, a station which housed three squadrons of Spitfires and one of Beaufighters (for night flying). Bader was given the responsibility of organizing the wing for offensive operations, sweeping over northern France in the coming summer rather than remaining on the defensive in English skies. Once again he had to work out new tactics and train the squadrons in formation flying. By 17 April they were escorting British bombers over the French coast to attack German defences and airfields. Soon they were penetrating as far inland as Lille. Bader continued to lead the sweeps of his wing in person. By the end of July 1941 he could claim to have shot down more than twenty aircraft in the past twelve months. In a single week that July he flew in ten sweeps across the Channel.

On Saturday, 9 August, he was flying his Spitfire back from a sweep over Béthune when a Messerschmidt 109 collided with the plane's tail. As he sought to escape from the crashing Spitfire, one of his artificial limbs became entangled in the cockpit cover and he had fallen some thousands of feet before the leather strap which attached the leg to the body snapped and he was able to complete the descent by parachute, breaking two ribs on landing. The Germans took him to hospital in St Omer. Such was the reputation of the 'legless fighter pilot' that they treated him as an honoured guest, broadcasting a message to England requesting that a spare right leg kept at his quarters in Tangmere should be dropped to him by an RAF aircraft. He was entertained in the officers' mess at Wissant, where the airfield was commanded by Colonel Adolf Galland, one of the three leading German air aces of the war. Galland allowed him to sit in the cockpit of a Messerschmidt, although another officer discreetly kept him covered with a revolver in case he sought to take off. Plans to escape were already in his mind: through a French girl who was

Colditz, the fortress where Bader was imprisoned after several escape attempts from other German prison camps.

serving as a nursing orderly, he established contact with sympathetic helpers in St Omer and, in the small hours of the Friday morning following his crash, he climbed down an improvised rope of knotted sheets from a window on the second floor of the hospital. Then, wearing British uniform and walking with difficulty because of his injuries, he was led into hiding in a peasant's house outside the town. Unfortunately one of the other girl workers in the hospital was a German informant and he was recaptured after taking refuge under stacked hay in a shed. His helpers were all sent to forced labour in Germany – remarkably, they survived this four-year ordeal and were able to return home in 1945. Bader himself, with the spare leg dropped by the RAF during a sweep on that same Friday, was immediately taken to a prisoner-of-war camp near Frankfurt-am-Main.

There followed three and a half years of frustration, intensified by the recurring pain to his injured limbs, for prison camp conditions aggravated the problems of a legless officer seeking to live a normal life. Yet Bader tried on several occasions to escape: once he managed to disguise himself as a private soldier and joined an outside working party on latrine duty near an airfield, hoping he would have the opportunity to steal a plane. But, though he went undetected for several days, the Germans foiled his plot: he was sentenced to ten days of solitary confinement, and moved to a special escape-proof prison camp, the notorious castle at Colditz, a sixteenth-century fortress, perched high over a valley in the ore mountains of Saxony, thirty miles south-east of Leipzig.

No surer testimony could have been given to Bader's triumph over his disability than the German decision to incarcerate a legless officer in so formidable a prison camp. Yet though such specialist treatment may have boosted his personal morale, imprisonment at Colditz intensified his physical suffering. The cobbles of the exercise yard were difficult for artificial legs even in summer: in the winter ice they were impossible. His German captors, respecting Bader's courage and will to survive, allowed him walks outside the castle on parole; but the days and weeks and months passed slowly for the inmates of Colditz. They knew by the winter of 1944–45 that the allies had landed in France. Since, however, the Channel coast was some 600 miles away, it seemed more likely that liberation would come, if at all, from the Russians in the east. Yet in the second week of April 1945 they heard that tanks of the United States First Army had reached the mountain valleys. On 15 April, Bader's imprisonment was ended by an American spearhead. It was a curious development: when he was captured, the United States was still a non-belligerent, and this was his first meeting with American troops. Within a week he was re-united with his wife in Berkshire. By the beginning of June he was back in command at Tangmere, with the rank of Group Captain. Later in the summer he was moved to North Weald, and given control over twelve fighter squadrons at the airfields of Essex and Suffolk.

Yet, although the countryside was familiar, the conditions were strange. So, too, were many of the aircraft: he flew a jet for the first time. He watched the RAF return to peacetime status with mixed feelings of satisfaction and regret. On 15

Bader with Air Chief Marshal Lord Dowding on 15 September 1945, just before the Battle of Britain anniversary fly-past which he planned and led.

September 1945 he was invited to plan and lead the inaugural Battle of Britain fly-past over London; and on that Saturday morning his Spitfire was at the head of 300 aircraft thundering through the hazy sky, for the first autumn of peace had few of the almost cloudless days of 1940. In 1946 he retired from the RAF and returned to Shell, for several years flying his own aircraft all over the world promoting the aviation business of the company. In Scandinavia, South Africa, the Far East and America as well as in France and Greece he was honoured as a hero. Much of the time he spent helping people who had suffered the amputation of legs and who found his presence, and advice, an aid in mastering their artificial limbs. In 1956 his services were recognized by the award of a CBE: and in 1976 he was knighted. To many it seemed an honour long overdue.

~ *Odette Sansom* ~

At the height of the Battle of Britain, King George VI announced in a broadcast to his empire that he had 'decided to create at once a new mark of honour for men and women in all walks of civilian life'. This distinction, the George Cross, would rank immediately after the supreme award for valour, the Victoria Cross, and would recognize a recipient's gallantry in conditions never foreseen when the terms of reference were drawn up for existing military honours. Three women were subsequently awarded the George Cross for their bravery in the course of the Second World War: Odette Sansom, Violette Szabo and Noor Inayat Khan. All three were agents serving with the British Special Operations Executive in France ('F Section of SOE'), a body responsible for organizing and co-ordinating sabotage and subversion across the Channel. Of these three heroines only one, Odette Sansom, survived the hell of the Nazi concentration camps to receive in person the George Cross which each had valiantly earned. Her survival was in itself a triumph of willpower, ingenuity of mind and courageous silence.

She was born Odette Marie Céline Bailly on 28 April 1912, the daughter of a bank official in Amiens. Her father joined an infantry regiment in 1914, won the Croix de Guerre and the Médaille Militaire for his tenacity and courage at the battle of Verdun, and was killed while tending two wounded members of his platoon. Odette, a delicate child, was educated at a convent in Amiens, settled with her widowed mother at Boulogne and came to know many English people, for in the twenties and thirties the French Channel resorts were popular with families seeking bargain continental holidays. In 1931 Odette married an Englishman, Roy Sansom, and settled in London a year later, after the birth of the first of her three daughters. By the outbreak of war in 1939 this girl from Picardy had become an English housewife, concerned like other mothers with the threat of bombing; and in 1940, when her native land was forced to make a separate peace with Germany and Italy, she evacuated her young family to Somerset. She was grieved to think of most of France in enemy occupation, with only a tenuous independence permitted in the central-southern and south-eastern departments and a right-wing authoritarian administration under Marshal Pétain established in Vichy. In the spring of 1942 Odette offered her services to the British War Office, thinking she might be able to undertake part-time translation work. She was persuaded that her proud Anglo-French patriotism could better be satisfied in a more gruelling enterprise. With her three daughters left at a convent school

Odette Sansom and her second husband, Captain Peter Churchill, her commanding officer in France.

242

at Brentwood, in Essex, she became a member of the Women's Transport Service attached to that élite corps, the First Aid Nursing Yeomanry, or FANY. This innocent-sounding appointment was a uniformed cloak concealing a highly effective dagger. In July 1942 she reported for training at the SOE school, a country house hidden in the New Forest, near Beaulieu, Hampshire. She learnt how to fire Sten guns, how to identify the insignia on German uniforms, how to send Morse signals, how to handle a canoe, how to evade answers under SS interrogation and all the techniques for appearing a perfectly normal person while engaging in alarmingly abnormal pursuits. By mid-September it was considered she was ready to be landed in France.

Women were employed by SOE for field work in France primarily as couriers and frequently as wireless operators: they were not expected to carry out acts of sabotage or to join in guerrilla operations, although Violette Szabo fought a rearguard action with German units before her capture near Limoges and another courier, Pearl Witherington, found herself in control of a Maquis force of some 2,000 young Frenchmen who specialized in cutting the main Paris–Bordeaux railway frequently and dramatically. Odette Sansom, like most women agents, was trained to serve as a courier and a circuit organizer, securing a flat in a specified town in France to which SOE might send other members of F group, either as part of an escape team or to encourage sabotage and unified action by the French resistance. It was intended that 'Lise' (for by now she had a code name) would land on the Mediterranean coast and work her way north to Auxerre, where SOE hoped to establish a new circuit. With several other agents (two of them women) she sailed from Gibraltar in the last days of October 1942 aboard a Polish-manned felucca, a small two-masted Mediterranean trading-vessel, which landed them a week later at Cassis, between Marseilles and Toulon in the un-occupied zone of France.

'Lise' arrived in France on the eve of a historic

Violette Szabo, one of the two other women awarded the George Cross for their brave work during the Second World War, with her husband. She was captured and died at Ravensbruck, the camp where Odette Sansom was also imprisoned.

turning-point in the war. On 8 November American and British forces landed in French North Africa, as part of a strategic pincer movement intended to link up with the Eighth Army advancing westwards through Libya after the victory of El Alamein. The Allied initiative prompted the Germans to enter the remaining 'unoccupied zone' of France on 9 November. The Mediterranean coast acquired a new significance in SOE's plans, presenting an additional area of subversion. Captain Peter Churchill, commanding officer of the Marseilles–Cannes SOE circuit (codename 'Spindle') per-suaded the authorities in London that in the changed circumstances he needed the presence of a talented Frenchwoman as his courier: 'Lise's' instructions to proceed to Auxerre were cancelled and she stayed at Cannes. Mounting pressure from German counter-intelligence induced Captain Churchill to move the centre of 'Spindle' activity from Cannes to Annecy, in Upper Savoy, in February 1943; and 'Lise' accompanied him northwards.

The prospect of a major resistance operation led Captain Churchill to return to England the following month, picked up secretly by a Westland Lysander of the RAF. During his absence German agents began to infiltrate 'Spindle'. He returned to Annecy on the night of 14–15 April, landing by parachute in a remote mountainous area and going into hiding with Odette Sansom at a hotel in St Jorioz. There, on the following evening, both Peter Churchill and Odette were arrested by Italian troops and a German security agent. They were escorted to Paris and housed in the notorious Fresnes Prison, where there were separate blocks for male and female criminals. During the train journey they had the opportunity of talking together and it was agreed that Odette Sansom should maintain she was Captain Churchill's wife, at the same time diverting attention from his mission to London, and the imminent outbreak of sabotage operations in south-eastern France. The Germans had not discovered the identity of Spindle's wireless-operator, or of a British officer who had landed from the Lysander which had taken Churchill to England in February. This officer – Captain Francis Cammaerts, son of a distinguished Belgian poet – was to build up a resistance circuit of great value to the allies in their invasion of southern France.

The Germans interrogated Odette Sansom repeatedly, seeking information about the remaining members of Spindle. On 26 May she was taken from Fresnes to the headquarters of the German security service (*Sicherheitdienst*) in Paris at 84 Avenue Foch for further interrogation. There she was systematically tortured: a red-hot poker was laid against the top of her spine and all her toe-nails were pulled out. But still she refused to say anything in answer to her questioner. Early in June she was brought before an improvised military court at security service headquarters and condemned to death as a British spy. She returned to Fresnes, expecting to be shot within a matter of days, if not hours. Even the technical attention to legal form accorded to Edith Cavell twenty-eight years previously was missing in Odette Sansom's case: she was given no chance to defend herself nor to hear in detail the charges against her. It seemed unlikely she would be spared.

Yet there was uncertainty in her captors' minds. She claimed to be the wife of this Peter Churchill, whom they had arrested with her: was she therefore a relation by marriage of the British prime minister? If so, should she not be held as a possible hostage to fortune rather than shot out of hand? There was, in fact, no known family connection between Peter Churchill and Winston Churchill, but the genealogical research facilities of Germany's security service were limited and no subordinate in occupied Paris was prepared to order the execution of an agent who might, later in the war, be of considerable interest and value to the authorities in Berlin. Both Captain Churchill and Mrs Sansom were, accordingly, retained in Fresnes and frequently interrogated for another eight months: occasionally they were able to meet and converse surreptitiously. Peter Churchill was moved to Germany in February 1944; Odette Sansom, with six other women agents of SOE, was taken in handcuffs by night train from Paris to Karlsruhe on 12 May 1944, twenty-five days before the allied armies landed in Normandy and only fifteen weeks before the resistance movement in Paris, financed and supplied by SOE, rose to liberate the city.

For some eight weeks the women appear to have been forgotten by the authorities and were housed, well apart from each other, in crowded cells in the civil prison of Karlsruhe. Orders arrived from Berlin in July. Three of the women were suddenly taken to the concentration camp of Natzweiler in Alsace and summarily executed.

Odette's other companions remained at Karlsruhe until September when they were taken to Dachau and shot. She herself was moved northwards, locked for almost a week in a cage at police headquarters at Frankfurt, brutally treated at Halle and brought at last to the concentration camp at Ravensbruck, amid the Mecklenburg lakes fifty miles to the north of Berlin. She arrived there on 18 July 1944, two days before the abortive plot to assassinate Hitler and create a non-Nazi government.

At Ravensbruck Odette Sansom was confined to an underground cell, small, solitary and dark. When the predominantly Franco-American Seventh Army landed on the Riviera on 15 August, her gaolers turned on the central heating of the cell and deprived her of all food to punish her for her work in Spindle and for silence over the identity and whereabouts of Francis Cammaerts. When, in October, her health seemed almost broken, she was taken to a cell above ground. Prisoners – including three SOE agents – were shot outside her window, which faced towards the entrance of the crematorium. In December 1946, giving evidence on oath at a war crimes trial in Hamburg, she described how she had seen women being driven 'screaming and struggling' to the crematorium doors as Red Army liberators drew near to Ravensbruck in April 1945. She was saved, once again, by her

The Allied army lands on the sunny, pine-fringed beaches of the French Riviera, 15 August 1944.

captors' belief that she was Winston Churchill's niece by marriage: for in the last days of the war the camp commandant personally drove her in his sports car to the American lines, hoping thus to save himself from execution as a war criminal. This calculated and belated magnanimity made no difference to his fate: he was hanged, as were all the top-ranking prison staff at Ravensbruck. So, too, was the officer responsible for Odette Sansom's torture in Paris: he was executed for ordering the shooting of British parachutists captured, in uniform, in July 1944.

Within a few days of her arrival in the American lines, Odette was re-united with her daughters in England. She was gazetted a member of the Order of the British Empire later that year and awarded the George Cross for 'courage, endurance and self-sacrifice of the highest possible order' in August 1946. In the following year she married Captain Churchill, and her story became widely known in 1949 when Jerrard Tickell's book, *Odette*, was published. A film version was first shown in 1950, with the title role taken by Anna Neagle, who had already played Edith Cavell and Amy Johnson on the screen. The public recognized the nobility of Odette's defiant silence after capture, and she was rightly hailed as a heroine. Yet she herself – Mrs Odette Hallowes, GC, as she became in 1956 – has always emphasized that she looked on the telling of her story as a tribute to those women who served with her but did not survive the war. Mrs Violette Szabo, a half-French girl from south London, won a posthumous GC for courage in circuits in Normandy and around Limoges: she was one of the agents shot at Ravensbruck. The part-American and part-Indian princess, Noor Inayat Khan, who had spent most of her life in France, played a vital role as wireless operator for a circuit in Paris: she was brutally interrogated and kept in shackles before execution at Dachau. There were others, too, who perished in the Nazi camps at Belsen and Natzweiler. In all, fifty SOE women agents were landed in France: fifteen of them were captured by the Nazis, of whom two escaped and Odette Sansom returned, a lone survivor of the long ordeal. No previous undertaking in British history ever called on a group of women to sustain such bravery or to offer such sacrifice.

～ *Martin Luther King* ～

On 15 January 1929 the wife of a Baptist preacher in Atlanta, Georgia, gave birth to a son who was named after his father, Martin Luther King. The boy grew up in an affectionate and closely-knit family circle. At school he was bright and popular; like his father, he went on to Morehouse College, Atlanta, where he was awarded his Bachelor of Arts degree. Briefly he thought of becoming a lawyer or a doctor but, at the age of seventeen, he felt called to the church's ministry, as had his father and his mother's father before him. To gain his Bachelor of Divinity degree he left Atlanta and studied at Crozer Theological Seminary in Chester, Pennsylvania, some twelve miles from downtown Philadelphia. So outstanding was his work at Crozer that the teaching staff urged him to take a doctorate at one of the New England universities. This raised for him a difficult personal decision: he had fallen in love with an attractive soprano from the small town of

Martin Luther King and his wife, Coretta, photographed on 26 March 1965 on a freedom march.

Marion, in central Alabama. He decided to seek the best of both worlds: he married Coretta Scott from Marion in 1953; and he enrolled at Boston University, becoming a Doctor of Philosophy in 1955. When not engaged in academic study, he served as assistant pastor to his father.

As yet, Dr King's career had been creditable, but with no hint of the compelling leadership which was to make him a national figure within twelve months. By temperament he was conservative, by conviction a supporter of the NAACP (National Association for the Advancement of Colored People), an inter-racial movement founded as long ago as 1910 to seek through education and political lobbying a society purged of segregation and white bigotry. But in 1955, when Martin Luther King accepted the pastorate of Dexter Avenue Baptist Church in

Montgomery, Alabama, the city was still strictly segregated by state laws enforced by white bigots. Shortly before Christmas that year a Negro seamstress, Rosa Parks, refused to give up her seat in a bus to a white man: she was arrested and jailed. It was this incident, typical of so many humiliations imposed on Negro communities in the past hundred years, that aroused in Pastor King the latent fire of Christ the Revolutionary. The harassment of Rosa Parks brought a specifically Christian leadership to the Negro revolt in the southern states. Ultimately it led to the triumph of the civil rights movement in 1964. Perhaps inevitably it led also, within thirteen years, to the martyrdom of Martin Luther King on a hotel balcony in Memphis, Tennessee.

Dr King persistently preached two basic doctrines of Christian social justice, racial brotherhood and non-violence. He was much influenced by the lessons of Gandhi's passive resistance movement in India which acquired impressive moral authority by its rejection of killing and bloodshed. In order to expose the inhumanity of municipal segregation Dr King founded the Montgomery Improvement Association soon after the arrest of Rosa Parks. The MIA then led a boycott of the city's buses which continued for 382 days, until at last the Supreme Court in Washington required the State of Alabama to desegregate its transport system. During the boycott Dr King was arrested on a legal technicality, while extremists wrecked his home with bombs and sought to terrorize his family. Yet, despite provocation, his followers held themselves back from a rampage of rioting. He had taught them that Negro violence would not only lead to reprisals from the rabid segregationists but would harden the white conscience outside Alabama; and they accepted his word.

By the end of the bus boycott Martin Luther King was recognized as spokesman for the southern Negroes. As founder-president of the Southern Christian Leadership Conference (SCLC), he encouraged the first prayer pilgrimage to the Lincoln Memorial in Washington (1957): the sincerity and moderation of his address on that occasion won him wide coverage by press, radio and television; and he was invited to Accra to help celebrate the establishment of Ghana, the first British colony in black Africa to gain independence. Yet, though by now a respected world figure, Dr King concentrated the energies of the SCLC on an arrowhead segment of the Deep South, principally from Atlanta down to the Alabama river at Selma and up to Memphis on the Mississippi, some 320 miles to the north-west. 'Sit-ins' at exclusive restaurants and 'freedom rides' in towns where the buses were

still not de-segregated provoked angry reprisals. In October 1960 Dr King was sentenced to four months' hard labour in the Georgia state penitentiary at Reidsville, an area of poor whites who were bigoted, resentful of educated blacks and reputedly inclined to reach for a lynching rope. With a presidential election due in fifteen days' time, both major candidates were informed that the Negroes had been deprived of their hero's wise counsel: the Democrat, John Kennedy, telephoned his sympathy to Mrs King while his brother, Robert, contacted the judiciary in Georgia and secured Dr King's release; the Republican, Vice-President Nixon, could not decide what to do. Negro votes a fortnight later were to tilt the balance of the election sufficiently in three key states to ensure Kennedy's victory and the prospect of new federal laws to safeguard the black man's civil rights.

The lawmaking process in a democracy seems intolerably slow to any minority suffering under social injustice. In the closing months of 1962 Dr King came to believe that the only way to quicken the pace of civil rights legislation was to shock the conscience of the nation by ensuring that millions of whites sitting comfortably in their homes could see on the television screen the true nature of a southern city's defence of its entrenched privileges. He therefore persuaded the SCLC to plan a campaign for the following Easter which would challenge 'the largest segregated city in the United States'.

From the air Birmingham, Alabama, was a depressing sight in the 1960s. Steelworks belched a smoky fallout over the homes of some half a million people, slightly more than a third of whom were coloured. Outside the city the names of suburbs – Bessemer in the south-west, Irondale in the east – underlined the industrial nature of this enclave in the cotton belt of the South. Birmingham was a town which had refused concessions to the blacks in its rest-aurants, snack bars and public places. It was a town of fear and violence, with 'nigger lovers' threatened by the Ku Klux Klan, whose headquarters were at Tuscaloosa, fifty miles away down Route 11. Here, in this city where the police force was notorious for racist brutality, Dr King and his followers led a prayer pilgrimage to city hall on Good Friday (12 April 1963). He was himself arrested and jailed; so, within the next three weeks, were more than 3,000 of his supporters. By 7 May there was no room for them in the prisons. America and the world watched as the accumulated hatred of the white extremists was let loose on peaceful demonstrators – police dogs, fire hoses, batons used on women and children as well as their menfolk. There were camera shots of State Troopers, the flag of the old confederacy painted on their helmets, trying to restore order – for, with Martin Luther King silenced and with high pressure hoses lashing their families, the blacks fought back despite their leader's creed of non-violence. Not until President Kennedy began to concentrate a fully mobilized 'battle unit' of the US army outside the city were the municipal authorities prepared to make token concessions over segregation in the cheaper eating-places. After five weeks in the headlines of the world, Birmingham became once more outwardly peaceful. A month later President Kennedy presented Congress with the text of an extensive civil rights bill.

To most Negroes, and to many liberal whites, the Birmingham campaign confirmed Martin Luther King's stature as a leader with a mission. From his jail he had smuggled out a letter in reply to white church leaders in Alabama who publicly criticized his encouragement of 'unwise and untimely' demonstrations. The letter, his 'long thoughts' when 'alone for days in a narrow cell', traced with pride the continuity of the Negro struggle from the days when 'our forebears, labouring without wages ... made cotton "king"' down to 'the opposition we now face': 'We will win our freedom,' he wrote, 'because the sacred heritage of our nation and the eternal will of God are embodied in our echoing demands.' The dignity of this letter stood out in contrast to

A verbal confrontation between a member of the National Association for the Advancement of Colored People Youth Council and white hecklers at a civil rights demonstration in Milwaukee in 1967.

the frenzied hatred shown on the streets of Birmingham. And it was this quality which inspired the visionary speech Dr King delivered to thousands of civil rights campaigners from the foot of the Lincoln Memorial in Washington on 28 August 1963: 'I have a dream that my four little children will one day live in a nation where they will not be judged by the colour of their skin but by the content of their character. I have a dream that one day in the red hills of Georgia, sons of former slaves and sons of former slave-owners will be able to sit down together at the table of brotherhood.' He became *Time* magazine's 'Man of the Year' for 1963. A year later he was awarded the Nobel Peace Prize.

President Kennedy was struck down by an assassin in Dallas on 22 November 1963, before his civil rights legislation was passed by the Senate. The Civil Rights Bill was finally signed by President Johnson on 2 July 1964. It was a victory for Martin Luther King's moderation; but not a complete one. So long as methods of

Dr King, winner of the Nobel Peace Prize in 1964, leads the Selma–Montgomery civil rights march in 1965.

electoral registration varied from state to state, it was possible for southern segregationists to deny the blacks their full political rights. And in the winter of 1964–65 Martin Luther King fought a new battle to make certain that his people were democratically enfranchised. 'Segregation is on its deathbed,' Dr King told university students in Pennsylvania on 20 January 1965. 'The question now is, how costly will the segregationists make the funeral?' He was soon to see the answer. The climax of the campaign came in March, in an area he knew well, the forty miles of central Alabama,

between Selma and Montgomery. On 9 March a white civil rights worker was murdered at Selma: on 21 March Dr King led a procession of 4,000 civil rights demonstrators from Selma to Montgomery (the state capital) to present a petition. He was personally assaulted and arrested; and, four days later, another white civil rights worker (Mrs Viola Luizzo) was shot by the Ku Klux Klan in Selma. Montgomery and Selma, it seemed, had learnt nothing and forgotten nothing from the experience of their northern neighbour, Birmingham. Once more there was a prospect of federal intervention; once more a civil rights measure came to the President for signature – the Voting Rights Bill of August 1965. 'The weapon of nonviolence, the breastplate of righteousness, the armour of truth,' as Dr King had once defined his resources, again emerged triumphant.

But for how long? In northern cities, where black communities suffered from economic as well as from social frustration, the SCLC had never carried much influence and militant leaders condemned Martin Luther King's efforts at bridging the gulf between black and white. Now in southern towns the formal restraint imposed upon governors and mayors played into the hands of underground extremists in the Ku Klux Klan and its even weirder offshoots. For many years Dr King had known he faced probable murder, either through lynch law or the assassin's bullet; and perhaps, as spring came in 1968, he had a premonition of disaster, for an apocalyptic tone began to ring through his public addresses. He was planning a 'poor people's march' on Washington. As a preliminary move, he crossed into Tennessee during the first days of April, intending to help the garbage workers of Memphis, struggling to improve their status. There, on the evening of 4 April 1968, a gunman with a long-range rifle shot him dead.

Political commentators had said for some time that Dr King was no longer the hero of his people: sophisticated intellectuals mocked the biblical diction of his oratory as something out of fashion, for he spoke English and not jargon. But in death he received the adoration of every liberal who hated racial prejudice and intolerance. The warmth and love won during the bus boycott and the prayer pilgrimages from his fellow Negroes was enduring and authentic. Unfortunately, however, grief at his murder made thousands forget his pleas for non-violence: rioting swept 125 cities of America, and at least forty-six people died because he had died. Yet mourners came to his funeral in Atlanta from across the nation and from all over the world, as though they were honouring a statesman who had held high office. At the last there was one final witness to his belief in passive simplicity: his funeral cortège was a mule train.

Dr King's funeral procession in Atlanta, Georgia.

~ Neil Armstrong ~

For many generations the fantasy of being 'first
man on the moon' has appealed to the creative
imagination of writers in differing lands. The
Greek parodist Lucian, the Englishman
Coleridge, Walt Whitman in America, Jules
Verne in France all dreamt of space travel and the
moon, while in 1901 H. G. Wells greeted the new
century with an exciting tale about the *First Man
on the Moon*. Since the moon is some 240,250
miles away, there remained about all such stories
an element of inventive improbability; they
seemed grown-up make-believe, compensation
for the discarded magic carpets of childhood. But
some scientists took the possibility of space travel
seriously. Dr Robert Goddard, for example,
invented and tested a liquid-fuelled rocket at
Auburn, Massachusetts; and on 16 March 1926
it travelled a full 62 yards at an average speed of
52 miles an hour. In the following year a group
of hardheaded American financiers suggested to
Lindbergh that, now he had flown solo to Paris,
he might consider backing a company which
would seek ways of sending him to the moon.
Very sensibly he declined: the spatial high jump
bar in 1927 was still only a mile or two above the
earth's surface. When, on 27 May 1931, the
Swiss physicist and balloonist, Professor
Auguste Piccard, flew 'higher into the upper air
than any man before him', he hit the headlines of
the world's press. To ascend ten miles into the
stratosphere made journalists write of future
space travel. Perhaps, they speculated, there was
already living somewhere the pioneer who would
set foot on the crater-pocked surface of the moon.

He was indeed alive and well and living in
Auglaize County, Ohio. But since Neil

Dr Robert Goddard, the 'Father of American Rocketry', in
1915.

252

Armstrong was a mere nine months old, the journalists could be forgiven for not readily identifying him. He had been born on 5 August 1930 in a farmhouse six miles from the township of Wapakoneta. His boyhood followed a familiar pattern: many homes in a short period of time along a belt through northern Ohio, for his father was an itinerant auditor. Not until 1944 did the family settle down finally back in Wapakoneta. By then Neil knew where his interests lay: for the past five years he had enjoyed building model aeroplanes which were powered by rubber-bands; and now he sought to make his games a reality. On Saturdays and in the vacation he worked for the local chemist ('Brading's pharmacy on Main Street'), receiving 40 cents an hour. If he helped Mr Brading for 22 hours, he could save enough money to afford a flying lesson at the airfield along the old brewery road. The working hours mounted up; and so did his time in the air. He flew solo at the age of fifteen, and on his sixteenth birthday he was granted a student pilot's licence. Two years later he joined the United States Navy and reported to Pensacola in Florida for training as a fighter pilot.

About the time the Armstrongs settled in Wapakoneta, an ominous change occurred in the aerial bombardment of Britain. On the evening of 8 September 1944 the first of nearly 15,000 V2 rockets was launched by German troops stationed near The Hague and aimed at the London area, 200 miles away. This bombardment continued intermittently until 27 March 1945: it caused 9,000 civilian casualties without the slightest effect on the outcome of the war. But the rockets showed mastery of a new technique, perfected at Peenemunde, a German research establishment on the Baltic coast, which fell into Russian hands during the last weeks of the war in Europe. The principal rocket specialist, Dr Werner von Braun, had, however, already left Peenemunde: he surrendered to the Americans and handed over to them surplus V2 missiles which had not been fitted with warheads. Dr Braun agreed to assist the Americans, and

experiments with his rockets were carried out in New Mexico between 1946 and 1949, while the US Navy developed a 'Viking' rocket of its own, which in May 1950 set up an altitude record of $106\frac{1}{2}$ miles. As yet, only writers continued to speculate on using a rocket to reach the moon. The army and navy experiments were prompted by the persistent cold war rivalry with the Soviet Union. For many years, however, the Russians had been interested in emerging from what one of their more poetic scientists described as 'the earth cradle of humanity'. If a space race developed between the powers, there could be no more prestigious prize than the moon.

Effectively the Space Age opened on 4 October 1957 when the Russians launched their 'Sputnik', the first artificial earth satellite. The Sputnik, bleeping its way in orbit round the earth for three weeks, seemed to mock America's efforts, although US scientists successfully put their 'Explorer' satellite into orbit eighteen weeks later. In an effort to keep ahead of the Russians, President Eisenhower authorised the establishment of NASA (National Aeronautics and Space Administration), a specialized agency to co-ordinate military, naval and civilian attempts to reach for the stars; and on 9 April 1959 NASA announced the names of the first seven American astronauts – three from the army, three from the navy, and Lieutenant Colonel John Glenn from the marines. Yet to the general public the Russians seemed ahead in the race: on 12 April 1961 Yuri Gagarin, travelling at more than 17,000 miles an hour, became the first man in space. Seventeen days later Commander Alan Shepherd responded to this challenge with a sub-orbital flight, 116 miles up in the skies, but his achievement did not capture the publicity enjoyed by Gagarin. At this point President Kennedy took a major decision: money would be spent on building a massive 'Saturn' rocket and a spacecraft capable of holding three astronauts; and on 25 May 1961, while the world was still marvelling at Gagarin's feat, the President sent a historic message to Congress: 'I believe that this nation should commit itself to achieving the goal, before this decade is out, of landing a man on the moon and returning him safely to earth.'

By now the lad from Wapakoneta was in his thirty-first year and serving as a civilian test pilot at Edwards Air Force Base in California. He had retired from the navy in 1952 with the rank of lieutenant, having flown 78 combat missions in the Korean War and won three decorations for skill and bravery. The President's announcement did not stir a response from Armstrong. He was, at the time, flying the X-15 rocket plane, sometimes attaining a speed of 4,000 miles an hour, and he felt that Kennedy's decision might cut funds for the winged rocket programme. It was only when, on 20 February 1962, Colonel Glenn became the first American to orbit the earth in space that Armstrong and other test pilots began to consider the possibility of joining the NASA team. On 26 April that year an American scientific probe craft, Ranger 4, at last reached the moon. Five months later Neil Armstrong joined the second group of astronauts selected by the experts of NASA's headquarters' staff in Houston, Texas.

Neil Armstrong (right) and Edwin ('Buzz') Aldrin, on a geological field trip, practise with the equipment they will use on the moon.

There followed for him intensive hours of physical and psychological training. Now he was watching the space race from beside the track. The Russians still had their successes: Valentina Tereschkova became the first woman in space on 16 June 1963; and a Russian craft landed on the moon, and sent back television pictures from the Ocean of Storms, on the last day of January 1966, four months before an American craft was ready for a soft lunar landing. But by then Armstrong was himself a participant in the race. On 16 March 1966 he was co-pilot of Gemini 8 spacecraft which successfully made the first docking in outer space. This achievement increased the probability he would be selected for the first moon landing flight. Everyone assumed, however, that command of that operation would be given to Lieutenant-Colonel Grissom, the first commander of a Gemini and the first astronaut to make two rocket flights into space. But on 27 January 1967 Grissom was killed, along with two other astronauts, when a flash fire on the pad at Cape Kennedy destroyed their Apollo 1 spacecraft during a simulated launch. This tragedy, which emphasized the unknown dangers of rocketry, grounded America's spacecraft for two years.

At the beginning of January 1969 NASA announced that three astronauts had been selected for the Apollo 11 mission to the moon. Armstrong would be in command of the flight, with Michael Collins as pilot of the command module and Edwin Aldrin as pilot of the lunar module. Both Collins and Aldrin were army officers: Collins had been born in Rome on 31 October 1930, and Aldrin in Montclair, New Jersey, on 30 January 1930. Collins had met Armstrong at Edwards Air Force Base, but did not know Aldrin until they both became members of the third intake of astronauts by NASA in September 1963. For six months after the NASA announcement the three men worked closely together at Cape Kennedy, accustoming themselves to conditions for space travel by living in simulators for ten or even fourteen hours a day. They had to study the evidence accumulated from exploratory flights by manned and unmanned spacecraft; an extensive photographic programme by the lunar orbiters; and the valuable experience of Frank Borman, James Lovell and William Anders who orbited the moon ten times over Christmas 1968 in the Apollo 8 spacecraft, returning safely to earth after six days and three hours in outer space. The intensive preparations for the flight of Armstrong's Apollo 11 reminded veterans of the build-up to the Normandy landings during the war. Nothing must go wrong. In Armstrong's case, D-Day had been fixed, months ahead, for 16 July 1969.

Armstrong entered the command module on its Saturn v rocket at eight minutes to seven in the morning. There followed an hour of checking controls, until at last, with the clock at 8.32, there came the awe-inspiring roar and flames of 'lift-off'. Thousands of people watched in Florida as the rocket climbed to twelve miles in eight seconds: thousands more watched on television. Radio contact allowed conversations to continue endlessly between the astronauts and Mission Control in Houston, silence coming only during prescribed hours of sleep and during the times when the spacecraft was behind the moon. Fifty hours out into space, the flight began transmitting live television pictures and millions in America, western Europe, Japan and South America were able to see the moon and earth and the inside of the command module as Armstrong and his two companions saw it themselves. By Saturday, 19 July, they were passing around the moon, on the first of twelve reconnaissance orbits to inspect the craters from between 60 and 170 miles above the lunar surface. On the fourth orbit Armstrong and Aldrin entered the lunar module landing-craft 'Eagle', leaving Collins to continue in the command module, 'Columbia'. After making nine more orbits, Eagle separated from Columbia

The moment of 'lift-off'.

and began a two-hour slow descent to the moon. The lunar landing was made on Sunday afternoon, 20 July 1969.

Around them, Armstrong and Aldrin could see for some four miles across a level plain, almost colourless: the Sea of Tranquillity was broken by craters and ridges. It was not an attractive vista, but a fascinating one; and all of it spread out on television screens in millions of homes throughout the world. That evening Armstrong lowered a ladder of nine steps from Eagle to the lunar surface, and set foot on the moon. 'That's one small step for a man, one giant leap for mankind,' he commented in a memorable phrase. Twenty minutes later, Aldrin backed out of Eagle to join Armstrong. They carried out seismic experiments, planted an American flag fitted with rigid wires so that the camera saw it apparently waving in an airless atmosphere, and collected moon rocks for scientific analysis. A plaque saying 'Here Men from the planet Earth first set foot upon the Moon, July 1969 AD' was embedded in some hard rock: it bore the names of the three astronauts and of the far-absent President Nixon. The only person who could not see this on television was the unfortunate Michael Collins, still orbiting in Columbia.

Fifteen hours after Neil Armstrong stepped on to the moon, Eagle began the ascent back to Columbia, safely docking on the afternoon of 21 July. Three days later their spacecraft splashed down in the Pacific, and they were brought aboard USS Hornet for a presidential greeting. Yet they had to wait for public acclaim. Spacecraft and spacemen alike were condemned to three weeks' quarantine at the Lunar Receiving Laboratory in Texas. Only then came the glitter: parades in New York, Chicago and Los Angeles; reception by both houses of Congress; and a trip around the world in thirty-eight days. For Armstrong, too, a special visit to Vietnam to boost the troops' morale at Christmas. Gradually life became almost normal: Collins accepted an appointment with the State Department; Aldrin

moved into industry; Armstrong took a professorial chair at the University of Cincinatti. In his home town, his days of glory will not be allowed to fade. For Wapakoneta now boasts a Neil Armstrong Drive, and the little airstrip along the brewery road has become the Neil Armstrong Airport. And small wonder: for whatever legends the Indians may have told of Big Chief Wapa and his Koneta, no one suggested even in fancy that they ever flew themselves to the moon and back, one holiday week in July.

President Nixon welcomes home the three Apollo 11 astronauts, (left to right) Armstrong, Collins and Aldrin, on board their rescue ship, the USS Hornet.

Index